Vehicles of Decolonization

In the series *Critical Race, Indigeneity, and Relationality,*
edited by ANTONIO T. TIONGSON JR., DANIKA MEDAK-SALTZMAN,
AND IYKO DAY

ALSO IN THIS SERIES:

Erin Suzuki, *Ocean Passages: Navigating Pacific Islander
and Asian American Literatures*

Quynh Nhu Le, *Unsettled Solidarities:
Asian and Indigenous Cross-Representations in the Américas*

MARYAM S. GRIFFIN

VEHICLES OF DECOLONIZATION

Public Transit in the Palestinian West Bank

TEMPLE UNIVERSITY PRESS
Philadelphia • *Rome* • *Tokyo*

TEMPLE UNIVERSITY PRESS
Philadelphia, Pennsylvania 19122
tupress.temple.edu

Library of Congress Cataloging-in-Publication Data

Names: Griffin, Maryam Susan, author.
Title: Vehicles of decolonization : public transit in the Palestinian West
    Bank / Maryam S. Griffin.
Other titles: Critical race, indigeneity, and relationality.
Description: Philadelphia : Temple University Press, 2022. | Series:
    Critical race, indigeneity, and relationality | Includes bibliographical
    references and index. | Summary: "This book considers collective
    Palestinian movement via public transportation as a site of social
    struggle through which Israel deepens its settler colonization of the
    West Bank and Palestinian communities refuse and transcend that project
    at quotidian, activist, and artistic registers"—Provided by publisher.
Identifiers: LCCN 2021003984 (print) | LCCN 2021003985 (ebook) |
    ISBN 9781439920787 (cloth) | ISBN 9781439920794 (paperback) |
    ISBN 9781439920800 (pdf)
Subjects: LCSH: Transportation—Social aspects—West Bank. | Freedom of
    movement—West Bank. | Settler colonialism—West Bank. | Military
    occupation—Social aspects—West Bank. | Decolonization—West Bank. |
    Palestinian Arabs—West Bank—Social conditions—21st century.
Classification: LCC HE268.47.A7 Z35 2022 (print) | LCC HE268.47.A7
    (ebook) | DDC 388.095694—dc23
LC record available at https://lccn.loc.gov/2021003984
LC ebook record available at https://lccn.loc.gov/2021003985

Printed in the United States of America

9 8 7 6 5 4 3 2 1

For Suleiman and our parents

Contents

Acknowledgments   ix

Introduction   1

1   The Im/mobilization Regime of the Israeli Enclosures
in the West Bank   21

2   The West Bank Borderscape   45

3   The People on the Bus: Routes (and Roots) of Mobile
Commoning   77

4   Public Transit Protests Traversing the Enclosures   101

5   Speculative Art and the Ghosts of Palestinian Transit:
Past-Present-Future   123

Conclusion   153

Appendix on Methodology   165

Notes   171

References   185

Index   201

Acknowledgments

The engine of this book, like many interdisciplinary projects, is collectively enabled and endeavored movement, both physical and intellectual. This book is the result of deeply meaningful and sustaining exchanges with the people who joined me on this journey over the course of many years. It is thanks to them that I took the routes I did to connect the ideas, commitments, literatures, and geographies that appear in this book. The due acknowledgments could have filled an entire chapter's worth of pages, but no amount of words would be sufficient to capture my gratitude to the people recognized here.

My eternal gratitude belongs to my Palestinian interlocutors and friends for contributing their insights and observations, for including me in their knowledge networks, for welcoming me into private spaces, for encouraging me, for feeding me, body, mind, and heart. It is deeply unfair that I cannot acknowledge them by full name here out of fear that the occupation forces to whose arbitrary rule they are subjected might punish them for any affiliation with the arguments expressed in this book. I am especially indebted to Hamza, Yasser, Aslynn, Khadr, Betty, Tanya, Vera, Rema, Naji, and Iyad. The Applied Research Institute–Jerusalem enabled some of the more challenging but fruitful aspects of this research and offered brilliant, energetic collaboration. Thank you to Zeina Chahid, Lena Saleh, Lara Hovsepian, and Marya Hannun, each of whom, in different ways, helped me to get to Palestine (sometimes quite literally to cross the border) and introduced me to invaluable people and places. I am grateful for the time with my "sister" Diana Hodali, which, whether in Palestine, Lebanon, or virtual space, is always re-charging. Thank you, as well, to my colleague and neighbor in the field, Fabio Cristiano, for scholarly exchanges and for once lending me his yellow-plated car, which was then promptly stolen.

My ability to pursue research about and in alliance with Palestinian life and struggle was enabled by generations of activism that has subverted settler colonial attempts to erase all traces of Palestine and Palestinians. I grew up surrounded by different scales of such activism (e.g., private conversations, cultural productions, political demonstrations, and other public events), and my experiences in higher education have been shaped by organizing efforts at multiple University of California (UC) campuses. For their successful work to preserve spaces that pursue Palestinian liberation in connection with many other struggles, the various chapters of Students for Justice in Palestine, the Palestinian Youth Movement, U.S. Campaign for the Academic and Cultural Boycott of Israel (USACBI), and similar groups, along with many other Palestinian organizers and intellectuals, have been met with relentless campaigns to harass, surveil, humiliate, punish, and criminalize them. This represents a global echo of the extreme political repression that Israel applies to Palestinians across historical Palestine, which has nonetheless failed and will continue to fail to undermine the Palestinian struggle. Any space to do intellectual work in relation to this struggle was hard-fought, and I remain full of admiration, gratitude, and commitment to everyone who continues to throw in with this fight.

In addition, the support of the following organizations made it possible for me to travel and conduct the research at the center of this book. I am grateful for research grants and support from the Palestinian American Research Center (PARC), the University of California Center for New Racial Studies, and the Flacks Fund for the Study of Democratic Possibilities. PARC in particular has been an ongoing support; special thank you to Penny Mitchell, who has provided me with invaluable connections and encouragement, and to Salim Tamari for early intellectual guidance. I also thank the School of Interdisciplinary Arts and Sciences at the University of Washington (UW) Bothell, and the UC Office of the President for research funds and time-off associated with my employment.

I am very fortunate to have had many opportunities to workshop the ideas in this book in different venues. During my postdoctoral fellowship at UC Davis, I benefited tremendously from a variety of opportunities to participate in scholarly spaces. Through the framework of their Comparative Border Studies Initiative, Sunaina Maira and Robert McKee Irwin orchestrated a symphony of politically engaged scholarly conversations that had a massive influence on the development of this book. I am grateful for the feedback I received from the affiliated writing group as well as the Cultural Studies and Middle East Studies colloquia. Sincere thanks to Maurice Stierl, the initiative's first postdoctoral scholar, for many generative recommendations and conversations. During the same years of my postdoc, there was a fortuitous opportunity to form the Palestine Studies working group in Northern California. My continued gratitude and admiration go to my fellow participants: Evyn Lê Espiritu, Keith Feldman, Sarah Ihmoud, Jenny Kelly, Sunaina Maira, Lila Sharif, and Magide Shihade. I owe another round of thanks to Jenny Kelly, who facilitated my participation in at least four professional opportunities to present my work that she organized. Thank you to Suad Joseph, Maile Arvin, Crystal Baik, and Omar Jabary Salamanca, among others, for organizing and inviting me to present my research and for offering their insights. I am grateful to many colleagues for their engagement and feedback, on conference panels or otherwise, and among them, those who have not yet been mentioned but had particular effect on my thinking are Su'ad Abdul Khabeer, Paul Amar, Moustafa Bayoumi, Arash Davari, Alex Lubin, Nadine Naber, Golnar Nikpour, Dana Olwan, Sherene Seikaly, Josh Stacher, Tiffany Willoughby-Herard, and Clyde Woods. The UW Bothell's School of Interdisciplinary Arts and Sciences, where I am now employed, provided fruitful spaces for me to advance the project in its later stages, including a faculty colloquium and a writing retreat. I am especially grateful to Lee Ann Wang, Thea Quiray Tagle, Karam Dana, Adam Romero, Christian Anderson, and José Fusté for engaging my research in these spaces. Thank you, as well, to my dear UW colleagues Chandan Reddy and Ben Gardner for their intellectual engagement and for advocating for me. I also thank Junaid Rana, who provided me generous feedback and guidance far beyond what was anticipated.

I have benefited from the tremendous mentorship of a number of people. I am deeply influenced—intellectually, politically, professionally, and personally—by Avery Gordon, whose mentorship and friendship are incomparable. Avery is uniquely talented at engaging people both critically and generously in ways that excavate the best version of whatever has been presented to her. I feel very lucky for our relationship. Sunaina Maira, Lisa Hajjar, and Richard Falk all carefully read early drafts of this project and shaped the direction I subsequently took. Special thanks to Sunaina, in particular, who offered me in-depth and influential feedback, growth opportunities, mentorship, and friendship during the transition of this project from Ph.D. dissertation to book. I am also thankful for Elizabeth and Cedric Robinson, both of whom, separately and together, shaped my intellectual and political development. Their house was a second home for me while in Santa Barbara, and I continue to meet people who are part of the extended family they've fostered.

I am very grateful to Iyko Day for supporting the publication of this book and its inclusion in the Critical Race, Indigeneity, and Relationality book series. This project was strengthened by the generous, careful, and insightful comments of the anonymous reviewers to whom I owe tremendous gratitude. Many thanks to the excellent editors Sarah Munroe, Ashley Petrucci, and Shaun Vigil of Temple University Press and the copyeditor Susan Deeks for a smooth, supportive, and enriching experience. Thanks also belong to my former student Alexander Montello for able research assistance related to obtaining image permissions.

Because I worked on it for many years and in many cities, this project has been enriched by intellectual and political conversations with countless individuals. Thank you to my dear friends and co-conspirators Amanda Batarseh-Sultan and Thea Quiray Tagle for reading and editing a full chapter and for making other crucial recommendations along the way. This project was enabled by the incomparable support and generosity of mind and spirit of two friends in particular: Carly Thomsen and Yousef Baker. Carly sustained me through this process with stunning friendship, brilliance, wisdom, generosity, and warmth, and that's in addition to the direct and illuminating feedback she provided on multiple drafts of this project. Yousef has been an unmatched writing partner—always ready for full-throated political exchange and unwavering encouragement while gently holding each other accountable to the writing time. I am also thankful for the profound friendship and guidance of Elizabeth Rahilly, who has quite literally seen it all. I am incredibly fortunate to have benefited from the brilliance and support of other friends and colleagues, as well, most notably: Abraham Avnisan, Tory Brykalski, Greg Burris, Karisa Butler-Wall, Esmat Elhalaby, Rana Jaleel, Gabi Kirk, Justin Leroy, Neda Maghbouleh, Jennifer Mogannam, Anjali Nath, Daniel Olmos, Steven Osuna, Jade Power Sotomayor, Cesar Rodriguez, Alex Shams, Mejdulene Shomali, Emily Tumpson Molina, and Lee Ann Wang.

My most profound admiration and love belongs to my extraordinary family. Thank you to my cherished in-laws for their affection, insights, warmth, patience, and remarkable generosity: Salah Alhourani, Suhela Aburezeq, Sharehan, Nareman, Rawan, and Mohammed. In addition to embracing me as family from our first moments together, they directly contributed to my research efforts. I am also grateful to my uncles and aunts, cousins, and grandparents for supporting and teaching me in many ways. In particular, thank you to my uncle Sami, aunty Hanan, and cousins Rayya and Karim (from afar) for allowing their Beirut home to become one of my homes, from which I then made my first visit to Palestine in 2012. It is difficult to capture in words the extent of my gratitude, esteem, and adoration for my mother Ranwa Haddad, father Edmond Griffin, and brother Philip. They live their fierce commitments to love, generosity, justice, learning, and laughter, and they've taught me that the best versions of each of those things are inextricably intertwined with the others. In addition to their provision of keen intellectual insights and patient moral support, my mother even provided me direct editorial assistance on the manuscript. Alongside my parents, no one deserves more thanks than my husband, Suleiman Alhourani, who has been my constant champion and unwavering partner. He was also in some ways my co-investigator in the field, coordinating with and accompanying me on key activities. He is a model of insightfulness, kindness, generosity, and support, and I remain in awe of him as we continue to navigate our journey together.

Vehicles of Decolonization

Introduction

Public transportation in the Palestinian West Bank, as elsewhere, is among the most mundane of daily affairs. People from diverse backgrounds with different itineraries come together in transit vehicles to move within and between cities. Yet like all aspects of Palestinian life, public transportation is severely affected by the policies and practices of Israeli settler colonialism, marked by the stops and starts of a capricious system of rule. The cumulative effect of Israeli interference in Palestinian movement is the annexation of Palestinian territory and the frustration of Palestinian life that, in turn, advances ongoing Israeli settler colonialism. But this advancement is continuously contested, and the vehicles of collective Palestinian mobility have become one site at which Palestinian self-determination is (re)claimed and practiced in mundane, spectacular, and creative ways.

This book offers the first study of collective Palestinian mobility and the decolonial power it represents. Through a focus on public transportation in the Palestinian West Bank as a site of social struggle, this study illuminates practices of Palestinian decolonization against and beyond Israeli settler colonialism. Employing a "viapolitical" approach (Walters, 2015), I take seriously vehicles, routes, and journeys and human interactions with them to bring into view the highly contested power dynamics of this particular settler colonial context and the role that mobility plays in constituting them. I present the specific logics and techniques of Israel's program to deny collective self-determined mobility to Palestinians, contributing insights about the ways that control of collective movement functions to enable Israeli settler colonialism. I also highlight the contested nature of this mobility control project, revealing that repeated practices of Palestinian self-determined mobility occur through people's interactions with public transit,[1] whether through everyday use, spectacles of protest, or artistic renderings. In arguing that Palestinian engagements with something as routine as transit contribute to decolonization, I bring together Palestine studies, Indigenous studies, resistance studies, and mobility studies. I consider some distinct but related modes of transit use that contribute to the process of decolonization, the significance of understanding these activities as decolonization rather than resistance, and the ways that the means of mobility condition the possibilities of these decolonial articulations.

An examination of public transit as a site of collective mobility, including its components and the actors that engage it—the system, the vehicles, the routes, the riders and drivers, the organizers, and so on—reveals a collective refusal of immobilization, fragmentation, alienation, and colonization at multiple registers and the collective practices of living alternatives to the settler colonial status quo. First, the quotidian operation and use of Palestinian public transportation enables movement and connection that constitute a rejection of the various institutions, physical structures, rules, and knowledges that were developed to control Palestinian mobility. In the process of enabling and enacting this quotidian mobility via public transportation, West Bank Palestinians dare to create a reality that asserts a kind of Indigenous self-determination over mobility that Israeli settler colonialism seeks to undermine and subvert. Second, Palestinian activists have featured public transportation, in physical and symbolic forms, in their actions because it enables them to reach and educate various international and domestic audiences, despite restrictions on the movement of their bodies and messages. And third, representations of public transportation vehicles appear in Palestine-based artwork as a way to envision self-determined movement across space and time in contravention of settler colonial logics.

A Brief Introduction to Public Transportation in the Palestinian West Bank

Public transportation in the Palestinian West Bank takes many forms. The Palestinian transit system in the West Bank involves a variety of vehicles, such as buses, shared vans, shared taxis, and private taxis, and is coordinated by the Palestinian Authority (PA) in a configuration it calls a "public-private partnership." While companies and individuals own and operate the vehicles and the stations, the PA determines the operating and licensing rules, the routes, and the fares of the system. According to common trade definitions, "public transportation" is a system of vehicles of collective movement that provides service to the public, whether by public or private agencies (or a combination).[2] In other words, the collaboration between the PA and private owners does not negate the "public" nature of Palestinian public transit; it is public because the vehicles operate in a way that provides service to the general public. I only partially include the use of private taxis or taxis for hire in this study. Trade practitioners and scholars differ on whether taxis for hire should be considered a component of public transportation because, while they are available to the general public, their hire tends to happen in an exclusive contractual relationship, such that the rider's engagement of the taxi necessarily excludes its hire by other would-be passengers. Private taxis do come into my analysis, however, in Chapter 3 when I discuss their collective engagement during the Palestinian uprising known as the second Intifada, in which small groups of passengers would contract with taxi drivers to make illicit trips to travel despite Israeli curfews and other mobility restrictions.

In addition to the public-private transit partnership that the PA administers in the West Bank, the book addresses, to different degrees, the Israeli-organized bus system that services Israeli settlements in the West Bank; the bus lines that run between the West Bank and Jerusalem that involve coordination among the PA, Israel, and the bus company; and the train system that has operated under Ottoman, British, and Israeli rule across Palestinian territory. Where these systems appear in the book, the discussions are limited to the ways that Palestinians have engaged them for mundane travel, spectacular political actions, or speculative artistic interventions.

Public transportation is a popular mode of travel in the West Bank, owing in part to the low rate of private vehicle ownership. For example, in 2013 there were 106,913 private vehicles registered in the Palestinian West Bank for a population of 2.643 million (Palestinian Central Bureau of Statistics, 2013, 2020). Since 2013, the number of registered private vehicles for the West Bank Palestinian population has more than doubled, to 226,301 (in 2019) for a population of 2.987 million (Palestinian Central Bureau of Statistics, 2019, 2020).[3] This may be related to the increase of personal debt in the territory, a point to which I return in the Conclusion. In the same period, the number of registered public transit vehicles also increased, but at a lower rate. Registered taxis increased by 9.6 percent, and public buses increased by 60.8 percent. While at first it might appear that the disproportionate increase in private vehicles suggests that public transportation is waning in importance, the number of vehicles per one hundred people in the Palestinian West Bank is still relatively low, at 7.5. Moreover, if the role of public transportation is indeed waning, it is important to trace precisely what may be lost with it. As the terrain of Palestinian movement in the West Bank continues to change in many ways, this book identifies some of the stakes of these shifts.

Settler Colonialism and the Im/mobilization Regime

Palestinian public transportation in the West Bank operates within the context of Israeli settler colonialism and thus becomes one among many sites where the Indigenous struggle against and beyond this project plays out. The goal of Israeli settler colonialism has been to annex the maximum amount of Palestinian land with the minimum number of Palestinian people while simultaneously undermining and invalidating their claim to the land. Over the course of the last century, the Zionist project took root in historical Palestine to establish a Jewish state on that land (Dana & Jarbawi, 2017; Sayegh, 1965). A settler colonial project forged in the crucible of nineteenth-century Europe, it was influenced by a mixture of Western European imperialism and the nationalisms of Eastern and Southern Europe at the time (Lockman, 1996, pp. 21, 23, 26–27). Israeli settler colonialism, like other versions, "is a set of hierarchical social relations that . . . facilitate the dispossession of Indigenous peoples of their lands and self-determining authority" (Coulthard, 2014, p. 7, emphasis removed). In the context of historical Palestine, Israeli settler colonialism has pursued the intertwined dual objectives of deterritorializing and denationalizing Palestinians from Palestine (see, e.g., Abu-Zahra & Kay, 2013; Barakat, 2018; Bhandar & Ziadah, 2016; Jabary Salamanca et al., 2012; Tabar & Desai, 2017). In this book, I examine how the Israeli colonial endeavor targets collective Palestinian movement and vehicles of collective Palestinian movement host rejections, obfuscations, and transcendence of settler colonial ambitions and logics.

While I use the term "settler colonialism" to describe the Zionist project in historical Palestine, I take up Rana Barakat's (2018) renewed call, alongside the critical interventions of Jodi Byrd (2011), Glenn Sean Coulthard (2014), J. Kēhaulani Kauanui (2016), and others, to apply the term in the context of Palestine through the framework of indigeneity. Centering indigeneity and Indigenous perspectives emerges as an imperative from the authority of Palestinians to narrate their history, present, and future (Barakat, 2018; Batarseh, 2019; Bhandar & Ziadah, 2016; Khalidi, 1997; Salaita, 2006). I recognize settler colonialism as a useful analytic to describe the Zionist project in Palestine, while I also underscore the "permanent incompleteness" (Barakat, 2018) of the structural attempt to disappear Palestine and Palestinians (Barakat, 2018, reading Wolfe, 2013). Approaching settler colonialism through the framework of indigeneity requires a careful and confrontational analysis of settler colonialism alongside a nuanced and alert recognition of Indigenous modes of living that exceed it.

Israel's direct occupation of the Palestinian West Bank began with the 1967 invasion sometimes called the Arab-Israeli War or Six-Day War. The invasion quickly turned into a long-term occupation with the creation and installation of physical and legal structures for permanent colonization. But the attempted annexation of the West Bank must be understood as an extension of the broader Israeli settler colonial project across the territory of historical Palestine. The original Zionist colonization of historical Palestine resulted in the displacement of approximately 75 percent of the Palestinian population, who then became refugees. Many of these refugees moved to locations in the West Bank and the Gaza Strip (WBGS), and in this way, the effects of Israeli settler colonialism reverberated across the WBGS long before they were officially invaded. Moreover, the drive to accomplish permanent annexation of the West Bank stems from the same settler colonial project that established the Israeli state on Palestinian land; they are different frontiers of the same expansionist endeavor. Thus, while the fragmenting effects of Israeli strategies vis-à-vis different segments of the Palestinian population have generated divergent experiences and subjectivities, they must be understood as echoes of the same sound—rhythmic repetitions of colonial violence in slightly distinct but resonant forms (see, e.g., Shihade, 2014). Even as Israel develops specific technologies for controlling Palestinian life in the West Bank, those technologies must be understood as part of this broader history of deterritorialization and denationalization.

One of the main approaches through which Israeli rule has advanced its settler colonial ambitions can be generatively described as "enclosures." Like other historical examples of dispossession regimes, the Israeli enclosures have involved the imposition of a mobility regime (what I call "im/mobilization" and discuss later in this introduction), a programmatic denial of autonomous movement, through the deployment of various physical impediments and legal tactics, such as the outlawing or permitting of forms of movement. The Israeli enclosures involve a mobility regime and accomplished the annexation of Indigenous land and the extraction of invented forms of value from it, economic reorganization and subjugation, political repression, and social alienation. This is reminiscent of the multiple dimensions of other historical examples of the enclosures (Bhandar, 2018; De Angelis, 2019; Federici, 2004; Fields, 2017; A. Gordon, 2018; Linebaugh, 2010; Midnight Notes Collective, 1990; Woods, 2009). These interrelated endeavors are well suited to advancing settler colonialism because they attempt to eliminate Indigenous commons, which, in their forms as accessible resources, gathering space, and knowledge exchange, provide a crucial foundation for collective Indigenous self-determination.

In their invitation to "rethink enclosures," Alex Jeffrey, Colin McFarlane, and Alex Vasudevan (2012) identify the commons and practices of commoning as "enclosure's 'other'" (p. 1248), and Peter Linebaugh (2010) refers to the commons as "enclosure's antonym" (p. 11). Across different contexts, examples of commoning have appeared both as targets of the enclosures and as responsive practices for resisting, undermining, or overcoming enclosures.[4] Similarly, the commons feature in this book in two ways. First, I note that the imposition of the Israeli enclosures has attempted to destroy Palestinian commons, resulting in not only the direct annexation of territory but also the destruction or confiscation of the bases for social, political, and economic autonomy, including knowledge of and access to Palestinian land. Second, the system of Palestinian public transit in the West Bank functions through practices that amount to "mobile commons" in opposition to and in excess of the Israeli enclosures (Papadopoulos & Tsianos, 2013; Sheller, 2018). In their study of cross-Mediterranean migration, Dimitris Papadopoulos and Vassilis Tsianos (2013) explain that the *mobile commons* are composed of living networks of shared knowledge about transnational movement, knowledge that passes informally and through social networks while it conveys dynamic information that can affect survival and quality of life.[5] Palestinian public transit in the West Bank also involves *mobile commoning* because it incorporates social interactions in its routine functioning to transport people to accomplish necessary elements of social reproduction.[6] I discuss West Bank public transit and mobile commoning in Chapter 3 but mention it here to signal that the Israeli enclosures are a reactionary response to the power of Palestinian commons, which, in turn, continue to evolve into forms appropriate for transcending the latest techniques of the enclosures.

I bring the idea of enclosures together with the framework of settler colonialism to assert that the Israeli enclosures impose controls over Palestinian mobility that have spatial, social, economic, and political consequences and that, in turn, facilitate the annexation of Palestinian land and the dispossession of the Palestinian people. Following the work of Coulthard (2014), I examine the enclosures as a mode of entrenching a *colonial* relation rather than a capital relation (although the concept of the enclosures has been particularly generative in understanding the emergence of capitalism, as many scholars have shown). Such an analytical shift centers the subject position of people subjected to colonization (pp. 10–11). For Coulthard, this shift reveals that, in the case of First Nations people and the Canadian state, it is "the history and experience of *dispossession*, not proletarianization, [that] has been the dominant background structure in shaping the character of the historical relationship between Indigenous people and the Canadian state" (p. 13). Similarly, I argue that dispossession has been, and continues to be, the dominant background structure shaping the relationship between

Israel and Palestinians and that dispossession has been partially accomplished through the enclosures strategy. The mobility regime imposed as part of the Israeli enclosures has enabled the confiscation of movement as a basis for indigeneity. In other words, as Israel denies Palestinian self-determined movement and monopolizes control over the means and terms of mobility, it attempts to eliminate Palestinian access to and familiarity with land as evidence of Palestinian indigeneity and to assert the entrenchment of freely mobile Israeli life on the same land as a permanent fact.

Scholars have traced the Zionist version of the enclosures strategy back through the British Mandate period and the early seeding of settler colonialism in Palestine, before (and often in service of) the formal establishment of the Israeli state (Bhandar, 2018; Fields, 2017). In this book, I focus on a particular chapter of the Israeli enclosures story that has unfolded in the West Bank since the 1967 invasion. As anti-Indigenous repression, the Israeli enclosures strategy was developed in tandem with emerging global technologies of border diffusion. The concept of diffused bordering processes accurately describes the physical impediments and legal tactics that Israel has used to impose its enclosures. Israel has developed a system of controlling Palestinian mobility by diffusing border processes across the territory of the West Bank (Tawil-Souri, 2012; Weizman, 2007). A number of factors contribute to the elasticity of those processes, including the construction or removal of physical impediments, such as roadblocks; the actual movement of their physical location, whether in the case of settlements whose edges continue to expand or that of "flying" checkpoints that pop up in different places along Palestinian routes; and the changing rules that govern engagement with these installations, such as different rules for who can cross certain checkpoints for what reason and when (see, e.g., N. Gordon, 2008a; Makdisi, 2008; Weizman, 2007). These processes have created a borderscape that is partially composed of actual encounters with Israeli military and civilian personnel, rules, and structures, as well as of the varying *possibility* of those encounters. But the borderscape is also shaped by the mobility strategies Palestinians develop in relation to and in the shadow of the possibility of getting ensnared in this net. I focus in the first part of the book on the development of the Israeli *border-enclosures* to describe the shape and function of Israel's mobility regime. The border-enclosures advance the annexation of land (and the extraction of settler colonial value from it) and the social, political, and economic degradation of Palestinian communities by using physical and legal forms connected to contemporary global trends of diffusing border technologies across a given territory rather than only around its edges.

The Israeli border-enclosures strategy manifests in *im/mobilization*. The reader may note throughout the book that I use "im/mobilization" to describe both the mobility regime to which Israel subjects West Bank Palestinians and the modality through which Palestinians experience settler colonialism. Julie Peteet (2017), Yara Sharif (2017), and others discuss Palestinian "immobilization" as constrained mobility and containment and their many consequences (Peteet, 2017, pp. 61–64; Y. Sharif, 2017, pp. 28–30, 47), and Helga Tawil-Souri (2012) advances the idea of "uneven im/mobilities" to describe how Israel's permits, alongside checkpoints, road systems, and other diffused bordering processes, enable Israeli mobility through the limitation of Palestinian movement. Hagar Kotef (2015) explains that this Israeli "'regime of movement' . . . subjects to Israeli control the circulation of people, goods, and services—and with them the economy, society, and polity—in the West Bank" (p. 27). Drawing from this robust scholarship, I use the term "im/mobilization" to capture the variety of ways that Israel denies Palestinian self-determined movement, whether to force, forbid, or otherwise create "uneven" experiences, means, and features of movement (Sheller, 2016; Tawil-Souri, 2012). While *limiting* Palestinian movement is a large part of the story, immobilization is also connected to other modes of controlling mobility, such as forcing people to move from their homes and their land or making travel so tedious or dangerous that it becomes a punishment unto itself. About Israel's siege of Nablus during the second Palestinian Intifada (2000–2005), Beshara Doumani (2004) writes, "The real story . . . is the slow and cruelly systematic asphyxiation of an entire social formation. The aim is to make the small routines of everyday life—such as working, going to school, visiting friends and relatives—so difficult as to precipitate major demographic shifts that, in turn, would break the Palestinian will to resist and make the colonization of their lands inevitable and irreversible" (pp. 48–49). Doumani's observation of the specific logic at play in that moment has also been the generalized logic animating Israel's im/mobilization program for the entire Palestinian West Bank, extending well beyond the end of the second Intifada. While the end of that Intifada brought about a loosening of outright closure, the infrastructural and strategic elements of Israeli control, as well as the ease and constant threat of their activation (Handel, 2015), continue to condition the possibilities of West Bank Palestinian movement until today.

The analysis in this book focuses on Israel's im/mobilization program in the West Bank as it emerged in response to the successes of the first Palestinian Intifada (1987–1993) and was subsequently refined and intensified through the Oslo years, the second Intifada, and to the present day. Kotef (2015) locates the "consolidation" of this mobility regime "sometime between the Oslo Accords (1993—the formal beginning of the ongoing 'peace process') and the years following the El Aqsa Intifada (2000)" (p. 28), while Tawil-Souri (2012) notes that the modern-day regime has historical roots in attempts to control Palestinian mobility throughout colonial history. Although I limit my discussion to the im/mobilization program that emerged after Israel's invasion of the West Bank in 1967, and especially the period of its refinement from 1990 to the present (slightly earlier than Kotef), I emphasize the function of im/mobilization to advance the broader project of Israeli settler colonialism, and I do so to connect this most recent modality of rule to previous iterations.

The im/mobilization program is composed of concrete Israeli practices that extend control over Palestinian movement in the service of its enclosure strategy, and, as suggested earlier, those practices can be understood as nodes in a diffuse border network. The border nodes in operation in the West Bank during the time of my fieldwork (2012–2016) involved shifting and static elements, physical structures and bureaucracies, immovable physical barriers, and unpredictably varying policies and practices. Some examples include a massive obstruction ("the Apartheid Wall"); hundreds of physical impediments; a regime of movement permits; static checkpoints and a program of "flying," or ad hoc, checkpoints; segregated roads and license plates; segregated settlements; segregated public transportation; and various military installations.

These im/mobilizing components work together to impose a racially inflected zero-sum logic on movement in the West Bank, generating a relational condition in which the ease, convenience, speed, and security of Israeli movement is conditioned on making Palestinian movement burdensome, unpredictable, slow, and dangerous (see, e.g., Tawil-Souri, 2012).[7] Through these dynamics, im/mobilization generates a "racial regime of mobility" in which Israel attempts to define a Palestinian subjectivity marked by its lack of self-determined mobility. As Cedric Robinson (2007) and Brenna Bhandar (2018) have demonstrated, racial regimes are created through cultural, economic, geographic, and political maneuvers that manufacture alibis for dispossession, justifying or even hiding it. Racial regimes are quite useful to settler colonial projects, which often involve appropriating indigeneity itself to naturalize the dispossession of Indigenous people (see, e.g., Freeman, 2010; Tuck & Yang, 2012, pp. 10–13; Wolfe, 2006). Lila Sharif (2016) reading Raja Shehadeh (2007), for example, identifies the Palestinian landscape as a site where Palestinian relationships to the land are confiscated and then claimed as the basis for Israeli indigeneity (see also Fields, 2010, 2017). Similarly, Israel's border-enclosures have sought to strictly control the *knowability* of Palestinian land, including who may know it and how. By attempting to impose this monopoly—one that, as I demonstrate in Chapter 3, is pointedly contested through the mundane operations of Palestinian public transit—Israel's racial regime of mobility frustrates spatial knowledge as one element in its contrived denial of Palestinian self-determined movement.

The racial regime of im/mobilization has generated a distinct social and territorial reality for West Bank Palestinians characterized by the shattering or fragmentation of territory and society. Fragmentation has occurred in many ways across the historical territory of Palestine, separating Palestinians from Israelis and Palestinians from one another within and among the areas in which they live (Gregory, 2004; Parsons & Salter, 2008; Tawil-Souri, 2012). As I discuss in Chapters 1 and 2, the territorial map imposed through the Oslo Accords and Israel's related diffusion of networked border nodes across the Palestinian West Bank have implemented a programmatic frustration of social, political, and economic connections across Palestinian enclaves, resulting in separation and alienation. But the *bantustanization* of the Palestinian West Bank is linked to a broader fragmentation across historical Palestine.[8] As the Israeli settler colonial project has expanded and contracted, it has taken on different social and physical textures in different segments of historical Palestine. In particular, these differences manifest in distinct but linked deployments of bordering as a way of separating and ordering Palestinian life. Israel's current ruling strategy vis-à-vis Palestinians appears to harness the global phenomenon of the multiplicity of the border as a set of practices that create difference (Mezzadra & Neilson, 2013). This has meant that the features of Palestinians' relationships to the Israeli state vary across space and time even as the overall orientation of the Israeli settler colonial project toward Palestinian denationalization (Abu-Zahra & Kay, 2013) and deterritorialization remains constant.

As Palestinians mounted anticolonial challenges, Israel physically fragmented the land of Palestine through technologies of mobility control, thereby separating Palestinians from Israelis but also separating Palestinians from one another (N. Gordon, 2008b). Furthermore, Israel has since developed increasingly distinct programs to deal with the Palestinian populations in each fragment. As a result, different categories of Palestinian subjects have been produced, formalized through identity documents, and defined in part by varying degrees of access to space and mobility (Abu-Zahra & Kay, 2013). For example, Palestinian citizens of Israel can move about with relative ease inside Israel but deal with direct discrimination in almost every aspect of their lives, including housing and education (Tawil-Souri, 2012, pp. 8–10, 12). Palestinian residents of East Jerusalem can move through some checkpoints denied to WBGS Palestinians but also, for example, experience discrimination and constant efforts to displace them from their homes. West Bank Palestinians deal with social institutions (at least nominally) run by fellow Palestinians but confront denials of self-determined movement virtually everywhere outside of their town of residence. One of the many consequences of this fragmentation is that there is no singular Palestinian experience of Israeli settler colonialism and therefore no singular Palestinian experience of mobility, as Israel has diversified its approaches to the fragmented Palestinian populations its practices have generated. For this reason, *Vehicles of Decolonization* focuses on mobility and public transportation in the West Bank in particular. Beyond illuminating the reasons for a methodological choice, this point about the fragmentation that results from enclosures illuminates one of the ways that collective Palestinian mobility via public transportation in the West Bank subverts settler colonial enclosures—by establishing, through mundane, spectacular, and artistic engagements, mobile connections across a fractured landscape.

Together, the racialized differentiation of im/mobilization and its fragmenting effects reveal the collective nature of im/mobilization. Certainly Israel's attempts to control Palestinian mobility frustrate both individual and collective movement. But im/mobilization is properly considered a collective issue. Im/mobilization is imposed on West Bank Palestinians as a group and, in turn, functions to produce that group as categorically ineligible for self-determined mobility. In addition, as explained earlier, the fragmenting effects of im/mobilization undermine Palestinian collectivity. Where im/mobilization is one modality through which West Bank Palestinians collectively experience Israeli settler colonialism, it is unsurprising to find that collective Palestinian mobility is also a site where Palestinian power is cultivated in opposition to and in excess of settler colonialism. In this context, the collective Palestinian exercise of self-determination over mobility can be understood as both the target of Israeli im/mobilization and a vehicle of decolonization.

Decolonization and Self-Determined Mobility

Despite Israel's imposition of im/mobilization through border-enclosures, West Bank Palestinians persist in moving around the territory. Certainly, travel for Palestinians, especially among Palestinian cities, towns, and villages, has become more cumbersome and dangerous over the past twenty-five years as a result of the border-enclosures. Yet Palestinian movement has not ceased entirely in the West Bank. Instead, it has become a viable means of challenging settler colonialism by moving around, against, and through it. In offering an account of engagements with public transportation as decolonization, I do not mean to trivialize the ongoing effectiveness of these enclosures; rather, I mean to identify the ways that transit as a mobile site and a site of mobility hosts the active cultivation of alternative relations of power that exceed and will outlast settler colonial domination and dispossession.

The cause of Palestinian liberation parallels other Indigenous struggles that focus on recovering land and the social relationships rooted in it (Coulthard, 2014, p. 13; Tabar & Desai, 2017, p. xi) to generate a decolonized future that transcends the networked domination of colonization. This book primarily analyzes the organized mobility of West Bank Palestinians, attending to the terms on which they can move about, access, and relate to and on their land, as a way of revealing assertions of Indigenous self-determination. I understand self-determination as the collective exercise of autonomy to shape the living present and future rather than only the rejection of alien rule.[9] This is particularly relevant in the context of the Palestinian West Bank. Through the Oslo Accords, Israel has abdicated direct responsibility for the welfare of Palestinians as the population of the West Bank that it has occupied in different configurations since 1967. Nonetheless, Israel has expanded its control across the territory, generating the material conditions of Israeli domination and the denial of collective Palestinian self-determination. This systematic denial appears in a number of social arenas, and in this book I focus on collective mobility as a terrain of struggle against and beyond this denial.

Self-determination requires the material conditions that enable Indigenous collective autonomy for multiple generations. Jeff Corntassel (2008) crafted the phrase "sustainable self-determination" to signify the process of sustaining meaningful Indigenous life, including its relational components, with and on Indigenous land (pp. 107–108, 116–121). In describing the first Intifada as itself an expression of Palestinian self-determination, Edward Said (1995) explained that the uprising "creat[ed] a model for communal life that is not based upon the exclusive authority of one party, one sultan, one representative state apparatus" (pp. 159–160). These illuminations of meaningful Indigenous self-determination point to the collective practices of autonomous world-making at its heart.

As such, meaningful self-determination and decolonization are thoroughly imbricated. Noura Erakat (2019) explains that

> the call for self-determination among Palestinians has increasingly ceased to refer to the desired national state alone, and has come to encompass a more abstract demand for freedom. It is a call that implicates an attachment to the land as a means of memory, existence, and dignity. . . . Palestinian self-determination has come to signify an ability to pursue a future, collectively and individually, as a natural condition of possibility and not as a form of resistance to the condition of social death. (p. 20)

Decolonization might be thought of as the ongoing process of asserting and exercising self-determination, and in settler colonial contexts this process necessarily centers the restoration of land and Indigenous relationships to and on it (Tuck & Yang, 2012, pp. 5–7). Eve Tuck and K. Wayne Yang (2012) emphasize that "decolonization in the settler colonial context must involve the repatriation of land simultaneous to the recognition of how land and relations to land have always already been differently understood and enacted; that is, *all* of the land, and not just symbolically" (p. 7).[10] The repatriation of land and Indigenous relationships to it requires the restoration of self-determined movement on the land. So the autonomous exercise of collective Palestinian mobility in contravention of settler colonial logics of domination makes up one significant dimension of decolonization.

The decolonization I illuminate in this book is a *process*; I do not claim that engagements with public transit have completed the work, but it is a process that has immediate significance rather than only gesturing toward some future condition. I consider three modes of engaging with public transit that contribute to this immediacy and material significance: routine participation, spectacular political organizing, and artistic interventions. The mundane participation of riders and drivers together in the Palestinian transit system generates a "mobile commons" (Papadopoulos & Tsianos, 2013) where a living network of collective knowledge about movement across territory operates and cultivates opportunities for communality. Activists' use of public transit vehicles and symbols transcend the fragmenting effects of the enclosures to forge meaningful political alliances. And artists creatively represent public transit vehicles as a way to practice and assert self-determined mobility through space and time. Each of these modes of engagement with public transit fosters collective Indigenous relationships mediated by land. Together, these three modes of engagement form a constellation of decolonial mobility. Tim Cresswell (2010) defines "constellations of mobility" as "particular patterns of movement, representations of movement, and ways of practising movement that make sense together" (p. 18). In the case of Palestinian public transit engagements, the three modes I examine work together to *make sense*—in other words, to generate alternative, decolonial mobility logics and relations.

Self-determined mobility might be generatively considered as one among many elements of "mobility justice." Mimi Sheller (2018) demonstrates the ways that mobility and justice coconstitute each other and offers an inclusive outline of the multiple and necessary components of a mobility justice agenda. She underscores that such agendas must emerge from the actual, situated practices of those already pursuing the cause of mobility justice (p. xv). In conversation with this work, I argue that examining multiple modes of engagement with Palestinian public transit through the lens of decolonization highlights the importance of self-determined mobility to the pursuit of mobility justice in settler colonial contexts. Proposing this connection is not without its complications; as Tuck and Yang (2012) have warned, social justice efforts and decolonization are often "incommensurable" in the sense that certain formulations of social justice may perform "settler moves to innocence" that retrieve or excuse the beneficiaries and institutions of settler colonialism from actively undoing its ongoing violence. I do not resolve this incommensurability between Indigenous self-determined mobility and the broader concept of mobility justice. Rather, by situating Palestinian self-determination in relationship to mobility justice, I invite the proponents of mobility justice to consider this incommensurability. For example, rather than celebrating Jerusalem's light rail as a mobility justice success because of its environmental effects, we might instead take cues from Palestinian civil society to understand it in terms of the annexation of Palestinian land it enables as it supports the circulation of Israeli settlers who live in the West Bank and work or shop in Jerusalem (Barghouti, 2009).

In proposing a relationship between Palestinian mobility practices and decolonization, the rich literature addressing Palestinian resistance is generative. This set of political and scholarly works consider armed resistance, nonviolent resistance, cultural resistance, transnational solidarity resistance, and other practices of various groups responding to many and changing modes of domination (see, e.g., Baylouny, 2009; Maira, 2013; Peteet, 2005; Qumsiyeh, 2011; Qutami, 2014; Tawil-Souri & Aouragh, 2014). Within this body of work, the Palestinian concept of *sumud* remains fertile if contested. The Arabic word *sumud* (steadfastness) is strongly identified with the Palestinian struggle, and it primarily represents a committed disposition to remaining on the land despite colonial efforts at displacement, but it also includes a wide repertoire of practices that enable staying and that symbolize survival.[11] The term has sometimes been associated with "passive resistance," "passive nonresistance," and even "aggressive nonresistance" (Tamari, 1991, p. 61), which reflects attempts to mark the political significance of seemingly nonpolitical action or inaction. Salim Tamari (1991) traces the history of the concept of *sumud* up to and through the first Intifada and, in so doing, connects previously passive expressions of steadfastness to the active organizing of popular committees. Rema Hammami (2005) asserts that, during the second Intifada, *sumud* took on a more "active connotation" and manifested in "continuing with daily life and movement" (p. 18). Similarly, in her ethnographic research among Palestinian activists in 1948 Palestine,[12] Nijmeh Ali (2019) challenges the association of *sumud* with passivity by identifying multiple "patterns" of *sumud* ("practical," "personal," "moral," and "cultural") and gathering them under the term "active *sumud*," which in Ali's formulation "means taking responsibility, constructing future initiatives, and moving from the traditional understanding of cultural *Sumud* . . . toward a transformative *Sumud*" (p. 100).[13]

The work to analyze multiple meanings and expressions of *sumud* describes a repertoire that is still ultimately tied to remaining on the land, including the cultivation of meaningful social and spatial relationships that give substance to that remaining. These collective practices are animated by what Sarah Ihmoud (2019) theorizes as *murabata*, "a politics of staying in place," a cultivation of meaningful *ties* to place through routine and repeated practices of being in and using it (pp. 519, 523). The linking of *sumud* with the practices of staying on one's land and "staying in place" illustrates the interrelatedness between this renowned Palestinian steadfastness and the concept of self-determined mobility, which must include autonomous decisions about *not* moving (in other words, *staying*). I put *sumud* and mobility into conversation and argue that collective exercises of freedom to move *and* to remain constitute a powerful force of decolonization that undermines settler colonial logics and dispossessions while also giving fuller meaning to the notion of *staying on* (and *returning to*) one's land. Connecting *sumud* and mobility contributes important nuances to our understanding of the concept and practices of *sumud* and locates the political significance of multifarious engagements with public transit in the context of settler colonialism.

Furthermore, discussions about *sumud* generatively intersect with social movements and resistance scholarship, which has grappled with questions about how to understand the significance of expressions of people power in mundane settings (see, e.g., Abu-Lughod, 1990; Bayat, 2010; Jeffress, 2008; Jones, 2012; Scott, 1985, 1990, 2009, 2012; Y. Sharif, 2017; Sharp et al., 2000). In exploring the significance of Palestinian use of public transit at mundane, spectacular, and artistic registers, I propose Palestinian transit as a site where the connections can be seen between everyday "nonmovement movement" (Bayat, 2010, 2017) and more direct forms of political intervention. In the Conclusion, I argue that Palestinian public transit hosts a range of manifestations of people power, which, in turn, demonstrates how mundane activities exist in relationship to more pointed forms of decolonization. It is for this reason that I have titled the book *Vehicles of Decolonization* rather than "Vehicles of Resistance."[14] I mean to signal my view that the politics of different modes of engagement with public transportation relate to and amplify one another while working together to decolonize mobile relationships among people and land.

A Brief Note on Research Methodology

Throughout this book I use the methodology of "viapolitics," a mode of inquiry coined by William Walters (2015) that attends to the routes, roads, and vehicles—the means of movement—and human interaction with them at literal and representational registers to uncover power dynamics that mediate human mobility. Walters developed his concept of viapolitics in relation to transnational migration, but Sheller (2018) has demonstrated that transnational migration must be considered only one component, albeit integral, in a broad agenda of mobility justice. "Viapolitics" can apply to examinations of "domestic" mobility, especially in a context in which border processes are diffused across a territory such that what counts as "inside" and "outside" is a constantly changing, contested, and subjective matter. Walters (2015) proposes three theses on viapolitics in which he asserts that representations of the means of mobility, such as media coverage of the arrival of refugee boats, articulate the conditions of possibility for mobility politics; that vehicles operate as "mobile sites of power" connected to broader mobility regimes, such as the role of inspecting commercial transport vehicles in the broader struggle over migration; and that the particular features of different means of mobility give rise to certain forms of political contestation, such as the case of deportations by commercial airlines that are sometimes challenged by passengers. Contributing to the "set of inquiries" outlined by Walters, I adopt a viapolitical approach to Palestinian transit in the West Bank to identify the role that the means of collective mobility play in the contestation between Palestinian self-determination and Israeli settler colonialism.

I collected the data featured in this book over the course of six trips to Palestine, amounting to twelve months in total, from 2012 to 2018, with the bulk of the fieldwork occurring during ten months in 2013 and 2014. I conducted participant observation of Palestinian public transportation in the West Bank. Based primarily in a suburb of the Greater Bethlehem area, I used transit to travel both within Bethlehem and from Bethlehem to all of the major cities of the West Bank. Until March 2014, I was also able to visit Jerusalem, Jaffa, Tel Aviv, and Haifa.[15] All of these trips were accomplished via public transportation, both bus and shared van. In addition to participant observation, I gathered information about collective Palestinian mobility through informal conversations in Arabic with approximately sixty public transit passengers and twenty drivers, most of whom were residents of the Greater Bethlehem area. In addition to speaking with drivers, I asked them to draw maps of their routes, which figure in my analysis in Chapter 3. I also interviewed, in Arabic and English, six transportation officials from the PA's Ministry of Transportation (Wizarat an-Naql w al-Muwasalat) and from the Bethlehem Traffic Department (Da'irat as-Seir). In 2014, I worked with the Applied Research Institute–Jerusalem (ARIJ) to meet with transit officials and drivers as part of an ARIJ project to draft a preliminary public transit map for the city of Bethlehem. I collected the cultural productions and artifacts generated by political activists, supplemented when necessary with interview data, and employed other cultural studies methods, including documentary research and textual and image analysis, which feature in Chapters 4 and 5. I discuss my research methods and methodology further in the Appendix.

Chapter Overview

To understand the politics of different engagements with Palestinian public transportation in the West Bank as a site of social struggle, one must first account for the context in which it operates. In Chapter 1, I present a detailed discussion of the phased development of im/mobilization as the mobility regime that imposes the Israeli enclosures strategy on the Palestinian West Bank in furtherance of settler colonialism. In response to Palestinian protests against the Israeli invasion and occupation of the West Bank and Gaza Strip, which began in 1967, Israel developed counterinsurgency technologies to contain popular resistance. During the ensuing fifty-plus years, these tactics have increasingly come to revolve around controlling Palestinians' movement. I start with the proposition that historical repertoires of enclosures can be understood as mobility regimes that target the commons in ways that degrade social, political, and economic life to accomplish land annexation and value extraction. Then I trace the development of im/mobilization against West Bank Palestinians, which emerged in the face of an uprising against the manifestly colonial nature of a purportedly temporary occupation as a way of retrenching Israeli settler colonialism.

As the Israeli enclosures in the West Bank developed and became more concentrated in the im/mobilization regime, they drew from and contributed to global trends of diffusing border processes. In Chapter 2, I examine the current state of im/mobilization through the lens of critical border studies, which recognizes borders as a set of practices that extend far beyond the site of a geopolitical line. Israel has contributed to the creation of a borderscape in the West Bank by diffusing border processes across the entirety of the territory even while it refuses to settle on its official, external borders. In the chapter, I describe physical structures such as the Israeli Apartheid Wall, the Jewish-only settlements inside the West Bank, a slew of barriers (boulders, trenches, earth mounds, gates, etc.), and stationary checkpoints, with other kinds of im/mobilization practices, such as Israel's system of segregated roads; the imposition of "flying," or moving, ad hoc, checkpoints; the complex permit system; heightened surveillance; and Israel's economic pressures and imposition of taxes on the Palestinian West Bank. But the West Bank borderscape is also shaped by Palestinian challenges to these border processes, particularly in the form of collective mobility via public transportation. For that reason, I outline the components of Palestinian public transportation, which manages to function in the West Bank despite Israeli im/mobilizations.

Having sketched the contours of the West Bank borderscape, I move to my analysis of engagements with Palestinian public transit at three registers—the mundane, the spectacular, and the artistic—to demonstrate that transit fosters and enables decolonial activity. In Chapter 3, I show *how* Palestinian public transportation manages to function in the West Bank despite the Israeli enclosures and discuss its significance. Even if ordinary Palestinians still suffer a great deal of hardship and inconvenience in trying to move around, this responsive system of public transit constitutes a quotidian but meaningful rejection and obfuscation of, and counterpoint to, the Israeli border-enclosures. I show here how local knowledge networks created and sustained by riders and drivers together attempt to ameliorate some of the unpredictability and disruptiveness of Israeli im/mobilizations. Where this mobility regime extends settler colonial power, irreverent Indigenous movement, enabled by this dynamic sociality, has become a kind of Palestinian mobile commoning. I trace the sociality embedded in the mundane Palestinian transit system back to the more overtly rebellious activities of off-road taxi drivers during the second Palestinian Intifada. The off-road Intifada taxis presented drivers with a way to resist the Israeli siege on the Palestinian West Bank economy and riders with a way to resist Israel's physical and social disruptions of Palestinian mobility. Through the social negotiation that fuels the transit system, Palestinian riders and drivers refuse confinement and fragmentation; reclaim spatial knowledge, the authority to create it, and the power to share it; and repeatedly practice decolonized relationships among people and land.

While routine participation in the Palestinian public transportation system involves mobile commoning against, around, and through the settler colonial enclosures, overtly political engagements with transit vehicles also contribute to decolonization. In Chapter 4, I examine the incorporation of transit vehicles into political protest actions. I analyze three political demonstrations that occurred in the decade just past and used public transportation, and specifically the bus, as both literal and symbolic vehicle. The protests on which I focus are the Palestinian Freedom Rides of 2011; the run of the annual mobile workshop known as the Freedom Bus in 2014; and the torching of a new segregated bus line in 2013. I argue that the bus uniquely enabled activists' communication of their messages both to fellow Palestinians and to international audiences. Their focus on the bus allowed the activists to move among a collection of terminological frames, invoking concepts of racial segregation, racism, and apartheid alongside occupation and colonialism. Through terminological movement, the Palestinian activists captured the many facets of Israeli settler colonialism in ways that resonate with global solidarity networks and that simultaneously educate them about the specifics of Israeli im/mobilization.

I round out my analysis of different kinds of public transit use by turning to artistic engagements. In Chapter 5, I analyze representations of public transit in Palestinian artwork as a vehicle for manifesting Palestinian self-determined movement across space and time in contravention of the logics of the Israeli colonial enclosures. I consider three creative renderings of transit vehicles by Palestinian artists: Decolonizing Architecture Art Residency (DAAR)'s architectural provocation *Right to Movement* of 2012; Mohamed Abusal's installation and photography project *A Metro in Gaza* of 2011; and Larissa Sansour's futuristic film *Nation Estate* of 2012. As these artists reimagine Palestinian transit, they create opportunities to reclaim Indigenous relationships to space and time, in opposition to the colonization of both, to exercise and anticipate collective self-determination. In doing so, they reveal the interconnectedness of autonomous mobility and decolonization.

Finally, in the Conclusion I argue that considering these various engagements with public transit in the Palestinian West Bank illuminates the interrelationship among different forms of people power. I offer a discussion of scholarly schemas for understanding expressions of people power in terms of the intentionality that animates it or its demonstrable effects on state control. By taking a viapolitical approach to studying collective Palestinian mobility in the West Bank, I note that public transit as a site of social struggle reveals that multiple registers of people power work in concert not only to resist settler colonial logics of im/mobilization but also to practice and preserve alternative relations of mobility. Having identified this repertoire of decolonization, I turn to the current, constantly changing landscape in the Palestinian West Bank, which is threatened with an intensified program of annexation, as well as the less visible changes induced by neoliberalism. In particular, I address the increase in private automobile ownership linked to an increase in private debt and suggest that, as time reveals the consequences of these trends, we should also consider their effects on collective mobility and the decolonial power it hosts.

1

The Im/mobilization Regime of the Israeli Enclosures in the West Bank

By 5:30 A.M. on any given weekday (Sunday through Thursday), Jameel would be sitting in a shared taxi blinking the sleep from his eyes as he headed toward Checkpoint 300 at the edge of Bethlehem.[1] The taxi—or sometimes it was a shared Ford transit van, depending on which vehicle had stopped for him that morning after he walked up the hill to the main road—would approach the gate of the checkpoint. Then Jameel would get out of the taxi and line up along with thousands of other Palestinians from the southern West Bank who were heading into Jerusalem for work. In 2013–2014, the entrance to the terminal had two fenced-in entry lanes (and a third exit lane): one for the "humanitarian line," which included those with medical permits, the elderly, the disabled, women, and children, and the other for everyone else, primarily adult men younger than sixty-five. Sometimes, the Israeli military would close or temporarily halt the humanitarian line; it appears to have been permanently deactivated since 2014.[2] In the early mornings when Jameel would cross, the large majority of those crossing with him would line up in the regular lane (nonhumanitarian), so it would be very crowded. While waiting in the congestion, young and able-bodied men in a rush would sometimes climb the outside of the corridor and drop down through the bars at the top to cut in the middle of the long and slow line.[3] The jeering and grumbling were audible. But the line cutting was not the main source of delay; the tempo of the line was determined by the first set of Israeli soldiers who checked documents before passing people through the turnstiles, perhaps in consultation with their colleagues in the next building, who operated the metal detectors or staffed the final kiosks where fingerprints and permits were examined.

After completing the trip through the multiple segments of the checkpoint, Jameel would crowd into one of the buses waiting on the other side of the structure. During these morning periods, the buses fill up quickly, passengers crowding to get into the space of the bus, whether into a seat or the standing room, and then depart in the direction of the Old City of Jerusalem. On their way, the bus would pass through predominantly Jewish West Jerusalem, making many stops as passengers, a few at a time, would deboard at the stop closest to their final destination. A college graduate in his mid-twenties, Jameel had worked for five years in local restaurants, barely able to earn enough to make his student loan repayments to the individuals from whom he borrowed, let alone enough to build a house or get married. When the opportunity arose to obtain an Israeli permit to enter 1948 Palestine, he left his job to work in construction in West Jerusalem. Jameel's permit was recreational, connected to a cultural organization, and did not authorize him to work. One of his coworkers had obtained a medical permit to seek treatment at a Jerusalem hospital, which he also used to access construction work opportunities in the area. Another interlocutor who worked in construction obtained his work-based permits directly from Israeli construction contractors for several decades. Yet other West Bank Palestinians who work in Jerusalem obtain permits through expensive brokers who connect permit seekers to Israelis pretending to be employers who make money from sponsoring permits without offering actual jobs. These are elements of what Cedric Parizot (2012) calls "a well-organized informal border economy" (p. 4). Of course many others, including three of my regular interlocutors, found ways to cross the Apartheid Wall to access job opportunities without any permit at all by joining others to accomplish illicit nighttime crossings.[4] This category of undocumented worker usually stays for several consecutive workdays, sleeping at the building site, to avoid the risk of repeating the illicit crossing every day. But because of his permit, Jameel did commute back and forth between Bethlehem and Jerusalem daily.

I open with the details of Jameel's morning commute to signal how West Bank Palestinians are subject to a mobility regime with social, political, and economic dimensions as part of Israel's efforts to colonize Palestinian land. Jameel sought work in Jerusalem due to the relatively higher wages and greater number of job opportunities available to him there, compared with the low pay and scarce work in the Palestinian West Bank economy. These features of employment are the result of Israeli efforts to induce Palestinian economic dependence on Israel to undermine political resistance. One of the ways Israel implemented its social and political strategy on the West Bank was through a mobility regime—more specifically, creating the pressure to direct the flow of Palestinian workers across the Green Line. This flow was then captured and disciplined through a connected system of checkpoints and permits, the current versions of which I discuss further in Chapter 2. This connected system of checkpoints and permits—what I identify as nodes in a network of diffused bordering practices—shaped Jameel's daily commute so that it involved multiple forms of public transit, long periods of waiting, and routine encounters with the unpredictable discretionary power of Israeli soldiers.

In this chapter, I examine the historical development of Israel's im/mobilization regime in the West Bank as an example of an enclosures strategy for advancing Israeli settler colonialism. I argue that controlling Palestinian mobility—denying Palestinians the self-determination to decide when, whether, how, and why to move—has allowed Israel to undermine Palestinian economic, political, and social life on Palestinian land. In turn, this multidimensional ruling strategy has enabled the annexation of the maximum amount of Palestinian land while disrupting and unearthing Palestinian life in the same territory. Israel has developed the enclosures strategy as a way to avoid deciding between complete annexation of the territory into Israel and full withdrawal from the West Bank while simultaneously preserving its overall settler colonial program.

Israel's strategy echoes historical examples of the enclosures. Gary Fields (2017) has carefully traced the historical resonances across the enclosures of fifteenth- through seventeenth-century England, the colonization of North America, and the establishment of Israel. He argues that across each of these three case studies, elite groups mobilized similar laws, architectural decisions, and cultural devices to impose enclosures on the subject population, which, in turn, manifested similar effects on the landscapes of each place.

There are yet other resonances across historical cases of "enclosures," particularly in terms of their dispossessive and subjectifying effects. For example, in her analysis of the English enclosures, Silvia Federici (2004) argues that the enclosures movement enabled the transition from feudalism to capitalism by targeting the commonly held land of feudal peasants—land that bolstered their capacity for self-sufficiency and thus their independence to resist the exploitation of feudal lords.[5] She demonstrates that the imposition of the enclosures obliterated the commons—the territorial basis for peasant self-sufficiency, political community, and social reproduction—with particular emphasis on the weaponization of gender in this process (pp. 61–115). In the context of Canadian dispossession of First Nations people, legal, spatial, and social tactics were also combined. For example, Brenna Bhandar (2018) identifies the invention of "the juridical category of the Indian" as one "binding together identity with access to land" (p. 150), and this has led to a "politics of recognition" that continues to advance "the dis-possession of Indigenous peoples of their lands and self-determining au-thority" (Coulthard, 2014, p. 25). These examples point to the political and social consequences of the enclosures that advanced broader projects of col-lective dispossession.

Stuart Hodkinson (2012) attempts to synthesize the diverse literature on enclosures into unifying themes, updating them to account for the spread of enclosures in the urban context. He proposes that three elements consti-tute enclosures: "privatisation," which is "the physical-legal process" of cat-egorizing "something" (such as "land, services or ideas") and assigning rights for access to it; "dispossession," representing the losses sustained by those who are now excluded from access; and "capitalist subjectification" or "the *encapturing* of people, place, space and culture" within extractive, alienating capitalist logics (p. 509, emphasis in the original). The enclosures, then, produce particular subjects and social relations as both method and result.

To these generative arguments about the multiple registers of enclosures that afford them their efficacy I add the perspective that we might consider enclosures to involve the imposition of a mobility regime, particularly when land (or space in general) is at stake. By involving physical structures, legal and bureaucratic instruments, and influence over labor flows, enclosures exert control over the mobility of the target population: restricting its move-ment onto or across lands that were once commons, criminalizing "purpose-less" movement through the creation of categories such as the "vagabond," and forcing movement into spaces of "encapturing" such as waged jobs, res-ervations, or prisons. Together, these effects contribute to enclosures, wheth-er the goal is to "seek out new spheres of life for accumulation, take place within spaces that have already been enclosed but where capitalist relations are under threat, or target spaces or networks that embody forms of com-mons, not just as natural resource pools, but also as socially constructed re-sources that provide degrees of protection from market forces and accumula-tion strategies" (Hodkinson, 2012, pp. 508–509). By shaping social, political, and economic subjectivities and relations, the mobility regime of the enclo-sures helps to accomplish their intended dispossessions.

Indeed, in the case of the Israeli enclosures, the settler colonial drive to fabricate settler indigeneity and erase Palestinian indigeneity has included the creation of a Palestinian subject defined by its lack of access to free movement and the territorial familiarity and national coherence that move-ment would enable. This subject becomes the necessary foundation on which an Indigenous Israeli subjectivity, defined in part by free (but "or-dered," as Kotef [2015] argues) movement and full territorial access, is con-structed and asserted.

True to form, the Israeli enclosures have imposed a mobility regime involving physical, legal, bureaucratic, and economic elements. Israel's twenty-first-century version of the enclosures relies on updated forms of spatial control—namely, the tactics of diffuse bordering. I examine the current features of this "im/mobilization" regime in the next chapter. This mobility regime has accompanied and contributed to the vitiation of the Palestinian economy, the frustration of autonomous Palestinian movement, the corroding of Palestinian politics, and the destruction of Palestinian social life. In doing so, the multiple registers of enclosures have advanced Israel's settler colonial project to permanently annex Palestinian land and eliminate Palestinian indigeneity. As I noted in the Introduction, I do not compare Israel's enclosures to other examples to make an argument about the emergence of a political economic system in Palestine.[6] Instead, I note the parallels between these different iterations of enclosures to connect the present case with similar *"economies of dispossession* . . . those multiple and intertwined genealogies of racialized property, subjection, and expropriation through which capitalism and colonialism take shape historically and change over time" (Byrd et al., 2018, p. 2).[7]

Im/mobilization, the mobility regime through which Israel's enclosure strategy has been most effectively applied, emerged in the aftermath of Israel's invasion of the West Bank and Gaza Strip (WBGS) in 1967 and was refined in the period after the first Palestinian Intifada (1987–1993). As I mentioned in the Introduction, a focus on the emergence of a particular ruling technique does not suggest a clean break from earlier approaches. This chapter describes the dynamics leading from the beginning of Israel's invasion and occupation of the West Bank through the emergence of the im/mobilization regime, but I also note that these developments continued a broader (and older) settler colonial program.

Israel's enclosure strategy was not a master plan developed and then implemented in one fell swoop. On the contrary, it cohered in a piecemeal fashion as a counterinsurgency strategy for dealing with Palestinian resistance to the unfolding but erratic reality of Israeli settler colonialism in the West Bank. I offer a historical account of the development of the Israeli enclosure's strategy to highlight the central role im/mobilization came to play in it. This im/mobilization regime conditions the possibilities for Palestinian collective movement in the West Bank, and for that reason it is important to understand how the regime advances settler colonialism to grasp the decolonizing power that Palestinian mobility exerts in the same context.

Before proceeding further, I want to pause to explain my terminological move to apply "enclosures" as a framework for understanding one of Israel's strategies vis-à-vis the Palestinian West Bank. Just as scholarship on Palestine continues to proliferate, so, too, do the many terms proposed to describe—

mostly, but not entirely, for scholarly circles—Israel's approach to Palestinian people and land. Intellectuals use various words and phrases to represent Israel's practices in the Palestinian West Bank and in historical Palestine more broadly: terms such as "occupation," "apartheid," "settler colonialism," "denationalization," "dispossession," "closure," "fragmentation," "separation," "imprisonment," "containment," "exploitation," "lawfare," "de-development" (Roy, 1995), "spacio-cide" (Hanafi, 2009), "politicide" (Kimmerling, 2006), "sociocide" (Abdel Jawad, 2013), "geography of disaster" (Handel, 2009), "matrix of control" (Halper, 2000), and more, each of which accomplishes significant elucidation.[8] Some of these terms are more useful as descriptors of Israel's apparent goals, while others seem to better describe Israel's tactics or strategies, although the line that separates those three categories remains terribly blurry, at best. Furthermore, Loubna Qutami and Omar Zahzah (2020) have argued that "the lexicon that Palestine is articulated through is becoming seemingly *less* familiar to the Palestinian collective condition and intellectual and political tradition. This lexicon is at times remarkably unfamiliar to Palestinians' nuanced understandings of their colonial conditions or of a political program that their collective ideals of freedom mandate" (p. 69). Given the wide variety of terms and their applications, I have several reasons for focusing on "enclosures."

First, by applying "enclosures" to Israeli settler colonialism, I mean to invoke a term that represents multiple layers of control: land annexation, movement restriction, economic reorganization and subjugation, political repression, and social alienation. The term "enclosures," I think somewhat uniquely, represents all of these simultaneous facets of Israeli power as they advance settler colonialism, highlighting the role of mobility regimes in doing so. Second, I conjoin enclosures with the notion of diffuse bordering practices in the next chapter to update the concept of enclosures in its twenty-first-century iteration. While hedges and fences, alongside legal and cultural devices, were the order of the day in the case of the English enclosures, Israel's enclosures today are being carried out through more advanced technologies of spatial control. Connecting the idea of diffused bordering processes to enclosures then updates our understanding of how enclosures work while putting them into the broader conversation about how bordering has become diffuse around the world. Third, invoking the term "enclosures" situates Israeli control as a reactionary force that is both responding to and threatened by Palestinian commoning, or forms of Palestinian collectivity that enable self-sufficiency and self-determination. I discuss the mobile commons later in the book, but here I mean to explain my adoption of the term "enclosures" as a way to think the commons' other (to flip the formulation of Jeffrey et al. [2012], who write about the commons as the enclosures' other [p. 1248]). In sum, I offer the application of the term "enclosures" in the hope of illuminating a nuanced, updated, and contextualized picture that reveals the central role of im/mobilization as a mechanism for advancing settler colonization. I also hope that the nuances the term signals enable an analysis that is more consistent with West Bank Palestinians' understandings of and experiences with Israel's approach to the Palestinian West Bank today.

Establishing Permanence: The Settler Colonial Occupation

To begin tracing the emergence of Israel's im/mobilization regime and its role in imposing enclosures on West Bank Palestinian life from 1990 to the present, it is necessary to understand the changing relationship between Israel and the West Bank that gave rise to this development. Israel's settler colonization of Palestinian territory in the West Bank is a frontier of the broader settler colonial project pursued in the name of Zionism. This frontier, like all frontiers, was and continues to be highly contested not only by the Indigenous population but also from internal challenges. The im/mobilization regime was developed as a way to navigate these various contestations. Controlling mobility in a way that denied self-determination to West Bank Palestinians enabled the piecemeal annexation of Palestinian land by coupling it with the anti-Indigenous, counterinsurgent effects of economic dependence, political destabilization, and social fragmentation.

The relationship between Israel and Palestinians living in the West Bank has shifted through various stages of the Zionist settler colonial project. The declaration of the State of Israel in 1948 precipitated the expulsion of 750,000 Palestinians in what is known as *an-Nakba* (the catastrophe); they became refugees and fled not only to neighboring countries but also to the West Bank and the Gaza Strip in a move they believed was only temporary. While their living conditions—many in makeshift camps, others living precariously in cities—were a direct consequence of the founding of Israel, the West Bank remained under Jordanian control until 1967. In June of that year, the Israeli military invaded the West Bank and the Gaza Strip in what is sometimes referred to as the Six-Day War or, in Arabic, *an-Naksa* (the setback). This invasion ushered in a new but related territorial relationship in which Israel's presence became intertwined with Palestinian geography.[9] What at first appeared to be a short-lived invasion never came to an end; instead it has continued now for more than half a century.

The first twenty years after the 1967 invasion revealed deep conflicts within the Israeli ruling class about how to approach the territory. These different factions were united by the primary concern of how to claim the max-

imum amount of Palestinian land while avoiding the absorption of Palestinian people into the Israeli national project (Farsakh, 2005b, pp. 52, 55;
Hanieh, 2003; Weizman, 2007, p. 58). However, as Leila Farsakh (2005b) explains, at the time of the 1967 war, the Israeli government was divided into
two camps that held differing opinions for how the newly occupied territories should be treated. One camp advocated for total annexation of the West
Bank and the Gaza Strip as Israeli territory, arguing that they "were an integral part of Israel, the 'promised land'" (p. 32). The other camp wanted to
selectively incorporate land that was not densely populated by Palestinians,
hoping to avoid absorbing a population that would threaten the Jewish identity of the nation. These two camps were oriented to more or less permanent
resolutions, both of which had troublesome implications for the settler colonial nation: either annex the entire WBGS territory and then face international sanction and the implications of absorbing a sizable Indigenous Palestinian population into the settler nation; or allow Palestinian national
independence, on a fraction of the territory, once and for all, which would
require dismantling all aspects of Israeli presence on that land (Andoni,
2001, pp. 209–210), not to mention dealing with the political ramifications.

To avoid choosing between these two tricky resolutions, Israeli leaders
proceeded with a long-term occupation that they characterized as "temporary." This claim of temporariness appeared to be an effective way of diffusing some early political opposition (N. Gordon, 2008a, pp. 34, 2008b, pp.
24–25). However, the temporariness of the occupation was quickly belied by
Israel's attempts to create "facts on the ground" to support "a de facto claim
over the WBGS" (Weizman, 2007, p. 93; Farsakh, 2005b, p. 53, respectively).
The "facts on the ground" approach sought to build as many inhabited Israeli structures in strategic places under the expectation that any future diplomatic negotiations would grant sovereignty over populated areas to the
state to whom the inhabitants belong (Khalidi, 2010). For example, shortly
after the 1967 invasion, the Israeli military began establishing institutions to
maintain itself over the long term, such as the military court system (Hajjar,
2005, p. 50). Physical structures also began to appear, including Jewish Israeli residential colonies (Figure 1.1), military bases to protect those settlements, and roads connecting them.

In June 1967, the same month that Israel began its occupation of the West
Bank, Yigal Allon, then Israel's minister of agriculture and a member of the
Labor movement, presented a plan to fortify the eastern edge of the West
Bank, newly under Israeli control. The Allon Plan proposed that Israel would
claim a corridor along the eastern edge of the West Bank because of its strategic location on the border with other Arab neighbors. This corridor had
been evacuated during the 1967 war by military brigades that destroyed Palestinian villages in the Jordan Valley to the north and south of Jericho and

Figure 1.1 Har Homa settlement on top of Jabal Abu-Ghnaim, as seen from the top of the neighboring Bethlehem hill. *(Photograph by the author.)*

drove out their residents (Weizman, 2007, pp. 57–58). One important feature of the Allon Plan—indeed, the feature that had the most lasting impact on Israeli policy—was Allon's proposal that the security zone be occupied by Israeli residential settlements in addition to military outposts. The idea was that "civilian" settlements would serve as strategically placed lookouts, able to alert military bases to oncoming threats, and would be expected to slow down invaders (p. 101). At the same time, the benefit of using civilian settlements in this context, rather than military outposts, was that they would express the Israeli intention of annexing the land permanently (p. 59).

The Allon Plan then provided for the return of approximately 50 percent of West Bank land to Palestinian control (connected to Jordanian rule) in two densely populated swaths in the northern and southern West Bank (Hanieh, 2003). While the intention to assume control over the territory of the West Bank was evident in the Allon Plan, it did not propose for Israel to maintain deep or permanent territorial involvement across and between the densely populated Palestinian areas. The Allon Plan was never formally adopted but was largely implemented nevertheless (Weizman, 2007, pp. 58, 80). Moreover, its reliance on civilian settlements as buffers along borders with Arab areas continued to influence subsequent developments of the occupation.

The cementing of the colony as the driving force behind Israel's occupation of the West Bank—in other words, the alignment between the supposedly temporary military occupation and the more permanent settler colonial agenda—occurred in the aftermath of the elections in 1977 in which the conservative Likud Party beat the Labor Party. Ariel Sharon, who had been appointed minister of agriculture, the position previously held by Allon, collaborated with Avraham Wachman on a plan to establish blocks of settlements (in which larger colonies could sustain new, smaller outposts) that would surround Palestinian areas and cut through them with restricted roads (Weizman, 2007, p. 81). His strategy was extended in 1978 by the World Zionist Organization, which outlined a five-year plan during which Israeli settlements would be built around and between Palestinian cities, cutting them off from one another. The anticipated result of the plan was that "the minority population [the Palestinians] would find it difficult to form a political and territorial continuity" (Hanieh, 2003). Again, a territorial strategy would enable political containment, this time with an eye toward fragmentation, not only of the population, but also of any future Palestinian state.

While none of these plans for settlement were carried out to the letter, their shared interest in proliferating and extending Jewish-only civilian colonies across the West Bank was thoroughly realized. In the four years after Likud's 1977 electoral victory, the number of Jewish Israeli settlements in the West Bank doubled and the settler population quadrupled. These settlements were built in an ad hoc, improvisational way, guided by different and sometimes opposing ideological concerns (Weizman, 2007, pp. 92–93). But after the 1977 election, the overall route of their expansion moved across West Bank land and between Palestinian cities.

The residential colony or settlement was the key to effectively establishing facts on the ground, and Israel quickly transformed its military occupation into a "civilian occupation" (Segal & Weizman, 2003; Weizman, 2007, pp. 57, 81). Furthermore, the central role of the settlement ensured the primacy of controlled movement and mobility in the settler colonial project and at this frontier in particular. Ann Stoler (2016) has noted that "a 'colony' as a common noun is a place where people are moved in and out; a place of livid, hopeful, desperate, and violent *circulation*. It is marked by unsettledness, and forced migration. A 'colony' as a political concept is not a place but *a principle of managed mobilities*, mobilizing and immobilizing populations according to a set of changing rules and hierarchies that orders social kinds" (p. 117). Indeed, as the colony became the driving political concept in shaping Israel's approach to the Palestinian West Bank, its *principle of managed mobilities* congealed in an enclosures strategy. The need to manage mobilities emerges out of the displacements, the imbalances, and the frictions that the colony causes because the people the colony displaces and dispossesses do not accept their domination. Similarly, im/mobilization, a mobility regime that enables the expansion of "the colony" (and settler colonialism) and is thus animated by the "principle of managed mobilities," developed as a strategy for undermining Indigenous resistance to denationalization and deterritorialization.

As Israel began laying down permanent structures across the WBGS, tension rose between the invading forces and the invaded people. From 1968 to 1970, Palestinian protest actions and strikes were held in the West Bank and Gaza. The Israeli military suppressed Palestinian resistance during this time with significant force, led by General Ariel Sharon, who earned the nickname "the Tank" for using aggressive tactics, such as home demolitions and the shelling of civilians. In the first six years of the occupation, hundreds of anti-occupation resisters were jailed, exiled, or assassinated (Qumsiyeh, 2011, pp. 118–120).[10]

This political unrest provoked the early expressions of the Israeli enclosures strategy, where we begin to see coordination among the imposition of control over movement; the annexation of Palestinian land; and the containment of Palestinian people spatially, politically, economically, and socially. To more permanently undermine the impulse to resist, and in response to Israeli economic pressures, Israeli leaders sought to induce Palestinian dependence on the Israeli economy (Kipnis, 1987, p. 135; Sayigh, 1986, p. 52). Soon after invasion, provisions were put into place to allow Palestinian workers to seek employment in Israel, particularly in the construction and agricultural sectors (Farsakh, 2005b, pp. 86, 93–94), and Palestinian markets were inundated with cheap Israeli goods that edged out more expensive Palestinian ones (Farsakh, 2005b, p. 36; Sayigh, 1986, pp. 47, 56). Thus, the Palestinian West Bank and Gaza Strip were unilaterally and partially absorbed into the Israeli economy to contain their populations politically. These early efforts to induce Palestinian economic dependence would be intensified in the coming years and had the immediate and lasting effect of coercing Palestinian movement, as Palestinian workers were put in the situation of having to seek gainful employment in Israel.

The goal of cultivating Palestinian economic dependence on Israel dovetailed with other Israeli economic interests. From 1965 to 1968, the years leading up to and just after the 1967 invasion, the Israeli economy experienced a recession as the result of planned economic restraint policies and an increase in wages for Israeli workers following demands by the Histadrut, the national labor organization (Greenwald, 1973; Nitzan & Bichler, 2002, pp. 123–127; World Bank, 1969). The 1967 invasion and occupation of the WBGS presented new opportunities and challenges in the wake of this recession. Israeli control over these Palestinian territories produced a population of low-wage workers who would drive down production costs and stabilize the Israeli economy (Farsakh, 2005b).

To advance this economic agenda, the military adopted a strategy of slow de-development in Palestine (Roy, 1995, pp. 4, 128). Establishing control over major swaths of land and water, the natural resources of the WBGS regions, Israel severely burdened Palestinian agriculture (Farsakh, 2005b, pp. 37, 109–10; N. Gordon, 2008a, p. 30). The Israeli government also imposed an asymmetrical tariff structure on the WBGS under which it limited the kinds of goods that could be exported from those territories into Israel and severely restricted exports to Jordan and other countries (Farsakh, 2005b, p. 36). The restrictions resulted in significant reliance on Israel for Palestinian imports and exports, which made up 95–99 percent of Palestinian gross national product from 1970 to 1991 (p. 39). During this period, Israel produced 90 percent of WBGS imports and absorbed 70 percent of its exports (p. 39); Palestinian employment inside the WBGS fell, while the percentage of Palestinian workers working inside 1948 Palestine (in other words, in the Israeli labor market) grew exponentially (p. 82). This growth in Palestinian employment in the Israeli economy, and the role of WBGS Palestinians as a semicaptive consumer market, presented the faltering Israeli economy with the opportunities needed to end the recession while simultaneously inducing Palestinian economic dependence on the Israeli market.

Yet these economic and political dynamics exacerbated the ambivalence within Israeli society regarding the question of annexing Palestinian land and absorbing Palestinian people. In these early years of the occupation we begin to see the uneven, and sometimes contradictory, approaches to biopolitical control that ultimately led to the im/mobilization regime.

For the first five years of the occupation, the West Bank and the Gaza Strip were declared closed military zones, and movement into and out of the territories was restricted (Parsons & Salter, 2008, p. 704). But by 1972, military directives known as "general exit orders" were issued to allow Palestinian movement into and out of the West Bank, Gaza, East Jerusalem, and 1948 Palestine. Israel had already begun to issue identity cards in orange cases to the Palestinians of Gaza and the West Bank, laying the groundwork for a system of tracking and restricting movement. A subset of Palestinians who were barred from entering 1948 Palestine or East Jerusalem received green ID cards (Tawil-Souri, 2011a, pp. 71–72, 2011b, p. 222). Even for orange-card holders, movement was not entirely uninhibited, as Palestinians from the West Bank or Gaza were not permitted to stay in Israeli-claimed territories or East Jerusalem between 1 and 5 A.M. (B'Tselem, 2017a).

The "general exit" orders permitting Palestinians to cross among the West Bank, Gaza, Jerusalem, and 1948 Palestine were still in effect through the beginning of the first Intifada and lasted until 1989 when they began to be restricted (and eventually were revoked in 1991) (B'Tselem, 2017a). During the general exit era, Israel began to cultivate Palestinian economic dependence on the Israeli market (Kipnis, 1987, p. 135). Sara Roy (1995) argues that Israeli leaders pursued this dependence plan to undermine Palestinian economic independence because it would destroy the basis for Palestinian national independence. Permitting Palestinian movement into Israel was advantageous because it allowed Palestinian labor flows into the Israeli market, and the integration of Palestinian labor was the first dimension of inducing Palestinian economic dependence on Israel.

The Emergence of the Im/mobilization Regime

As a counterinsurgency strategy, inducing Palestinian economic dependence was not entirely successful, and Palestinians continued to protest during the first fifteen years of Israel's occupation of the West Bank. During this period, Palestinian resistance was largely (though not exclusively) directed from outside—by the Palestinian Liberation Organization (PLO) living in exile and fighting from the Jordanian and Lebanese fronts. After the Black September War of 1970, King Hussein expelled the PLO from Jordan, forcing the organization to concentrate its activities in Lebanon, particularly in the south (Khalidi, 2007, pp. 136–138). Then, in 1982, Israel invaded Lebanon and drove the PLO from its last holdout in an area adjacent to Palestine. The PLO relocated its headquarters to Tunis, making it more difficult for the exiled leadership to effectively coordinate on-the-ground resistance. For Palestinians living under military occupation, though, this turn of events dashed the hopes that relief would be brought to them from outside (Johnson et al., 1989, p. 32). They took up the mantle of organizing resistance, and soon thereafter the first Palestinian uprising, the Intifada, began (Andoni, 2001, p. 209; Qumsiyeh, 2011, p. 134).

Late in 1987, a series of incidents in which Palestinians were killed by Israeli soldiers provoked popular demonstrations in the WBGS. As Mazin Qumsiyeh (2011) argues, these protests are properly viewed as the beginnings of the first Palestinian Intifada (p. 135).[11] At the heart of the Intifada was a challenge to the sustainability of the 1967 occupation and specifically to its tangible aspiration for perpetuity (Khalidi, 2007, p. 198). The rebellion opposed the building of Israeli outposts and settlements in the WBGS, the establishment of the Israeli civil administration to control everyday Palestinian life, the annexation of Jerusalem, and other aspects of the occupation (see, e.g., Andoni, 2001, p. 210).

The spatiality of military occupation at the time also influenced the possibility and success of the popular rebellion. By 1987, the Israeli military operated as the dominant authority in the WBGS, which, in its attempt to subordinate Palestinian life to the Israeli state in a relationship reminiscent of "direct colonialism," maintained a presence throughout the territories (Hammami & Tamari, 2000, p. 3). For the Palestinian resistance, this meant that its opponents could be found everywhere and, thus, expressions of opposition could take place anywhere. Indeed, the uprising manifested on every street corner, city square, and rural hillside, all over the WBGS (e.g., Andoni, 2001, p. 211).

The Intifada was a popular, grassroots mobilization that deployed a diverse array of tactics. It involved a high level of participation from all sectors of Palestinian society, and local leaders coordinated actions within their communities. Furthermore, because Palestinian areas were still somewhat connected, and because the Israeli military still exerted singular authority in the region, life in the Palestinian refugee camps, urban centers, and rural areas did not vary sharply in terms of exposure to Israeli rule (though, of course, there were distinctions in other facets of life; Andoni, 2001, p. 211). This diffuse and popular mass mobilization registered its opposition to military occupation in many creative ways: "Popular committees challenged Israel's Civil Administration; an underground school system was established after the Israelis closed the schools; Israeli products were boycotted; people threw out their military identity cards; and there was a tax rebellion, most famously in Beit Sahour" (Andoni, 2001, p. 212; see also Qumsiyeh, 2011, p. 141).[12] Among the endlessly diverse actions, students and other residents resorted to traveling on foot or donkey to circumvent the Israeli military's repressive curfews and roadblocks.[13]

In 1988, after the first Intifada began, Israel faced the dilemma of how to reconcile the emerging military demands to impose control on the rebelling Palestinian population of the WBGS with the existing economic integration of Palestinian labor (Farsakh, 2005b, p. 121). Israel responded by developing tactics for conditioning WBGS Palestinians' mobility on Israeli permission, revoking Palestinian self-determined movement primarily from the West Bank and Gaza Strip into Jerusalem and 1948 Palestine. In January 1990, Israel began to issue identity cards containing a magnetic strip to Palestinian residents of Gaza and the West Bank who were allowed to enter Jerusalem or 1948 Palestine. At first, such cards were widely issued, and the most common category of WBGS Palestinians barred from entry were those who had been arrested or detained by the Israeli authorities for any reason, even those against whom charges were never filed (Tawil-Souri, 2012, p. 14). Still, the ID card system was predicated on subjecting Palestinians to a thorough bureaucracy of surveillance.

At this time, the Israeli government also attempted to revise its earlier efforts to drive Palestinian labor flows from the WBGS into Israeli-claimed territory by pressuring Israeli employers to reduce their reliance on Palestinian workers. In 1990, Israel's legislature, the Knesset, passed a law to harshly penalize any employer caught employing undocumented Palestinian workers, as well as to fine the workers themselves a sum that amounted to roughly half of their monthly income (Farsakh, 2005b, p. 121). The government acted at a time when Israel was beginning to see an influx of Jewish migration after a long period in which it had hit its lowest levels (Farsakh, 2005b, p. 127), a salve for the demographic anxieties of the settler colonial project. The disintegration of the Soviet Union in 1991 provided most of these newcomers: between 1989 and 2000, approximately one million Jewish people from the former Soviet Union immigrated to Israel (Friedberg, 2001, p. 1373; Sabella, 1993).[14] As economic refugees, these immigrants were expected by Israel to be willing to work in the same low-wage sectors as WBGS Palestinians (e.g., agriculture and construction) and thus serve as a possible replacement for Palestinian workers in the Israeli economy. Naomi Klein (2008) explains the anticipated significance of the arrival of these immigrants: "They bolstered Zionist goals by markedly increasing the ratio of Jews to Arabs, while simultaneously providing a new pool of cheap labor. Suddenly, Tel Aviv had the power to launch a new era in Palestinian relations. . . . [Closure] quickly became the new status quo, with territories sealed off not just from Israel but from each other" (p. 546). However, Farsakh (2005b) contends that, in the end, an influx in foreign workers did *not* significantly replace Palestinian laborers. In the same period, and likely because of Israel's plan to build public housing for the new immigrants, there was a boom in the Israeli construction sector, which increased the demand for workers across the board (Farsakh, 2005b, pp. 128, 138), a demand that could not be met entirely by the new immigrants. Still, the availability of new and, most important, non-Palestinian immigrants enabled the Israeli military command in the WBGS to exercise more control over Palestinian mobility, such that it was able to impose closure on Palestinian territories during periods of intensified conflict, and the proportion of non-Palestinian workers in the labor pool would pick up the slack (p. 138).

With the onset of the Persian Gulf War in 1991, Israel further tightened restrictions on Palestinian movement, this time citing Palestinian solidarity with Saddam Hussein's threats against Israel as a pretext. For six weeks, the West Bank and the Gaza Strip were "closed," meaning effectively that no movement at all was allowed into 1948 Palestine (Nakhal, 1996). Subsequently, the "general exit" orders that had been in place for almost two decades were revoked entirely, and movement of WBGS Palestinians into Jerusalem and 1948 Palestine was restricted to those able to obtain Israeli permission (B'Tselem, 2017a). The cancellation of the general exit orders in 1991 marked the beginning of what is known as Israel's "Closure Policy"

(Hass, 2002).[15] Closure was accompanied by the imposition of the permit system that required any WBGS Palestinian who wanted to cross into Jerusalem or 1948 Palestine to obtain a permit, or *tasreeh* in Arabic. The Israeli-issued magnetic ID cards mentioned earlier in this chapter were a prerequisite for obtaining a permit for any reason (Tawil-Souri, 2012, pp. 14–15). Palestinian workers could apply for an Israeli permit to work in 1948 Palestine *only* if they managed to meet the combined requirements of a formal request by an Israeli employer, registration with the Employment Service offices, *and* security and tax clearance by the Israeli military (Farsakh, 2005b, p. 121). The interlinked systems of ID cards and travel permits began to resolve the tension between Israeli demand for Palestinian labor and the need for repression against an occupied Indigenous population through control over Palestinian mobility. In fact, despite its purported justification as a security measure for Israel, the permit system has become an invaluable tool for manipulating Palestinians into becoming informants for Israel, with the granting of a permit offered as incentive or the revocation of a permit threatened as punishment (see Berda, 2018).

Regardless of the official starting point of the closure policy, we might consider it a cohesion of Israel's then emergent strategy of controlling Palestinian movement to enact its settler colonial enclaves. The introduction of a regime that premised Palestinian movement on Israeli-issued identity documents in 1990 provided the foundation for the closure policy because closure was administered through the ID cards. Moreover, we might consider the official policy to condition WBGS Palestinian mobility on Israeli permission alongside the ongoing efforts to compel WBGS labor flows into the Israeli market. By generating pressures for movement and simultaneously disciplining that movement, the Israeli im/mobilization regime and its denial of Palestinian self-determined movement began to cohere.

This mobility regime breathed new life into the Israeli enclaves after the significant challenges from the Intifada. Certainly, as described earlier, Israeli policy advisers were drafting plans to separate Palestinians spatially (a form of controlling mobility) to undermine their political cohesion as early as the mid-1970s. But their experience with the wide scale of popular participation in the grassroots political mobilizations of the first Intifada demonstrated the dangers of Palestinian unity for the future of Israeli settler colonialism. Imposing control over Palestinian mobility allowed Israel to subject the Palestinian population to a condition of *fragmentation*, breaking Palestinian territorial connections both between and within the West Bank and Gaza. The closure policy was one element of this emerging program. By the end of the first Intifada, Israel had also installed checkpoints and roadblocks, periodically imposed curfews, and instituted a system of travel permits, all of which increasingly worked in concert.

Fragmentation and Im/mobilization

If the first Intifada is understood as a demonstration of the unsustainability of a permanent Israeli occupation and the advancement of settler coloniza- tion, it was thoroughly successful. The diffuse, creative, and popular forms of resistance cost the Israeli economy dearly. As Qumsiyeh (2011) notes, in the first three months of the Intifada alone, Israeli revenues declined by 30 percent from the year before; tourism suffered; exports to the West Bank, Gaza, and other countries fell; and military spending skyrocketed (p. 157). The peace talks that resulted in the Oslo Accords came out of the moment of possibility opened up by the Intifada. The PLO approached the Oslo pro- cess as the beginning of a path toward Palestinian national independence. They also saw an opportunity to formally relocate their leadership to the West Bank and Gaza after so many years of trying to lead from outside Pal- estine (Andoni, 2001, p. 210; Khalidi, 2007). Israel joined the process with a recognition that its approach to the West Bank and Gaza could not con- tinue on its existing course indefinitely. However, Israeli officials did not retreat from a settler colonial agenda. Instead, they leveraged the process to implement a different approach that relied more heavily on controlling Pal- estinian mobility.

Having never resolved the issue, Israel still faced the same conundrum as before: whether to completely annex the WBGS and thereby absorb large numbers of Palestinians or cede a small portion of the territory for Palestin- ian national independence as dictated by United Nations Security Council Resolution 242. While the success of the Intifada forced the Israelis to alter the course of the occupation, it was not successful in forcing them to make a choice between those two options. Instead, as Helga Tawil-Souri (2011a) explains, "The Oslo 'peace' agreements helped 'normalize' the occupation, resulting in a Palestinian landscape that has experienced a *shift* in the meth- od of Israeli control, but *not its withdrawal*" (p. 76). Preferring to postpone the decision indefinitely while simultaneously creating favorable facts on the ground, the Israelis pursued an agenda of preserving Israeli presence in the WBGS, with a focus on imposing strict and endlessly complex separa- tion between Jewish Israelis and Palestinians in the territory (Andoni, 2001, p. 210; Farsakh, 2005b, p. 69; N. Gordon, 2008a, p. 35; Weizman, 2007, p. 10). This would remain the primary theme in the Israeli attitude toward negotiations with Palestinians, most famously articulated in a slogan by Prime Minister Ehud Barak in his 1999 electoral campaign: "Peace through separation" (Pacheco, 2001, p. 195).

Indeed, Israel appeared to pursue territorial separation between the Pal- estinian West Bank and 1948 Palestine through the construction of its Apartheid Wall.[16] However, the reconfiguration of Israel's relationship to the West Bank and to West Bank Palestinians through the Oslo Accords reveals a more complex and partial separation that in turn evidences Israel's enduring colonial motivations. Because of the advancement of civilian outposts, settlements, and the civil and military infrastructures they necessitate across West Bank land, the territorial separation of Israelis from Palestinians has become a tricky affair, involving micromanagement of space and mobility (Peteet, 2017; Weizman, 2007). This is precisely the interwoven spatial reality that has necessitated a reliance on diffused bordering tactics, discussed in the next chapter.

What did become clear from the *type* of separation pursued through the Oslo Accords was a manifest settler colonial motivation to pursue "the political imperative for more land with fewer people on it, more expulsion and less population to control" (Khalili, 2012, p. 184). A key element of this program was the abdication of responsibility for civilian affairs to the Palestinian Authority (PA) while retaining for Israel control over the land without consideration for the Palestinian people on it (N. Gordon, 2008a, pp. 35–37). Yet Israel only reconfigured rather than completely withdrew their involvement with Palestinian civilian affairs, particularly with respect to identity documents and the operations of the Israeli Civilian Administration Office in the West Bank. Thus, it appears that if the Israelis genuinely wanted to extract themselves from Palestinian civilian life, they have failed. Instead, the situation can be described as "the double process of inclusion and exclusion," the total denial of rights to Palestinians while subjecting them to a system of Israeli control and inducing dependence on that system (Tawil-Souri, 2012, p. 8).[17] Of the system of identity cards on which WBGS Palestinian mobility came to be conditioned, Tawil-Souri (2011b) writes, "ID cards . . . achieve a central goal: supervising the Palestinian population, neither (immediately) liquidating it nor integrating it into the fabric of Israeli society, but controlling it and rendering it manageable to state power" (p. 224). Her argument can be applied to the whole im/mobilization regime, as it enabled a continued program of managing the Palestinian population being dispossessed of their land.

Still, while separation has been only partially and dubiously pursued, Israel succeeded through the Oslo Accords in negotiating a comprehensive *fragmentation* of Palestinian life into distinct segments vulnerable to isolation.[18] The 1995 Interim Agreement on the West Bank and the Gaza Strip (also known as Oslo II or the Taba Agreement), divided up territorial sovereignty in the West Bank between the Israeli and Palestinian authorities into areas A, B, and C. Areas A and B are composed of noncontiguous parcels under PA civil control, but only Area A falls under sole PA security control; Area B is subject to joint Israeli-Palestinian security control. Area C, which is under Israeli civil *and* security control, was and is the only contiguous territory in the West Bank (World Bank, 2008). The Oslo schema created a Palestinian territorial configuration that scores of scholars have described as an "archipelago" composed of municipal islands, now separated from one another by Israeli roads, settlements, checkpoints, roadblocks, walls, military bases, and an encompassing bureaucracy (Khalidi, 2005; Makdisi, 2008, p. 92; Nusseibeh, 2011, p. 14; Weizman, 2007, pp. 7, 11). In addition to "archipelago," other frequently used terms that convey similar meanings are "bantustans" and "cantons" (see, e.g., Farsakh, 2005a; Pappé, 2008; Reinhart, 2006). Israel's success at imposing fragmentation is now visible on the map (Figure 1.2).

With this complex constellation of territorial fragmentation in place, Israel intensified its enclosures strategy in the West Bank, including its economic, political, and social dimensions. Having achieved some flexibility from the control of labor demands, as explained in the previous section, the Israeli military was free to periodically impose closure on the WBGS Palestinian population. From 1994 to 1999, WBGS Palestinians endured 443 days of active Israeli closure, resulting in an average of ninety days of unemployment per year for Palestinian workers relying on employment inside Israeli-controlled areas (Farsakh, 2010). In addition, the Israeli settler population and number of housing units for settlers on WBGS land increased by nearly 50 percent (Farsakh, 2002, p. 20). Farsakh (2005b) notes that the theory of immigrant workers replacing Palestinian labor did not bear out in the numbers (with some notable exceptions during the 1990s) in part because Palestinian labor was still needed and, in fact, was preferable for work in settlement construction (p. 139).[19] Absorbing Palestinian workers into settlement construction was appealing for many reasons: it continued the policy of inducing Palestinian economic dependence, thereby undermining Palestinian political activity and the viability of a self-sufficient Palestinian state; it posed less of a compromise for Israel's regime of movement restrictions because (for the most part) it did not require Palestinians to cross the Green Line; and it enabled a larger profit margin because employers were not required to pay benefits for workers on settlements, and commuting costs for Palestinian residents living close by were low (Farsakh, 2005b, p. 139). Moreover, it recruited Palestinians to build some of the structures of their own confinement. Here we can see an illustration of Stoler's concept of the "colony" as a "principle of managed movement"—where the control over Palestinian mobility, including the influencing of Palestinian labor flows—plays a central role in advancing Israeli settler colonialism in and across the West Bank.

Through the Oslo Accords, Israel managed to solidify this mobility regime to overcome the formidable challenges of the first Intifada to its settler colonial agenda. The Oslo era allowed Israel to "reorder" its colonialism

United Nations Office for the Coordination of Humanitarian Affairs

occupied Palestinian territory

West Bank: Area C Map

February 2011

Border

- - - International Border

- - - Green Line

Israeli Unilaterally Declared Municipal Area of Jerusalem[1]

1. In 1967, Israel occupied the West Bank and unilaterally annexed to its territory 70.5 km of the occupied area

Barrier

——— Constructed / Under Construction

- - - - - Planned

Oslo Agreement[2]

Area (A), (B)

Area C & Nature Reserves

Oslo Interim Agreement

2. Area A : Full Palestinian civil and security control
Area B: Full Palestinian civil control and joint Israeli-Palestinian security control
Area C: Full Israeli control over security, planning and construction

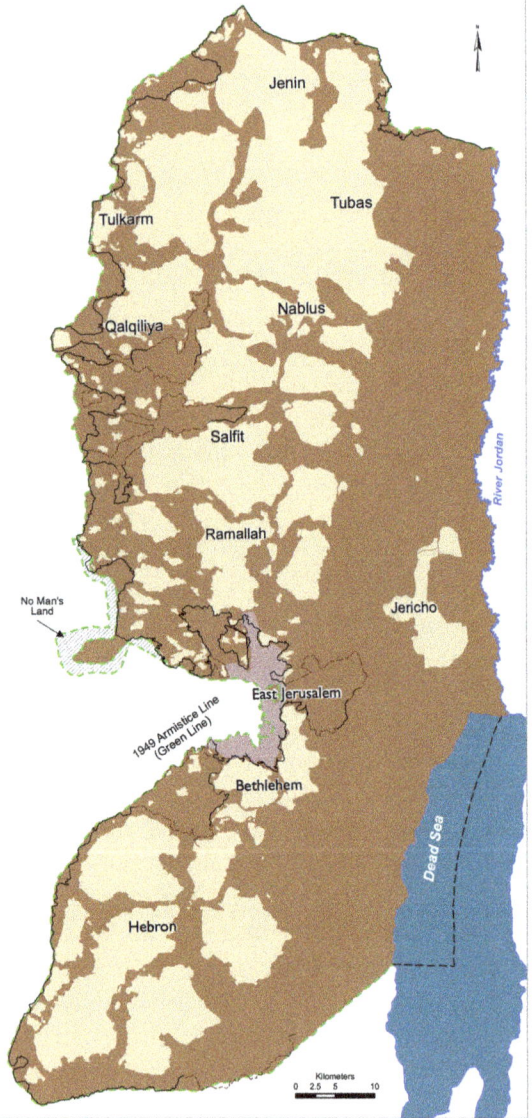

Mediterranean Sea

West Bank

Gaza Strip

ISRAEL

EGYPT   JORDAN

Jenin

Tubas

Tulkarm

Nablus

Qalqiliya

Salfit

River Jordan

Ramallah

No Man's Land

Jericho

East Jerusalem

1949 Armistice Line (Green Line)

Bethlehem

Dead Sea

Hebron

United Nations Office for the Coordination of Humanitarian Affairs

Cartography: OCHA-oPt - February 2011. Base data: OCHA, PA MoP, JRC update 08. For comments contact <ochaopt@un.org> or Tel. +972 (02) 582-9962   http://www.ochaopt.org

Kilometers
0 2.5 5   10

Figure 1.2 Map of West Bank Areas A, B (together) and C. *(Source: OCHA/ReliefWeb.)*

through an emphasis on im/mobilization and its fragmenting effects (Dana & Jarbawi, 2017, p. 210). In the 1990s, Israel further developed multiple elements of its mobility regime, including the ID cards, travel permits, checkpoints, physical barriers, and settlement construction. Oslo's geographic jigsaw puzzle fostered settler colonial expansion in the West Bank. Meanwhile, widespread Palestinian disappointment with the failures of the Oslo Accords to allow for meaningful independence deepened. It is in this context of exasperation that the second Intifada began.[20]

This second mass uprising is often said to have begun after Ariel Sharon, flanked by approximately one thousand Israeli police, entered the Aqsa compound in Jerusalem's Old City on September 28, 2000, reportedly shouting, "The Temple Mount is in our hands," invoking the phrase broadcast around East Jerusalem after the Israeli military seized it in 1967. Following this incitement, on September 29, a Friday and the Muslim holy day of the week, a battalion of the militarized Israeli border police descended on Al-Aqsa Mosque at the behest of Prime Minister Ehud Barak (Said, 2001b). Clashes ensued, and the Israeli police killed seven Palestinians and injured many more. Then, on Saturday, September 30, news spread—along with a now widely recognized image—of the shooting of twelve-year-old Muhammad Durrah in the Gaza Strip. Certainly, these events constituted colonial provocation, but, as Diana Buttu, former legal adviser to the Palestinian Liberation Organization, notes, "The groundwork [for the Intifada] was laid in the years before" (Adam, 2020). A generation of Palestinians, outraged by those gruesome deaths, was fueled by mounting alarm at the territorial dispossessions that the Oslo period (1993–2000) had advanced. They took to the streets in protest. But Israel met these initially peaceful civilian demonstrations with extreme military force, resulting in more than four times the Palestinian deaths than had occurred during the entirety of the first Intifada (Adam, 2020).[21]

By the time the second Intifada began, the Israeli military had already deployed some tactics of im/mobilization, such as the permit system, an expansion of settlements, segregated roads, and checkpoints, to quell eventual political unrest. Anne Marie Baylouny (2009) argues that this spatial fragmentation caused Palestinian resistance in the second Intifada to take on a more violent character than the first because it reduced the spaces available for collective, public protest. No longer able to rely on the effects of turning out large numbers of people who participated in the demonstrations of the first Intifada, protesters of the second uprising included violent tactics in their repertoire to register their message (Baylouny, 2009). But it is also clear that Israel's extreme violence toward the Palestinians was part of the instigating spark for the second Intifada, setting a most violent tone for the new uprising. In the context of this Intifada, Israel further intensified im/mobilization.

During, and partially because of, the second Intifada, the Israeli economy plummeted into a recession from 2000 to 2003, leading to $10 billion–$13 billion losses (Graham, 2011, p. 144).[22] But the Israeli military's reaction to the uprising provided an economic opportunity. Its innovations in counterinsurgency became popular on the global market. From 2002 to 2005, the Israeli economy bounced back from the recession because of its participation in this global arms and security trade, due in no small part to an almost 350 percent increase in foreign industrial investments into this sector (Graham, 2011, p. 144).

The lucrative laboratory in which new "security" products were developed for the global market produced or modified many of the tools of im/mobilization and its fragmenting effects. As the im/mobilization regime was refined, the physical hallmarks of enclosures also proliferated. The expansion of the settlements imposed physical borders across the territory of the West Bank, not only at their edges, but also around the military installations established to protect them and the roads built to serve them. Given that they combined the annexation of Palestinian land with the control of Palestinian mobility, and economic, political, and social dispossession, the settlements exemplify the multiple dimensions of an enclosure strategy that relies on the management of mobility.

But the expansion of settlements was also accompanied by other im/mobilization developments through the years of the second Intifada. In 2000, the passage that connected the West Bank and the Gaza Strip was permanently cut off (Bennett et al., 2003). Then, in 2002, the Israeli cabinet announced plans to construct a wall between 1948 Palestine and the West Bank to restrict Palestinians' physical movement across the Green Line. The Apartheid Wall (which I also refer to as the Separation Wall or simply the Wall, terms I discuss further in Chapter 2) would come to be composed of tracts of eighteen- to twenty-four-foot-high concrete slabs, electric fencing, barbed-wire fencing, and trenches (B'Tselem, 2017c). The structure would wrap around, and through, Palestinian areas as much to annex territory as to im/mobilize and fragment the West Bank population. During the second Intifada period, the Israeli military also subjected large numbers of WBGS Palestinian communities to lasting curfews. Twenty-four-hour curfews could be applied for days on end, and, the World Bank (2003) notes, at their peak, curfews affected 900,000 West Bank residents at one time. In addition to the Wall, a varying number of Israeli checkpoints were installed, imposing unannounced, random closures of major arteries of Palestinian traffic. The World Bank (2003) also estimated the existence of 140 Israeli checkpoints inside the West Bank and twenty-five to thirty in the Gaza Strip. In addition, there is no indication that these figures include impromptu, or "flying," checkpoints, whose locations and activation are neither permanent nor predictable. Beyond checkpoints, the military erected all manner of physical barriers to block roads, at times effectively sealing off entire villages. In the same report, the World Bank estimated the number of unmanned obstructions at approximately two hundred in 2002. A year and a half later, in December 2003, the Israeli military had installed 735 obstructions, which included everything from staffed checkpoints to boulders blocking the way, throughout the West Bank (United Nations Office for the Coordination of Humanitarian Affairs, 2006). All of these forms of Israeli control—the Apartheid Wall, the checkpoint, and roadblocks—would come to inform U.S. military strategy in Iraq (Graham, 2011, p. 139).

Certainly, the repressive function of im/mobilization tactics intensified during the period of the second Intifada, but Israel did not decommission those tactics after the Intifada ended. Ariel Handel (2015) notes that Israel's restrictions on Palestinian movement "peaked" in 2001–2008, the years of and immediately following the second Intifada. Some of the impediments have been removed since the end of the uprising. The West Bank has not been put under routine curfews; some road impediments have been removed (even though new ones have been introduced); and checkpoints sometimes let traffic through relatively unburdened. But, he observes, all of the mechanisms of closure are still there, ready to be activated at a moment's notice, and thus continue to *condition* Palestinian movement (pp. 74–75). In fact, for the past decade, the physical and bureaucratic elements of im/mobilization have become more "professionalized" and elaborate (Braverman, 2010; see also Mansbach, 2009). The result is a more polished masquerade that still aims to deny Palestinian self-determined movement.

I opened the chapter with a vignette describing the daily commute of one of my interlocutors, Jameel, in 2013–2014. Indeed, it has been in the years since the end of the second Intifada that Checkpoint 300, through which Jameel had to pass each morning, has been developed and converted into the commanding fixture that filters Palestinian movement from much of the southern West Bank into Jerusalem and 1948 Palestine. Jameel's commute across the checkpoint revolved around the intertwined system of ID cards and travel permits, the bureaucracies that accompany them, and the personnel and equipment deployed for checking them. These, too, have become routinized features of Israeli rule in the West Bank. His decision, along with that of thousands of other West Bank Palestinians, to seek better-compensated construction work building Jewish Israeli homes in Jerusalem must also be understood as a result of the enclosures strategy that has sought to undermine the Palestinian economy as one of its tactics, encouraging the movement of Palestinian labor while simultaneously ensnaring it in multiple layers of control and exploitation. Yet Jameel's commute is not only a result of compulsion. While the Israeli enclosures have attempted to influence the direction, speed, and quality of West Bank Palestinian movement, mobility remains a contested terrain, where Palestinians attempt to exercise self-determination in, against, and beyond the confines of im/mobilization.

In the next chapter, I turn to the present-day components of the im/mobilization regime to illustrate how they function to impose a diffused network of border processes across the territory of the West Bank. This "borderscape" is coconstituted and challenged by the functioning of the Palestinian public transportation system, among other elements of Palestinian mobility, opening up spaces for mundane, spectacular, and creative challenges to settler colonialism.

2

The West Bank Borderscape

Many shared van (or *Fordaat*, the Arabicized plural of the English word "Ford," one of the typical makes of such vehicles) journeys on the well-traveled route between Bethlehem and Ramallah, two prominent Palestinian cities in the West Bank, include a seemingly trivial pair of acoustic events that nonetheless express crucial information. The first is a syncopated series of reluctant clicks as passengers slide one end of their seatbelt into its buckle on the other end. The second, maybe fifteen minutes later (depending on traffic), is a cascade of reverse clicks as the driver and passengers liberate themselves from their seatbelts in rapid succession.[1] The first event is often preceded by instructions from the driver to buckle up. The second is not preceded by any directive but is occasionally followed by a barely audible sigh. These dual sonic phenomena do not bookend the trip but, rather, take place right in its middle.

During the trip from Bethlehem to Ramallah, the point in the road at which passengers and drivers fasten their seatbelts occurs as the van passes through Al-Eizariya, before reaching the roundabout at the entrance of the gigantic Israeli settlement, Ma'ale Adumim, which lies just to the east of Al-Eizariya (and the small Bedouin village of Arab al-Jahalin). Al-Eizariya is a Palestinian city that falls under the Oslo Accords designation of Area B, territory whose civilian affairs are the responsibility of the Palestinian Authority (PA) but that is otherwise under predominantly Israeli security control. The belts come back off around the time the van passes through the long shadow of the massive Israeli checkpoint at Qalandiya.

The seatbelt clicks on the shared van are an ephemeral but reliable marker of space for West Bank Palestinians. Riders and passengers typically buckle up where their route takes them onto a road controlled by Israel, and they unfasten their seatbelts when they have crossed back onto a Palestinian road. Should Israeli military personnel stop a Palestinian driver on that stretch of road and find that one of his passengers is not wearing a seatbelt, the driver could be fined, among other consequences. The second set of clicks also evinces a rejection of Israeli control over Palestinian life. About the unfastening of seatbelts in this context, Yazan Al-Khalili (2011) elaborates, "The drivers liberate themselves from the seat belts, in the same way that they liberate themselves from the occupation" (p. 45). Al-Khalili notes that the PA also demands the fastening of seatbelts but is not accorded the same compliance. In this way, the unfastening of seatbelts is not only a rejection of Israeli domination but of the PA's role in brokering Israel's technologies of im/mobilization in the aftermath of the Oslo Accords (Al-Khalili, 2011).

Embedded in these miniature concertos of clicks is the story of the Palestinian Intifadas, the Oslo Accords, and the effects of the ongoing Israeli settler colonial project on Palestinian self-determined movement. These infrapolitical practices (Scott, 1985, 1990, 2012) constitute an irreverent, limited obedience that wears a cloak of mundanity while still asserting the traveler's agency in negotiating invisible borders: Israel may have claimed control over these strips of road, but Palestinian riders will comply only during the exact minutes they move on those roads, and not a second more.

I begin with the seatbelt story as an example of what William Walters (2015) calls *viapolitics*—a "set of inquiries" that takes vehicles, routes, and roads as a vantage point for understanding the salience of mobility in society. Walters explains that viapolitics "treats the interaction of humans and vehicles as an irreducible feature of migratory struggles" (p. 478). Collective Palestinian movement via public transportation in the West Bank, the primary focus of the book, is not "migration" as such. And yet the distinction between transnational migration and internal collective movement begins to dissolve when one considers the extent to which Israel has developed a ruling strategy in the West Bank that parallels the global proliferation of "new spaces of border control" (Walters, 2006, p. 193). Because Israel's im/mobilization regime in the West Bank incorporates multiplying, diffused bordering processes, the everyday collective movement of Palestinians across the space shaped by those processes can properly be considered alongside more traditionally recognized forms of cross-border migration. Applying a viapolitical approach to this context illuminates the contestations of power that happen over and through the specific means and mechanics of mobility.

The seatbelt click concerto is an example of the politicized interaction between humans and the means of mobility. A viapolitical approach to examining the terrain of struggle in the colonized West Bank treats the geography of wearing and not wearing the seatbelt on public transportation as a node on the map of power relations. The way that the sounds burst into and recede from the sonic field of the *Ford* ride traces the strings of Israel's flexible border net cast onto the Palestinian West Bank. The breaking of the space's silence reflects the breaking of the territory by the Oslo Accords' territorial mosaic. But the audible disruption also reflects the fact that collective Palestinian mobility is itself an influential force, shaping the map of power relations as it negotiates the "elastic geography" of the colonial occupation (Weizman, 2007).

In this chapter I identify some of the defining features of this dynamic map of power to recognize collective Palestinian mobility in the West Bank as a site of decolonial struggle. The features that shape this map are Israel's diffuse bordering tactics and the vehicles, personnel, and routes of the Palestinian transit system. I describe the West Bank as a "borderscape," drawing from critical border studies and mobility studies that have developed this term to represent how modern states use diffused bordering processes across internal and external territories (rather than only at geopolitical boundary lines) and how people contest and reshape those processes through mundane and spectacular activity (see, e.g., Brambilla, 2015; Mezzadra & Neilson, 2013; Papadopoulos & Tsianos, 2013; Walters, 2006, 2015). Indeed, the diffusion of bordering practices across the West Bank corresponds with a similar phenomenon occurring in many places around the world. In a marked global trend, the logics and force of borders, through which states exert their power to include and exclude but also to compel, forbid, surveil, and discipline mobility, have been diffused across a variety of points within and beyond the territory of a particular state (Mezzadra & Neilson, 2013; Walters, 2006). These points include more than just the operation of governmental border control agents at places such as airports, but also the expression of state power in subtler places, such as in the physical surface of commercial transport trucks designed to repel migrant stowaways (Walters, 2006, p. 195).

Helga Tawil-Souri (2012) has observed that Israel's approach to borders is instrumentalist: while on the one hand, it has resisted setting final borders with a Palestinian state, on the other hand, it diffuses bordering processes across the territory of the West Bank (pp. 2–3, 12–13; see also Parsons & Salter, 2008, pp. 703–704). Israel has established internationally recognized borders only with Egypt, to the southwest (in 1979), and with Jordan, to the east (in 1994), although these borders might be affected by future political negotiations. Its northern and northeastern borders have remained unfixed, not to mention Israel's refusal to commit to any borders with remaining PA territory. Paradoxically, Israel manages to avoid an actual and final declaration about its borders with the Palestinians by extending bordering logic (primarily the notion that Israel is the sovereign vested with the authority to determine the parameters of mobility) and border processes (namely, the physical and bureaucratic exercises of mobility control) *across* the West Bank. It is this diffusion of the border that allows Israel to continue its settler colonization of Palestinian land without assuming full responsibility for the West Bank and the Palestinian people living there.

The strategy of ruling through the diffusion of border processes is dynamically contested, where Israel attempts to orchestrate a variety of confrontations in Palestinian space and Palestinians endure, avoid, or reject those encounters. Tawil-Souri (2012) demonstrates that Israel "borders" West Bank Palestinian life not only through multiple "contact points," which include physical impediments, but also through "more dynamic administrative bureaucracy," such as the system of ID cards on which some important features of Palestinian life are predicated (p. 13). Similarly, Julie Peteet (2017) refers to checkpoints as "encounter spaces" and describes the effects of Israel's spatial control in the West Bank as creating dynamics of "filtering" and "funneling" Palestinians. Indeed, the multimodal border web that Israel imposes on the West Bank constitutes an im/mobilization regime that attempts to deny self-determined movement to Palestinians.[2] This network of encounter points creates multiple, moving, and sometimes unpredictable moments—as well as anticipation—of encounter between Palestinians and Israeli colonial power. Together, the linked set of actual and possible encounters creates an "elastic territory" (Weizman, 2007, p. 7) that imposes uncertainty onto Palestinian mobility (Handel, 2015, pp. 74–75). But in the same territory, these border points are negotiated, endured, obfuscated, and avoided by Palestinians on the move. Thus, the plasticity of the West Bank territory not only derives from the unpredictable and constantly changing nature of Israel's bordering processes; it is also shaped by the collective movement of Palestinians that makes Indigenous claims to the same space.

In what follows, I review some of the bordering mechanisms that Israel uses and show that they function to impose an im/mobilization regime on West Bank Palestinians in furtherance of settler colonialism. I also introduce in detail the components of the Palestinian transportation system in the West Bank, which I identify as an important coconstitutive force of this particular borderscape.

The Components of Israel's Diffuse Bordering Program

While the Israeli government has not officially declared its borders with the Palestinians, it has undertaken to build a physical structure, the Apartheid

Wall, that might at first blush appear to mark a border with the West Bank. In fact, the Wall is a key element in the West Bank borderscape that is advancing Israeli settler colonialism. In 2002, during the second Palestinian Intifada, the Israeli government began to construct the Wall along a path that was loosely near the Green Line (the 1949 Armistice Line) that separated Israel from the territories of the West Bank (and the Gaza Strip) prior to Israel's invasion of these remaining Palestinian territories in 1967. Much of the Wall is composed of massive eight-meter concrete slabs, but electric fencing, razor wire, small cement blocks, and other barriers serve as placeholders where the project remains incomplete. The Wall's proposed final length illustrates how distinct it is from the Green Line: while the latter is only 350 kilometers long, the Wall, when completed, will be 712 kilometers long. As of its last update in 2018, the United Nations Office for the Coordination of Humanitarian Affairs in the Occupied Palestinian Territory (OCHA OPT) reported that 465 kilometers, or 65.3 percent, of the Wall had been completed, and of this completed portion, 85 percent has been built inside the West Bank, well east of the Green Line. The Wall's route also snakes and undulates in irregular ways to the advantage of the Israeli state. As a result, upon its completion, Israel's Wall, due to its physical location, will have annexed 9.4 percent of Palestinian land in the West Bank.

The Wall goes by many other names that range from the evocative to the euphemistic and the deceptive. They include the Apartheid Wall, the Security Barrier, and the Separation Fence. I use "Apartheid Wall" to represent how the structure mixes racial spatial segregation, territorial fragmentation, and colonial domination and annexation. (Interchangeably, I also use the simplified version "the Wall," following the Palestinian use of *al-Jidar*.) There is compelling evidence to suggest that construction of the Wall was undertaken to preserve and extend Israeli control over the maximum amount of West Bank land rather than for the stated purpose of restricting the entry of West Bank and Gaza Strip (WBGS) Palestinians into Israel (see, e.g., Reinhart, 2006, pp. 157–173). The construction of the Wall has separated West Bank Palestinians from one another, from other cities in the West Bank, and, in some cases, from their own land. In fact, these effects formed the bases for Palestinian legal challenges to the construction of the wall in the Israeli High Court of Justice (HCJ). In a few cases, petitioners' limited success caused the Israeli government to redraw the map of the Wall's proposed route (B'Tselem, 2017c; Weizman, 2007, p. 171). However, they failed to prevent the Wall's construction or expansion, and the HCJ's ruling afforded the rerouted Wall "judicial and moral legitimacy" (Weizman, 2007, p. 173). However, on the international stage, concerns about the colonial character and annexationist consequences of Israel's Wall led the International Court of Justice (ICJ) to issue an advisory opinion in 2004 that described the Wall as in violation of international law and recommended that it be dismantled. The ICJ (2004) explained that its opinion was based specifically on the fact that the Wall would "create a 'fait accompli' on the ground that could well become permanent . . . [and that] would be tantamount to *de facto* annexation."

In addition to directly annexing Palestinian land, the route of the Wall dispossesses Palestinians by impeding Palestinian movement in a number of ways. The Wall's immobilization function undermines Palestinians' political unity and social cohesion by generating fragmentation and alienation (Dana, 2017).[3] This is particularly true for those 7,500 Palestinians who live between the separation barrier to the east and the Green Line to the west, an area known as the "Seam Zone." That number is expected to increase to thirty thousand when the wall is completed (Landau, 2013). "Seam Zone enclaves," as they are called, are often severely isolated. Al-Walaja village, for example, is now surrounded on all sides due to the building of the Wall (Rainey, 2010). Although it is only four kilometers from Bethlehem and 8.5 kilometers from Jerusalem, its only current connection to the rest of the West Bank is a single access road that leads to Beit Jala, part of the Greater Bethlehem area (Rainey, 2010). There is no longer any direct access to Jerusalem from Al-Walaja; what once might have been a ten-minute drive may now take more than an hour (Rainey, 2010). Al-Walaja is just one of many Seam Zone cities whose residents are imprisoned by the Wall and the accompanying regime of road restrictions (see, e.g., Lien, 2013).

Notwithstanding the construction of the Wall, there is a growing presence of Israelis inside the West Bank: settlers who set up and expand Jewish-only enclaves deep into Palestinian territory and the military personnel sent to protect them. Israeli settlements are gated suburban colonies (Handel, 2013) located almost exclusively on hilltops across the West Bank. They are considered illegal under international law (UN Security Council, 1979, 2016; ICJ, 2004). The project of Israeli settler colonialism in the West Bank predates the building of the Wall by nearly four decades, but in the current period, settlement building has intersected with Wall construction in a way that reveals the colonial goals of both: "The logic being that by seeding the terrain with 'anchor points' in strategic places, state planners would reroute the Wall around them in order to include them on the 'Israeli' side" (Weizman, 2007, p. 3, see also p. 87). Settlement building aims to annex territory on the Palestinian side of the Green Line, but it also seeks to fragment Palestinian areas into isolated enclaves, simultaneously establishing "control of the interstices of an archipelago of about two hundred separate zones of Palestinian restricted autonomy in the West Bank and Gaza" (Weizman, 2007, p. 11). This fragmenting consequence of Israeli settlements reveals their role in the im/mobilization regime, as the location of the settlements interrupts, elongates, and frustrates the routes of Palestinian movement in the West Bank. As existing settlements expand and new ones appear, their effects on Palestinian movement also change, highlighting one of the ways that Israel's bordering processes are not stationary but mobile.

One element of the settlement apparatus is the system of segregated roads, which extends territorial control from the actual settlements into the surrounding landscape by designating some roads as accessible only to Israelis. Dubbed the "forbidden roads regime" (Figure 2.1), this system includes three kinds of road designations according to the Israeli human-rights organization B'Tselem: "completely prohibited roads," which are accessible only to Israeli citizens and to which access is strictly regulated by checkpoints that will not allow non-Israeli citizens to pass; "partially prohibited roads," which are inaccessible to Palestinians except for those who have the required permits or who come from villages that would be entirely cut off, if not for the partially prohibited road; and, finally, "restricted use roads" on which Palestinians are allowed to drive but have to pass through Israeli checkpoints for access (B'Tselem, 2004, pp. 13–18). Beyond restricting the use of these roads, the "forbidden roads regime" restricts Palestinian movement in a different way.

As Hagar Kotef (2015) explains, "Since Palestinians are not allowed to travel on [these roads], and often even to cross them, they become a technology of separation, even if they were originally built for other purposes" (p. 54). Importantly, the rules of this road segregation system are not formally recorded anywhere—not in legislation, military orders, public records, or even signs (Kotef, 2015, p. 55). Based on the discretionary orders of Israeli military leaders in the West Bank (B'Tselem, 2017b), the segregated roads system illustrates the occupation's characteristic arbitrariness that is primarily animated by the logic of denying Palestinian self-determined movement.

Despite being the most physically prominent, the Apartheid Wall is just one of the formidable obstacles to movement imposed by the Israeli government in the West Bank. The deepening of the occupation, which has been occurring since the beginning of the second Intifada, has been chiefly accomplished through physical separation of Palestinians and restrictions on the means of movement by which they might otherwise physically connect. As of January–February 2020, OCHA OPT (2020) reports, 593 physical impediments to movement had been put in place by the Israelis in the West Bank.[4] These impediments include checkpoints, partial checkpoints, roadblocks, road barriers, road gates, earth mounds, earth walls, and trenches. Some of these obstacles are moving or impermanent, which means that their activation is neither predictable nor reliable. Weizman (2007) notes that these hundreds of barriers have "splintered the West Bank into a series of approximately 200 separate, sealed-off 'territorial cells' around Pales-

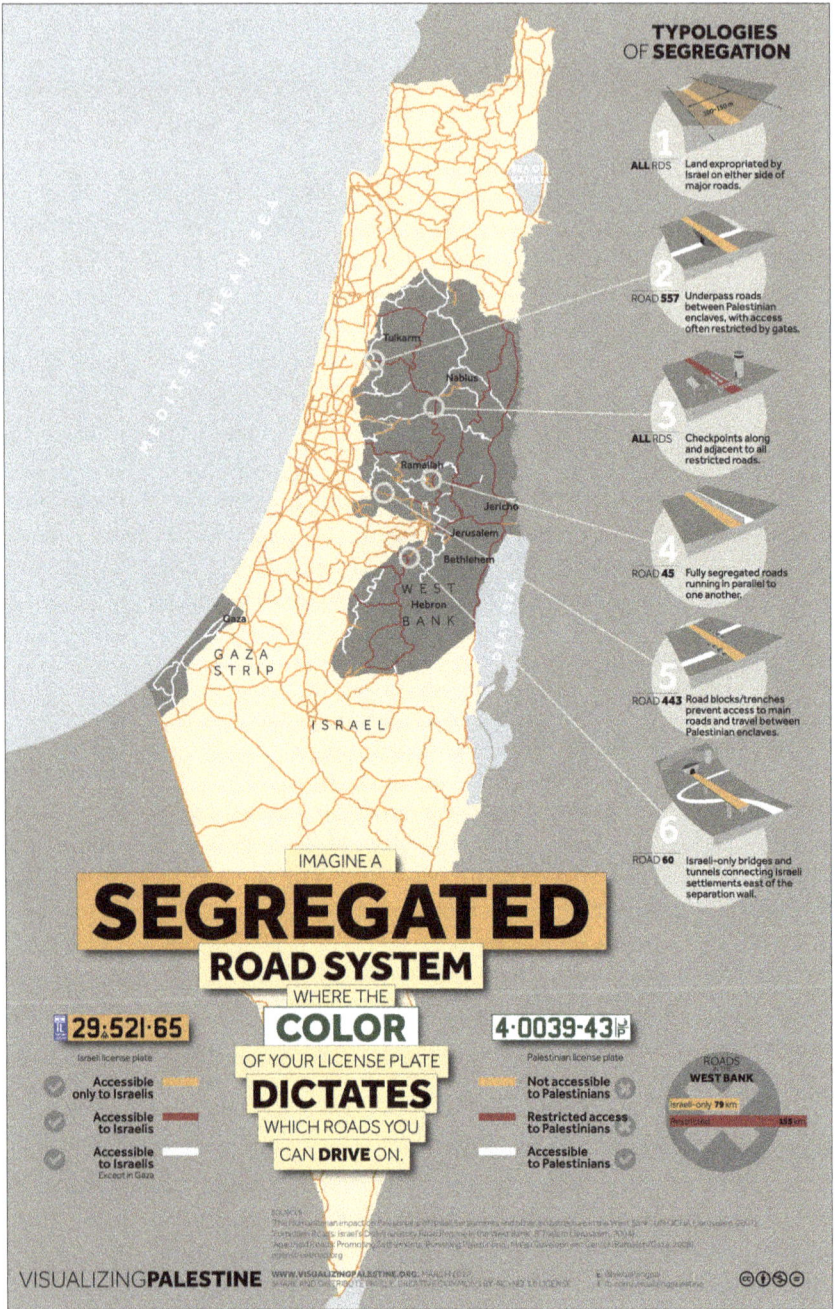

Figure 2.1 Segregated roads infographic. *(Source: Visualizing Palestine.)*

tinian 'population centres' . . . with traffic between these cells channeled through military-controlled bottlenecks" (p. 146; see also Handel, 2009, p. 183). None of them affect the coming and going of the Jewish population in the West Bank (Makdisi, 2008, p. 41). Rather, they ensure settler mobility that is faster, easier, and more efficient.

Along with the Wall, the Israeli checkpoint is the most notorious type of im/mobilization structure imposed on the West Bank. B'Tselem (2017b) reports that, as of January 2017, Israeli forces had established ninety-eight fixed checkpoints in the West Bank, thirty-nine of which are identified as "points of entry to Israel," even though these, too, are located inside West Bank territory.[5] Of the thirty-nine checkpoints that regulate the movement of Palestinians from the West Bank into 1948 Palestine (and back),[6] all are staffed regularly and completely closed when unstaffed (B'Tselem, 2017b). In addition to these ninety-eight permanent checkpoints, there are a number of "flying" checkpoints—impromptu encounter points where Israeli soldiers stop traffic and subject people and vehicles to scrutiny—whose shifting locations are unpredictable and unannounced. From April 2019 to March 2020, OCHA OPT estimates, the Israeli military deployed 1,500 flying checkpoints. Permanent checkpoints operate according to changing rules about who and what can pass through them. At some checkpoints, only men (or sometimes men and women) below a certain age (the limit can be set anywhere between forty and sixty-five) are subjected to search; at others, everyone must pass inspection. These rules are also mediated by the discretion of the soldiers administering the checkpoint. For example, in 2012 I boarded a bus from Ramallah to Jerusalem that stopped at the Qalandiya Checkpoint. Many of the passengers began to stream out of the bus and into the walk-through inspection line in the checkpoint's building. I stood up to follow the two other U.S. passport holders with whom I was traveling when an elderly Palestinian woman gestured for us to stay seated. After ascertaining that we spoke Arabic, she explained to us that we, as foreign tourists, were not expected to submit to the walk-through inspection; she was also exempted because of her age. She stopped talking as two young, heavily armed Israeli soldiers boarded the bus and began checking the remaining passengers' papers. They merely glanced at the covers of our passports and continued on to the next passengers. In 2013, the shared taxi in which I was riding from Bethlehem to Ramallah was stopped at a flying checkpoint somewhere beyond Al-Jab'a. This time my U.S. passport and visa were thoroughly checked. I note this small difference just to demonstrate the role that soldiers' individual discretion plays in the uneven application of paperwork inspection at checkpoints.

There are also rules about which vehicles can pass through a given checkpoint. The determinations rely in part on a segregated license plate system. Israeli license plates are mustard yellow in color while current Palestinian license plates are white with green writing. (Some are green with white writing.) Cars with Palestinian plates are not permitted to cross through checkpoints into 1948 Palestine or East Jerusalem, while Israeli-plated vehicles are. However, even among the cars with yellow plates, West Bank Palestinian drivers are not permitted to drive through checkpoints; Palestinians with Israeli citizenship, residents of East Jerusalem, and foreigners are. At some checkpoints, travelers arriving on public transit are required to leave vehicles on one side, cross through on foot, and board another vehicle (bus or taxi) on the other side. Saree Makdisi (2008) explains that "those kinds of checkpoints are surrounded by scenes of chaos and confusion: massive, slow-moving traffic jams of taxis, cars, buses, minivans, and trucks, some trying to find a place to park; others, to get out of the parking spaces they had been wedged into; still others just trying to get through the mess" (p. 43).

The network of checkpoints interacts with a complex system of travel permits and the segregated identity cards that are a prerequisite for the permits. Whether a Palestinian is allowed to cross a given checkpoint depends in many cases on whether she has obtained the necessary permit, but even for some checkpoints that do not require a particular travel permit, proof of identity in the form of a sanctioned identity card is required. According to a document obtained from the Israeli Civil Administration in the West Bank by the newspaper *Ha'aretz*, there are 101 distinct types of travel permits that affect WBGS Palestinian movement that differ based on the authorized purpose, crossing location, destination, time, and duration (Levinson, 2011).[7] The biggest category of travel permits issued to Palestinians are those that authorize work inside 1948 Palestine, Jerusalem, or Israeli settlements in the West Bank (Al-Qadi, 2018, p. 9). The Israeli administration of this system is complex and inscrutable. As Yael Berda (2018) thoroughly illustrates through her study and legal representation of countless cases of Palestinians seeking permits, "Administrative flexibility, wide discretion, conflicting decisions, and changing decrees create constant administrative friction and uncertainty" (p. 35).

Furthermore, the Oslo Accords provide that Palestinians' applications for travel permits must be submitted to the PA as the government of the Palestinian people, even though final decisions about the travel permits are made by Israel. However, since 2000, Israel has expected Palestinian permit seekers to submit their applications directly to the local office of the Israeli Civil Administration, while the PA has stridently contested this policy (BADIL Resource Center for Palestinian Residency and Refugee Rights, 2003; Al-Qadi, 2018, p. 17). The permit system is tethered to the underlying identity card system that Israel has developed since its establishment, and in its modern manifestation, the ID card system is divided into categories that distinguish among Palestinians based on where they reside (Alqasis & Al-Azza, 2015; Tawil-Souri, 2011b, p. 221). While the PA has taken over administering ID cards to WBGS Palestinians, their serial numbers are the same as those originally in the Israeli population registry (BADIL Resource Center for Palestinian Residency and Refugee Rights, 2003). The travel permits and ID cards constitute a bureaucratic network that features an incredibly complex application system involving a wide array of formal and informal Israeli, Palestinian, and international actors (Berda, 2018; Parizot, 2018). These interwoven bureaucracies illuminate the monopoly Israel claims over the authorization of Palestinian movement across the territories through which it has diffused its bordering processes. Together they *collectively* subjectify WBGS Palestinians as ineligible for self-determined mobility.

By disrupting the flow and tempo of traffic in an unpredictable manner, the network of checkpoints burdens Palestinian movement. In this way, it not only enables the annexation of land via settlements but also accomplishes the annexation of Palestinian time. While stolen *land* is a phenomenon that many call to reverse, stolen *time*, such as the time lost waiting in long lines at checkpoints or on a long detour, is something that cannot be reversed (B'Tselem, 2007; Hass, 2005). Peteet (2017, 2018) has theorized the way that control over time, and specifically "imposed waiting," has been weaponized by Israel as "a purposeful and willful deprivation of mobility and temporal autonomy" (2018, p. 44). Makdisi (2008) comments that, due to the arbitrary administration of security measures at checkpoints, "A routine trip can quickly turn into a living nightmare of waiting and immobility" without any prior warning (p. 43). The Israeli journalist Amira Hass (2005) elaborates on the harms that extend from the dispossession of Palestinian time, harms that align with the multipronged effects of the Israeli enclosures:

> Time . . . is a precious resource for every human being. Time that is robbed while waiting at checkpoints, or waiting for permits, cannot ever be returned. The loss of time, which Israel is stealing every day from 3.5 million people, is evident everywhere: in the damage it causes to their ability to earn a living; in their economic, family and cultural activity; in the leisure hours, in studies and in creativity; and in the shrinking of the space in which every individual lives and therefore the narrowing of their horizon and their expectations.

Considering the annexation of time relates to what Anderson et al. (2009) refer to as the "when" of the border, a dimension of mobility control that undermines the temporal nature of social relationships by, for example, pre-

Figure 2.2 Traffic outside Qalandiya Checkpoint on the road from Ramallah
to Jerusalem. A vendor hawks prayer beads and belts to waiting drivers.
(Photograph by the author.)

venting people from regularly or reliably reuniting with loved ones. As border processes deny Palestinians self-determined mobility, they are "suspended in time" (p. 7). Such a suspension recalls Reem Fadda's (2009)
reading of "not-yet-ness," where Palestine appears to be suspended in the
colonial time of the present, violently detached from its Indigenous past and
future (p. 230). Indeed, Israel's im/mobilization regime, composed of diffused border processes, attempts to annex both "kinds" of Palestinian time:
mundane and historical.

The Qalandiya Checkpoint, for example, which lies on the road between
Jerusalem and Ramallah, creates an unpredictable amount of traffic for
those heading in either direction at various times of day and night (Figure
2.2). Heading into Qalandiya from the West Bank, nonexempt passengers
(determined by the prevailing rule of the day) are all expected to exit their
public transportation vehicles and pass through a long corridor surrounded
by metal bars and into the heart of the checkpoint, where they are asked for
identification and travel documents and their belongings and person are
subject to search.[8] Sometimes buses are not permitted to pass through, forcing passengers to find another bus on the other side of the checkpoint, to
take a micro-bus through a different checkpoint, or to hire a very expensive
taxi to complete their trip. This is just one of the many delay-causing im-

pediments Palestinians encounter daily as they move by public transit through the arteries of the West Bank. In this context, the cost of movement is not only the price of bus fare. It also always entails a variable expenditure of time.

Checkpoints are also a way of exposing Palestinian residents of the West Bank to the arbitrary scrutiny and discretion of Israeli soldiers. In addition to the obvious dangers that encounters with an occupying military force pose, such as rather unpredictable threats to life and liberty, exposure to the threat of Israeli violence, surveillance, and detention can also have a chilling effect on Palestinian political expression. Checkpoints are reputedly dangerous for known activists and for young people who live in refugee camps throughout the West Bank. The refugee camps have a reputation for being highly politicized, and some refugee youth actively participate in anticolonial protests. A popular perception expressed by my interlocutors is that, when one of the checkpoints strewn across the interior of the West Bank is activated, Israeli soldiers may arbitrarily arrest refugee youth on suspicion of participation in political activities based solely on their refugee status. Relatedly, on the occasions of Palestinian political demonstrations anywhere in the West Bank (not necessarily nearby), Israeli officials will suddenly close checkpoints or intensify screening procedures to such an extent that the delays create a de facto closure. The checkpoint then becomes a space for disciplining and punishing the entire West Bank Palestinian population through exemplary violence against Palestinian political expression, whether active or suspected.

Israel's "Container Checkpoint" is a militarized intersection on the only road connecting the Palestinian cities of the southern West Bank (e.g., Bethlehem and Hebron) to those in the central (e.g., Jericho) and northern (e.g., Ramallah and Nablus) parts of the territory. It sits atop a hill and disrupts the flow of traffic that passes between the dusty undulations of the Wadi in-Nar (Valley of Fire) road to the south and three roads to the north. During my time in the West Bank between 2012 and 2014, I heard many stories that featured the Container Checkpoint, which surprised me because of its seeming modesty during those years. At that time, the Container Checkpoint was hardly remarkable, consisting of rather unassuming structures: a few guard kiosks positioned on the side of a different traffic gate (a striped yellow wooden arm attached to a rotating gear that lifts the arm to allow traffic through and lowers the arm to stop traffic) and a handful of stray dogs that seemed always to be basking sleepily in the sun, oblivious to the young, armed soldiers smoking cigarettes a few steps away. In those years, I was lucky enough to get caught only once in the excruciatingly slow-moving traffic that results when the soldiers lower the traffic arms to search vehicles in one direction or another. Regular commuters know that such a decision, always unannounced, can add many hours of delay to their travel. In 2015, Israel expanded the checkpoint's structures to include terminals to more thoroughly inspect people and vehicles, along with imposing gates surrounding the checkpoint, lending it a much more permanent appearance.

But these developments have not changed the fact that the "Container" is an ominous encounter point with Israeli forces in the middle of a Palestinian West Bank route. As such, it represents not only the possibility of unpredictable delay and the personal and social costs that always accompany a loss of time, but also the possibility of serious danger, of sudden colonial violence. The murder in 2020 by Israeli soldiers of Ahmed Erekat, an unarmed young man driving from Abu Dis to pick up his sister and mother from a hair salon in Bethlehem on the day of his sister's wedding, occurred at the updated Container Checkpoint. Erekat momentarily lost control of his vehicle as he maneuvered the tight and disorienting space of the precariously perched checkpoint, rolling into the curb next to one of the kiosks. He got out of his car with his hands up and was shot dead on the spot. In 2013, Israeli forces at the Container killed Anas al-Atrash, who was on his way home to Hebron with his brother, with whom he ran a shoe store in Jericho. Al-Atrash had been asleep until the car stopped at the Container Checkpoint behind a vehicle whose passengers were being detained; rousing from sleep to find the red light of an Israeli gun moving around inside the car, he groggily stepped out of the car and was immediately shot to death (Ehrenreich, 2013). Perhaps Erekat and al-Atrash were executed for simply being Palestinian and moving their bodies in a way that was not ordered by the Israeli personnel.[9]

The dangers of the checkpoints are multiple. While the loss of life marks one extreme, they enact many other forms of violent dispossession, as well. I heard one of the Container Checkpoint stories from Karim, a refugee resident of a Bethlehem suburb and a recent graduate of Al-Quds University in Abu Dis.[10] Each day, he would take public transportation to school, typically a shared transit van, that would cross through the Container Checkpoint. One day, he headed to campus to take a final exam. Planning for the possibility of delay at the checkpoint, he left home an hour early and caught a shared van from the main road. Sure enough, the checkpoint had been activated that day, and the traffic was backed up all the way down the mountain into the valley below. Once Karim's van finally arrived at the checkpoint, the soldiers decided to collect the ID cards of all of the van's passengers and direct the van to pull over while the soldiers took their time examining the documents. Fearing he would be irreversibly late for his exam, Karim decided to leave the van and find another car to take him the rest of the way to the university. He knew that typically the soldier would return the stack of IDs to the driver who would then distribute them to the passengers, so Karim asked the driver to bring his ID to the university. He then carried out his plan and made it in time to take the exam. After completing it, Karim left the classroom and found the driver wandering on the campus looking for him. The driver beseeched Karim to return with him to the checkpoint. He explained that an Israeli soldier had discovered that Karim had left without being cleared, confiscated the driver's ID card, and ordered him to bring Karim back to the checkpoint. Karim obliged.

Once Karim and the driver returned to the checkpoint, the Israeli soldier directed the driver to leave. He refused, however, feeling responsible for this fellow Palestinian young man, but the soldier pointed his gun at the driver and forced him to leave. The Israeli soldiers were furious with Karim for circumventing their asserted monopoly over authorizing Palestinian movement. As punishment, they kept his ID and left him to stand in the sun for what he said felt like an eternity, even pointing their guns at him when he asked to go to the bathroom. According to Karim, the punishment was not only the monotony and discomfort of standing and not knowing when he would be released. The checkpoint is very busy, and each traveler who passed him would see him standing there, perhaps wondering whether he might be collaborating with the Israelis. After about an hour, Karim was finally allowed to leave. He flagged down another transit van to take him home to Bethlehem.

While the Container and the checkpoint system to which it belongs are only one element of Israel's diffused bordering processes in the West Bank, these incidents represent some of the dangers and dispossessions to which Palestinians are exposed at any of the encounter points in the West Bank borderscape. The ultimate colonial violence of taking a life exists in relation to other consequences, such as irreversibly wasting time stuck in traffic or being held on the side of the road, enduring public humiliation, missing special occasions or mundane affairs, and experiencing fear and collective punishment. Israel's diffusion of border processes across the territory of the West Bank creates an im/mobilization regime that inflicts this violence through the systematic denial of self-determined mobility. The physical and bureaucratic components of this regime condition the terrain of Palestinian mobility, but they do not determine it entirely. Instead, various forms of Palestinian mobility contribute to shaping the West Bank borderscape. I now turn to one of those forms—public transportation as the means of collective mobility—to describe its components and extend the viapolitical inquiry mentioned at the beginning of this chapter. In addition to asserting that vehicles, roads, and routes should be taken seriously to illuminate the fact that mobility is a terrain of struggle between the power of states and people, Walters (2015) argues that understanding the specific elements and characteristics of the means of movement in any given context reveals the possibilities for resistance they might enable. Following this approach, I offer an overview of the elements of Palestinian public transit in the West Bank to form the basis for my arguments in Chapters 3–5 about their decolonizing potential.

The System of Palestinian Public Transit in the West Bank

Like those in most urban places, residents of the West Bank choose from a number of individual and shared methods of transportation to travel within and among cities for a variety of social reproduction purposes, including commuting to work or school, accessing health care, making social visits, engaging in tourism/recreation or shopping trips, and so on. While private car ownership in the Palestinian West Bank is increasing with the increased availability of private loans, an issue I address in the Conclusion, the number of private cars per capita in the West Bank is still low.[11] In this context, reliance on public transportation is still widespread.

Palestinian public transportation in the West Bank comprises converted tour buses, school buses, and micro-buses that transport people among and within cities; eight-seat shared Ford transit vans that run intercity routes and transport intracity riders along the way; five-seat shared sedan taxis that drive routes within cities; and private sedan taxis that transport individual passengers wherever they want to go (typically within a city). The Ottoman-turned-British train system that used to cross through the West Bank and Gaza is no longer functional in Palestinian areas, and the new Jerusalem light rail crosses into West Bank territory, but only to connect Jerusalem with some Israeli settlements. There are no subways or metros for Palestinians, and, notwithstanding an interesting history, there is currently no functioning Palestinian airport.[12]

I differentiate between movement "inside a single city" (*daakheli* [internal] in Arabic) and movement "among cities" (*khaareji* [external]) because these are operative distinctions in the transit system. By "city" I mean something that might also be considered a "county" or "greater metropolitan area" in the U.S. context—that is, a collection of cities and neighborhoods that blend together into one large urban area. In Arabic, this kind of space is called a *muhafidha*. In Bethlehem, for example, the *muhafidha* includes the three major subcities of Greater Bethlehem—Bethlehem, Beit Jala, and Beit Sahour—as well as surrounding neighborhoods and villages. The forms of public transportation that are confined to operation "inside" Bethlehem might travel among these internal neighborhoods, or even out to one of the surrounding villages, and still be considered internal (*daakheli*) transit.

The distinctions among the kinds of public transportation available to West Bank Palestinians partially conditions the possible engagements with them, so I now turn to describing the specifics of each type. Buses are one component of West Bank public transit. According to a PA Ministry of Transportation official interviewed in 2014, there were 867 Palestinian buses running in the West Bank, owned by eighty-six small, private companies, the largest of which had forty-five buses. Since then, the number of registered buses in the West Bank has steadily increased to 1,055 in 2019 (Palestinian Central Bureau of Statistics, 2019). Bus companies operate routes inside and among major cities. Some bus companies have routes that operate completely inside one specific greater metropolitan area (*muhafid-ha*) and routes that connect two different urban centers. Within large metropolitan areas such as Bethlehem and Ramallah, special bus companies run particular routes between residential neighborhoods and the city center. They can stop anywhere along the way, according to the requests of passengers or to pick up people on the street who wave them down. Each company also has starting and ending points where they park their buses and wait for approximately fifteen minutes before continuing again. Usually, these bus companies collect fares from passengers as they board but do not issue tickets to them.[13]

In Bethlehem, where I was primarily based during my fieldwork, there are seven bus companies. In June 2014, the Beit Sahour Bus Company, for example, was operating twenty-eight buses (Figure 2.3). One of its lines ran back and forth between the Bethlehem suburb known as Beit Sahour and the famous Manger Square up a very steep hill. It also ran a few other intra- and intercity routes, including one round trip per day to and from Ramallah. Another bus company runs from the large Dheisheh refugee camp neighborhood in the southern area of town to Manger Square in the center, picking up passengers along the busy streets on the way. Still other companies serve different corners of the greater Bethlehem area (Figure 2.4).

A separate fleet of buses connects Bethlehem and Ramallah to East Jerusalem. They belong to a company that was created by a Beit Jala Palestinian who holds Jerusalem residency after the Wall was built. Because the company provides service to Jerusalem, on the other side of the Wall's route, and thus passes through Israeli military checkpoints, the company must coordinate its operation with the Israelis. Its fleet includes large tour-size buses and small micro-buses, often comfortable and air-conditioned, and issues tickets. Line 21 leaves from Bab az-Zqaq, a busy intersection between Bethlehem and Beit Jala, and transports passengers through the Tunnel Checkpoint (*an-nufuq*) all the way to the Damascus Gate of Jerusalem's Old City. However, only passengers who hold Jerusalem residence cards or foreign passports are allowed to take Line 21 and pass through the Tunnel Checkpoint. The rest of the southern West Bank residents who want (and are permitted) to take transit to Jerusalem must find their way to the Bethlehem Checkpoint—also known as Checkpoint 300 (Figure 2.5)—and cross

Figure 2.3 Beit Sahour Bus Company bus. *(Photograph by the author.)*

Figure 2.4 Microbus on the Beit Jala–Bethlehem–Doha route.
(Photograph by the author.)

Figure 2.5 Collection of private taxis waiting at Checkpoint 300 in Bethlehem. The section of the Apartheid Wall behind the taxis was freshly painted just before the photograph was taken; it is usually covered with anti-occupation murals. *(Photograph by the author.)*

on foot. On the other side, they will find Line 24 of the same bus fleet waiting to take them the rest of the way to the Damascus Gate. From Ramallah, the same company operates buses that cross the Qalandiya Checkpoint, although quite often buses from Ramallah are not allowed to continue beyond the checkpoint and must drop off their passengers, who then must cross through the inspection terminal of the checkpoint and board a different bus to continue to Jerusalem.

Two kinds of Palestinian sedan taxis operate in the West Bank. The first is the private for-hire taxi (*taxi Tulub*), which picks up patrons and takes them to their desired destination without stops along the way. Private taxis are permitted to travel both inside and among cities. They are easily identifiable because their body paint is solid yellow. Taxis are either owned and operated individually or through taxi companies. For example, in Bethlehem in 2014, there were twenty-eight private taxi companies.[14] While these taxis are allowed to pick up patrons who hail them from the side of the road, many people also call taxi drivers directly to arrange to be picked up. Some drivers have such a strong client base that they work exclusively by phone, rushing from one client's house to another.

Figure 2.6 *Service* taxi with black side panels, parked near the "Cinema" area of Bethlehem. *(Photograph by the author.)*

The second kind of taxi is the shared taxi, referred to as *service* (pronounced *ser-vees*).[15] The *service* is a four-door sedan vehicle with yellow body paint but can be differentiated from the solid-yellow private taxis by black side panels at the front and rear of the vehicle (Figure 2.6). The intracity *services* used to be stretch-sedan Mercedes-Benzes with seven passenger seats, but the older vehicles were phased out for new five-seat models.

Services circulate on intracity routes that have been predetermined by the Ministry of Transportation and are permitted to pick up any passengers who hail them. If they are stopped by Palestinian police outside their designated route, they can be cited and fined. *Service* drivers will typically stop for any passenger going along their route, as long as there are enough empty seats in the vehicle. Indeed, they will continue to pick up riders, hoping to fill all four passenger seats. Sometimes, *service* drivers will stop their vehicles in one of the designated areas in town to wait for enough passengers to completely fill their vehicles. While drivers must pay a fee to stop in these areas, they may opt to do so to guarantee a full car before heading out. If they do not pay to stop in a designated area, they are still permitted to pick up passengers from the street, but they are not allowed to stop and wait for passengers along the roadside. These *services* are not permitted to operate among cities (i.e., in greater metropolitan areas) but might have routes that travel through multiple neighborhoods or subcities within the larger city. In other words, the sedan *services* run routes that are confined to their *muhafidha*. For example, in Bethlehem there is a *service* line that circulates between Beit Jala and Bethlehem, both of which are subcities or neighborhoods of the Greater Bethlehem area. Another line transports people to Al-ʿAbediyya, a village on the outskirts of Beit Sahour, which is considered part of the Greater Bethlehem area (Muhafidhat Beit Lahem) but is nonetheless a distinct village from the neighboring city of Beit Sahour.

In addition to the taxis for hire and *services*, shared vans operate throughout the West Bank. The fleet consists of vans with seven passenger seats and solid orange (or sometimes yellow) body paint (Figure 2.7). The shared vans are sometimes referred to as *service* or *Fordaat* (the Arabicized plural of "Ford," in reference to a common make, although, as noted earlier, *Fordaat* include vans made by Volkswagen, Mercedes-Benz, and others). Like the internal *services* and buses, the *Fordaat* are confined to predetermined routes and can be fined for straying from them. *Fordaat* routes run between major cities, such as Bethlehem–Ireeha/Jericho, and connect neighborhoods, villages, or subcities within a single *muhafidha*.

In Bethlehem, there are *Fordaat* that connect villages around the edge of the city to its center, where some of the village residents come to work or shop.

Figure 2.7 *Ford* van parked near the "Cinema" roundabout in Bethlehem. *(Photograph by the author.)*

The *Fordaat* are permitted to drop off and pick up passengers anywhere along their route. Pickups are *not* permitted off their official routes but still frequently occur. For example, it is common for drivers coming from Dar Salah, a village on the outskirts of Beit Sahour, to pick up passengers along YMCA Street in Beit Sahour on the way to Bethlehem's transit center, the Mujama' (Complex), even for drivers whose official routes only begin *at* the Mujama'.

Drivers do not typically collect fares from passengers right away. Especially on the longer intercity hauls, passengers spontaneously decide to pay when they are near their destination (but well before they get off). Once one passenger hands her money to the driver, the rest tend to follow suit. After informally consulting with friends and fellow riders about why people opt to pay mid-route or toward the end, I frequently heard the explanation that they wait until after they have passed known problem spots in the road. Obstructions such as the Container Checkpoint outside Bethlehem or Qalandiya outside Ramallah might be closed or cause so much traffic that the ride will not be completed. In such cases, passengers would still pay the driver something, but a negotiation would ensue about how much. Most passengers prefer for such negotiations to take place before money has been exchanged, so they hold their fares until they seemingly have passed the danger. For short rides inside the city, though, passengers will usually hand their money to the driver promptly after taking a seat. As with most of the West Bank–only buses, *Fordaat* passengers are not issued tickets.

The schedules of the *Fordaat* vary by route, but they generally operate on the principle that they do not depart until all the vehicle's seats are occupied with paying customers. For busy routes, such as Bethlehem–Ramallah during the typical workday rush hours of 6 and 10 A.M., vans may leave every five or ten minutes. On the routes that connect the outer villages to downtown Bethlehem, the vans typically take village residents to work or shop in Bethlehem in the morning, wait in town for a few hours, then transport the returning villagers home in the afternoon. In a series of visits to each of the van stations around Bethlehem in 2014, drivers reported that morning and afternoon business had been good: from 6 to 9 A.M., a full van might leave the villages every ten or fifteen minutes, and the same kind of schedule applied in the opposite direction from 1:30 to 4 P.M. The Beit Fajjar–Bethlehem line reported leaving every half hour, and this is sometimes the case for other lines, too. During the midday, most routes slow down, and the routes to the villages practically stop. The midday schedules of the busy intercity lines vary wildly, and the drivers were hard-pressed to give me an estimate—runs depend entirely on passenger flow. Most of the village route drivers reported very little activity between 9 and 10 A.M. and between 12 and 1 P.M.

If a single village-bound passenger does show up for a van at midday, the driver has the discretion to decide whether to make the trip; if he chooses not to, the passenger will have to wait several hours until enough people arrive to fill the van at the end of the workday. One morning at 11:30 I came upon Im Ahmad,[16] surrounded by full shopping bags and waiting alone in the van to Beit Fajjar, doors open to maximize the cross-breeze. She told me she had been waiting for approximately an hour, and the driver had just agreed to take her. He had hoped another passenger would show up if he waited, but luck was not on his side that day. In the absence of fixed schedules, there are recognizable daily travel patterns, but luck or chance play a significant role. Such is to be expected from a transit system that is not centrally owned and operated. Drivers and passengers alike are at the mercy of market-demand flows.

The PA categorizes Palestinian transportation in the West Bank as a "public-private partnership." Buses and some private taxis are generally owned and run by companies, while *services* and *Fordaat* vehicles are often owned individually. The PA Ministry of Transportation (Wizarat an-Naql w al-Muwasalat) determines the routes and sets fares and rules for vehicle licensing, numbering, and appearance. The ministry coordinates with regional Da'irat es-Ser offices (basically, traffic and motor vehicle departments), which license vehicles and drivers and communicate with local owner-operators.

To operate a transit vehicle in the West Bank, one must register the vehicle for public use and obtain a special public transportation license plate. In addition, one must obtain a line permit number, which grants permission for the vehicle to be operated along a predetermined route. The line permit number is emblazoned inside a black square painted on the side of taxis, *services*, and *Fordaat* (Figure 2.8). Vehicle owners must complete the licensing process and then proceed to a body shop equipped to paint the vehicle according to the standard. Finally, public transportation drivers must ob-

مجمع بلدية بيت لحم

مجرى الخط

بيت لحم – بيت فجار – جورة الشمعة وبالعكس

رقم البرميت 15-0522

SERVICE سرفيس

Figure 2.8
Line permit box emblazoned on the side of a *Ford* van assigned to the Bethlehem, Beit Fajjar, and Jurat ash-Sham'a route. *(Photograph by the author.)*

tain their own transit driver's licenses, which are distinct from regular driver's licenses. In other words, each public transit vehicle in operation requires all three of these numbers to operate legally.

Since many drivers cannot afford to purchase line permit numbers, they instead opt to rent a number from the Ministry of Transportation or from a third party. Only one-line permit number can be rented at a time, and the driver must register as renting that number with the local transportation agency. Private citizens who can afford to may purchase line permit numbers and then rent them out for use by people who have their own cars.

There is no limit to the number of line permit numbers that can be purchased (as opposed to rented). In this configuration, the owner of the permit number collects a monthly flat fee from the driver without having to involve himself in the complications of maintaining a vehicle. Others rent out permit numbers and transit-approved vehicles together. In other words, they employ drivers to use their permits. In this scenario, the vehicle owner and driver split the amount that is earned—sometimes down the middle; sometimes two-thirds to the driver and one-third to the owner. The earnings are divided after the cost of gas, parking, and, sometimes, coffee, a sandwich, or a pack of cigarettes is deducted. A vehicle owner who employs a driver assumes responsibility for all internal repairs, while the driver is responsible for body damage to the vehicle.

Figure 2.9 Vans at the Batarseh lot headed for Jurat ash-Sham'a.
(Photograph by the author.)

Figure 2.10 From the al-'Ain lot in Bethlehem, vans go to Tuqu'. *(Photograph by the author.)*

Figure 2.11 At the al-'Ain lot, drivers rest in the shade, share drinks, and wait for passengers to fill their vans. *(Photograph by the author.)*

Inside many of the major cities of the West Bank, such as Hebron, Bethlehem, Jericho, Ramallah, and Nablus, there are multiple stations, lots, or corners where public transit vehicles congregate. Typically, there are separate lots for each route or set of routes that travel in the same direction (Figures 2.9–2.11). Many such lots are unmarked, and there are few signs for guidance. To come across them, a potential traveler would need to ask around.

In Ramallah, amid the many different transit lots around town, the two central hubs are located on the same street, one of the six or so that branch out from the main roundabout and central landmark, al-Manara (the Lighthouse). The Ramallah central bus terminal is actually a small, fenced-off parking lot with buses of various sizes—tour buses, school buses, fifteen-seat micro-buses, all converted into public transit vehicles—parked in rows on both sides. A canopy provides shade for resting drivers, but most of the drivers mill around near their buses, calling out to people who enter the lot to advertise their bus's final destination. "Nablus!" "Beit Lahem!" "Ireeha!" they call for travelers to Nablus, Bethlehem, and Jericho, respectively. Most of the buses have numbers, but one does not need to know the number to get on the correct bus. Any of the ebullient drivers will point you in the right direction as soon as you say where you are going.

Just down the street, toward al-Manara, is the Mujama', which operates as the central station for the shared vans known as *Fordaat*. Drivers park scores of big, orange vans in rows corresponding to their final destinations. The *Fordaat* wait on a dedicated level of an indoor, above-ground parking structure. Here, too, when you walk up the long, curved driveway ramp to the Ford level, the drivers call out their destinations until you find the right van. In both cases, whether taking a bus or a van, passengers wait for each vehicle's seats to fill before departing. This indicates one reason some people choose to ride *Fordaat* instead of buses; since *Fordaat* have fewer seats, they fill more quickly.

A similar arrangement can be found in Bethlehem, where different forms of transportation congregate and wait to pick up passengers in a structure called the Mujama' of Bethlehem. The building is located on the main road in Bethlehem, known as Manger Street (Share' al-Mahid) because it leads to the major tourist destination, Manger Square. Bethlehem is marked by hills, and the Mujama' perches on the side of a slope leading to Beit Sahour. As in Ramallah, the shared intercity *Fordaat* vans line up by destination, but in Bethlehem the *Fordaat* level is several floors below the main street entrance (Figure 2.12). Again, passengers need only show up, and they are quickly swept into a vehicle headed for their desired destination. If they face a wait, they can buy coffee, tea, or a snack from one of the handful of small shops and carts set up next to the parked vans (Figure 2.13).

Figure 2.12 Mujama' transit center of Bethlehem from the *Ford* level below. *(Photograph by the author.)*

Figure 2.13 View of the Hamada restaurant and pastry shop next to the *Ford* vans at the Bethlehem Mujama'. *(Photograph by the author.)*

Figure 2.14 Mujama' of Bethlehem from the *service* level above.
(Photograph by the author.)

Travelers arriving in Bethlehem at the *Fordaat* level, whether coming from Ramallah or next-door Beit Sahour, will take an elevator up to the Manger Street level of the Mujama', which doubles as a commercial center (Figure 2.14). Here the building hosts an array of shops selling the latest fashions in clothing and accessories, as well as small corner stores where shoppers can buy some snacks or top up their cell phone minutes. There is also a fast-food restaurant called "Kentucky Fried Chicken," whose massive sign brands the back of the building for all of the approaching vehicles below. On the same level, Bethlehem residents come to the local office of a Palestinian phone company to pay their bills and otherwise manage their accounts.

Just outside the doors of the Mujama' on the Manger Street level, intra-city *services* wait in line to fill their vans with passengers coming from Manger Square or out of the Mujama'. From there, passengers might jump into a *service* and head toward Fawanees, the dessert shop adjacent to Beit Jala that is famous for its Nablus-style *knafeh* and many varieties of baklava or down the hill toward Souq ash-Sha'ab, the major grocery store and landmark in Beit Sahour. During the time of my fieldwork, those willing to wait and enjoy a rather antiquated ride for a less expensive fare of 2.5 shekels (about 60 cents) could walk to Manger Square and take the blue-and-white

Beit Sahour bus down the hill to the Souq ash-Sha'ab corner. Passengers traveling a greater distance to one of the nearby villages might catch a ride in one of the intercity *Fordaat* on the downstairs level of the Mujama' and get out along the way; if they prefer a roomier ride, they can hail a private *taxi Tulub* and ride to their destination alone.

The price of a bus, van, *service*, or taxi ride predictably depends on how far one is going. Bus and van fares are set in advance, and they vary based on whether the bus can convey people only to the major checkpoint along the way or beyond. There are also different fares for youth, adults, and seniors. Van fares tend to be about 20 percent higher than bus fares going the same distance, but van rides are very popular and considered faster than the bus. Passengers can get off the bus or the van at any point along the road, and their fare may be reduced depending on how much of the route they are riding. If one passenger gets off early, the driver will likely pick up a passenger waiting on the side of the road to refill the emptied seat. Passengers are often waiting along the main routes, possibly from villages that are far from the departure points in the major transportation centers. Taxi fares in the West Bank are negotiated between the passenger and the driver, although for oft-traveled routes, the typical price may be assumed by both parties, as I observed during my fieldwork.

Fares tend to increase slightly in response to gas price hikes, but the tension is felt by drivers and passengers alike. As one driver explained to me, the fares to take a *Ford* from Bethlehem to Ramallah (or Jericho or Hebron) are too high for passengers and too low for drivers. Operators incur various expenses beyond gas. They must pay for their licenses, and they must pay a fee each time they park in the central transit station of either of the major cities they drive between. Drivers can be held liable for traffic violations they commit, especially if they are stopped on Israeli-controlled roads with passengers who are not wearing seatbelts. These bureaucratic incidentals may contribute to the conviction among some drivers that they did much better business illicitly shuttling (and price gouging) passengers through the countryside during the second Intifada, which I discuss in the next chapter.

Passengers are presented with a choice among various forms of transportation, and they perform ad hoc calculations that consider convenience and cost in making their decisions. For example, one of my interlocutors, Muhammad, occasionally travels from his job at a nongovernmental organization in Beit Sahour to his ancestral village on the outskirts of town. At the time of my fieldwork, he could take two shared taxis, pay 6 shekels (about $1.50), and possibly wait on the road for either, or he can take a private taxi and pay 10 shekels to avoid unpredictable waiting times. Passengers who wanted to travel from Beit Sahour to Ramallah could try to catch the Beit Sahour bus that departed only once—in the morning—and cost 16 shekels (about $4), or they could take a 2.5 shekel (about 60 cents) *service* ride to the Mujama' of Bethlehem and get in a *Ford* to Ramallah for 22 shekels (about $5.50). While more expensive, the *Ford* is more comfortable and smaller, meaning that passengers spend less time waiting for the vehicle to fill up. Among my interlocutors of all ages in Greater Bethlehem, it was widely agreed that passengers find private taxis and shared vans (*Fordaat*) expensive; buses, cheap; and shared taxis (*services*), fair.

These cost-benefit analyses that riders routinely perform are affected by fare rates, as well as availability. As one way to improve employment, officials at the PA Ministry of Transportation told me, they raised the number of permits granted to *Ford* drivers, increasing their numbers on the street to a level that some people found excessive. The increased availability of *Fordaat* running routes that pass through Beit Sahour to Bethlehem, for example, resulted in the hobbling of the local Beit Sahour Bus Company, which used to have more business shuttling passengers up the very steep hill to Bethlehem. From 2012 to 2014, this bus service slowed and began running only a couple of times a day, commonly transporting fewer than eight passengers in its entire school-bus length. Ministry officials confirmed that the reduced service offered by the Beit Sahour Bus Company was a direct result of the increased availability of *Fordaat*, which run constantly up and down the hill and are therefore much more appealing for travelers who do not want to waste time waiting for a bus to leave. By 2016, the Beit Sahour Bus Company had closed, and the company subsequently sold its route licenses and vehicles to two other companies that now use them.

One common feature of official public transportation systems in developed nations is the availability of route maps. In the context of Israeli public transit, route maps are available for the bus and train systems, including those that connect to the settlements, but no route map is publicly available for Palestinian public transit in the West Bank. In part, this situation exists because a printed route map can become obsolete at any moment due to the shifting Israeli rules that govern the terrain on which Palestinian transit operates. During an interview in 2013, I asked the outgoing general manager of road transportation in the Ministry of Transportation whether there was a route map and a timetable for any of the transit lines under the jurisdiction of the PA. He pointed me to a large map affixed to the wall, which he used to plan the intercity transit routes in an effort to coordinate among the various transit owners and operators in the West Bank. But the map was not publicly available or widely distributed as an official route map for transit riders. When I asked why, he chuckled with frustration and explained there would be no point in printing route maps or time schedules because both can change due to the whim of a single Israeli soldier or Israel's shifting colonial tactics. Israel's diffused bordering processes impose delays on Palestinian movement, randomly or inconsistently closing off or rerouting routes, imposing intensified levels of scrutiny, and changing access and use rules for various roads and entrances. For this reason, when I asked the general manager what could improve the public transportation system in the West Bank, he replied, matter-of-factly, "An end to the Israeli occupation."

While the Palestinian public transportation system in the West Bank offers coordinated, recognizable, and readily available transportation to the public, it also features unpredictable delays, inconsistent service, and perilous exposure to Israeli military authority. Due to Israel's diffused bordering practices, which have embedded the Israeli military into the quotidian landscape of the West Bank, an unavoidable characteristic of transit ridership is that it moves Palestinians through direct encounters with surveillance, state violence, and dispossession of time and other social resources, all of which make up the broader Israeli border-enclosures strategy that enacts settler colonialism in the territory. Despite myriad disincentives to movement, Palestinians manage to move about the West Bank on public transportation every day, which often provides the only way for them to connect with certain opportunities for social reproduction. The service gaps that result from the unpredictability of Israel's diffuse borders are converted into opportunities in which the practice of democratic spatial negotiation flourishes, amplifying a formidable power of local knowledge networks and Palestinian communality against which colonial forces must contend. From these dynamics, it becomes evident that public transportation in the West Bank is a terrain of struggle on which Israeli colonial power imposes itself and Palestinians build local knowledge networks to carry on living everyday life. To this latter point the next chapter turns.

3

The People on the Bus

Routes (and Roots) of Mobile Commoning

Despite the burdens and dangers of movement in the West Bank, Palestinians still manage to organize their lives around expectations of collective mobility via public transit. They do so by building communal knowledge networks based on constantly updated information transmitted as a routine part of the transit system. This network involves real-time interactions among transit participants, whether across open car windows or while inside a vehicle waiting for it to fill up, that help people make decisions or just prepare themselves for the road ahead. Sometimes the interactions are just friendly socializing and other times they are heated negotiations over price or route. But the repeated social interactions generate and strengthen relations among people and space that defy the organizing logics of settler colonialism.

For example, infrequent riders or those headed to new destinations need only show up to a city's central transit terminal to be quickly guided in the right direction by drivers or fellow passengers. Or they might instead ask a local store owner, taxi driver, or friend. In fact, asking others is the only way to learn the locations from which most buses and vans depart, the destinations to which they travel, and how long the trip will take. These interactions make up a web of local knowledge networks that alleviate some of the system's inconveniences and dangers. This component of sociality built into the transit system is what allows users to gain relevant information in the normal course of the interactions required to use the system when unexpected changes to the route or schedule occur. The practices of producing and sharing knowledge about how to use the public transportation system in the West Bank contribute to mobile commoning that enable Indigenous reclamation and use of space. Mobile commoning, in turn, represents an active if quotidian exercise of *sumud* that holds together fragmented Palestinian communities and fosters meaningful relationships in and to Palestinian space (Figure 3.1).[1]

In any public transportation system, users' experiential knowledge can enhance and ease their experience. But what distinguishes the Palestinian case is that it operates in and interacts with a settler colonial project attempting to "monopolize the legitimate means of mobility" (Torpey, 2000) in order to extend itself. Against this backdrop, one of the important characteristics of Palestinian public transit is that it is not possible to use the system as an isolate. One must interact with others to obtain the information necessary to get by, and this communal knowledge sharing has a strong if implicit political valence. While squarely located in the realm of everyday life, mundane engagements with public transit and the sociality they necessitate constitute powerful practices of decolonization for three reasons. First, Palestinian transit fosters social connections, both in the course of normal transit use and by conveying Palestinians from one place to another, that subvert the fragmenting effects of Israel's im/mobilization regime. Second, Palestinian transit functions through the creation and dissemination of spatial and temporal knowledge over which Israeli settler colonialism seeks to claim a monopoly through its diffused border processes. And third, Palestinian transit cultivates and draws from exercises of self-determined mobility, where the system's participants assert and fulfill expectations of moving that exceed the domination of the im/mobilization regime.

The political valence of these mundane engagements with transit exists in relation to a wide array of organized, concerted civil resistance. From local protests against dispossession in particular villages to internationally coordinated campaigns, such as the Boycott, Divestment, and Sanctions Movement (BDS Movement, 2005), Palestinians continue to resist Israeli settler colonialism broadly and the elements of its im/mobilization regime specifically (Peteet, 2018, pp. 169–200). Yet coordinated political actions do not make up the entire field of Palestinian power. Quotidian activities undertaken repeatedly in the course of everyday life, often for reasons other than self-conscious political resistance, also contribute to the Palestinian struggle (see, e.g., Seidel & Tartir, 2019, p. 9).

In Chapters 1 and 2, I analyzed the development and features of the Israeli im/mobilization regime as contributing to a border-enclosures strategy for advancing settler colonialism in the West Bank. Now I turn to an examination of routine engagements by riders and drivers with public trans-

Figure 3.1 Man carrying full bags of groceries toward a *Fordaat* station in Nablus. *(Photograph by Avery F. Gordon.)*

portation and the sociality that emerges. I argue that these interactions represent Palestinian mobile commoning, which poses a counterforce to the Israeli enclosures. Dimitris Papadopoulos and Vassilis Tsianos (2013) advance the notion of the "mobile commons," which represents a living network among refugees, primarily those who move across the Mediterranean toward Europe, of shared knowledge about transnational mobility. The mobile commons are not enclosed in the realms of public or private life; rather, they are composed of the continual, quotidian, cooperative production (or reclamation) and sharing of spatial knowledge. Similarly, I argue that the way Palestinians navigate the Israeli border-enclosures as they use public transportation to move around the West Bank can be considered practices of mobile commoning.[2] The notion of commoning has resonances in Palestine: Alessandro Petti, Sandi Hilal, and Eyal Weizman (2013) write about "al-masha'," a form of common land in Palestine that involves collective ownership and cultivation and that continues to survive colonial encroachments. They demonstrate a "re-activation" of the notion of al-masha' through its application beyond the agricultural context to represent "cultivation of life [that] is concerned as much with forms of living as with life itself" (pp. 183–184). Taking inspiration from their multiple applications of the concept, I argue that mobile commons can be understood as a moving form of al-masha' because they involve repeated, collective practices of communal care and social connection as Palestinians move across Palestinian land.

Both particular and general resonances of the concept of commoning matter. Mimi Sheller (2018) identifies a global repertoire of mobile commoning as the basis for a global movement for mobility justice (p. 167). Mobile commoning in a variety of places represents characteristic practices of the "utopian margins," where people both enact and anticipate modes of living that are alternatives to forms of domination (A. Gordon, 2018). These global resonances suggest common modalities of people power even while the particulars of each context indicate distinct significances. In the case of Palestinian public transportation, mobile commoning represents quotidian practices that enable self-determined movement, modes of living that exceed the limiting conditions of settler colonialism. I now turn to an examination of the specifics of how Palestinian mobility is commoned in the West Bank.

Transit Sociality, Flexibility, and Communal Care

Due to the impracticality of printing route maps and schedules for a transit system that operates under military occupation, as noted in Chapter 2, drivers and passengers rely heavily on direct conversations and word of mouth for the most up-to-date information about routes, fares, and approximate timetables. These exchanges constitute living, dynamic communal knowledge networks. Drivers on intercity routes, which are likely to cross through or near Areas B and C and thus to bring them within the purview of Israeli military control, may encounter unexpected obstructions as a result of the occupation. To deal with such situations, transit drivers keep in touch with one another through cell phones or across open windows as they pass one another. The first few drivers on any given route to come across either an activated checkpoint or a flying checkpoint will quickly spread the word to other drivers passing that point. In some cases, prior knowledge about the checkpoint will allow the driver to take an alternative route. For example, a common location for flying checkpoints is on the road below Beit Sahour, after the main road passes under a bridge on the way to the village of Dar Salah. On the Beit Sahour side of this impromptu checkpoint location, the road forks in two directions that lead either to Bethlehem or to Hebron, the two main cities of the southern West Bank; on the Dar Salah side is the main road to Ramallah. This is a strategic location because it marks a point that West Bank Palestinians must cross on the route between the northern and southern districts. However, locals and transit drivers know about a detour that avoids the checkpoint. I omit the details of the detour because it might compromise the safety of drivers and passengers, although when I asked one of my interlocutors, a long-time *taxi Tulub* driver, whether he thought the occupation forces knew about such detours, he waved his hand and said, "Of course. They just want to inconvenience us." While this remark may appear to suggest that these elongated detours are the intended result of the flying checkpoints rather than resilient movement around them, I have demonstrated that the ultimate goal of the inconvenience is to discourage Palestinian self-determined mobility altogether. Thus, because the detours represent Palestinian knowledge of the territory and enable Palestinian movement directed by Palestinian priorities, they are properly considered part of mobile commoning.

Upon learning about activated or flying checkpoints on the road, the drivers will, in turn, notify their passengers if they are already on the road; if they have not yet departed, they will warn boarding passengers in advance. This can be crucial information for some riders who are vulnerable to Israeli detention, perhaps because they are known political activists or come from a refugee camp, whose youth are often targeted as part of Israel's collective punishment of the camps. It is also important information for travelers with appointments or time constraints at their intended destination; if they learn in advance about a checkpoint, which can sometimes cause several hours of traffic delay, they can send word or opt not to board at all. While these are seemingly small decisions, they can allow passengers to protect time or opportunities that might otherwise be confiscated by settler colonial im/mobilizations.

The transmission of live-update information is easily accomplished because the transit system has sociality built into it. Amahl Bishara (2015) recognizes the "sociality of travel" practiced by drivers of private cars navigating Israeli im/mobilizations across the West Bank, noting that this sociality "consolidate[s] a sense of Palestinian collectivity" (p. 34). Relatedly, the routine functioning of public transit creates opportunities for sociality and relies on it. Use of Palestinian transportation in an atomized, anonymous, and mechanical way is not possible. To even locate the right vehicle headed in their direction, passengers must interact with the drivers calling out their destinations. Beyond these initial interactions, Palestinian transit use is a thoroughly social affair for cultural reasons. For example, greeting strangers is a typical cultural practice, and it is common for passengers boarding a vehicle to greet those already inside by saying, "As-salamu alaykum" (Peace be upon you). Sometimes early exchanges develop into boisterous conversations among passengers and drivers, recounting the events of the previous night's Barcelona or Madrid football match or commiserating about the morning traffic at the checkpoint (see Hany Abu-Assad's artistic interpretation of the political valence of this social space in his 2002 film, *Ford Transit*). In this way, transit ridership is another venue for the extension of the sociality of Palestinian public life, integral to maintaining a sense of community against the fragmented territorial backdrop.

Moreover, opportunities for sociality emerge from the transit system's necessary flexibility. While Israeli im/mobilizations disrupt transit predictability, the Palestinian system functions in a somewhat flexible way to respond to those disruptions on the fly. It is precisely this flexibility that presents opportunities for the repeated practice of communality and mutual aid. One common way this plays out is through the negotiations that occur when a passenger wants to stop somewhere between a vehicle's departure point and destination. The passenger may want to stop along the route or at a location that might cause a change in the route. Since both negotiations are common, interactions between passengers and drivers are necessary.

According to interviews I conducted in 2014 with officials from the Palestinian Authority (PA) Ministry of Transportation, there were no permanent "bus stops" on routes *between* different cities or *muhafidhat*.[3] By the summer of 2018, though, this seemed to have changed, with sheltered metal-frame benches, emblazoned with corporate advertisements, appearing across the landscape. Still, these bus stops do not mark the sole permissible stops on a given route; rather, stops are still negotiated in real time. Whether on a bus, *Ford* van, or *service*, passengers can ask that the vehicle stop anywhere along the way by simply saying, "Ya'teek al-a'fiyeh" (a common blessing for anyone working), to the driver or making a more direct request. Especially in the case of the *Ford* van, when a passenger gets off the vehicle mid-route, she frees up a seat that the driver may fill by picking up someone waiting on the side of the road ahead. For some people in small villages strewn among Palestinian urban centers, this may be their only way to catch a ride.

In some cases, a passenger might request that a *Ford* driver take a detour or a different route to deposit her closer to her destination. For example, on three trips from the Jericho arrival terminal to Bethlehem, I observed a passenger saddled with luggage asking the *Ford* driver to leave the main route and transport her across hilly terrain to her home. This negotiation may be done without the knowledge of the other passengers. Certainly, such an agreement can (and did) cause annoyance and even provoke spirited opposition from other travelers, but given a prevailing ethos of communal care enforced through gentle scolding from others, the opposition ultimately obliged.

From Bethlehem to Ramallah, it is possible for shared vans to stop in Abu Dis to drop off students of Al-Quds University, but this elongates the route into an area that can be plagued by traffic. So passengers headed to Abu Dis have to negotiate with the driver and passengers in order to get there. Instead of organized stops and signs, the kind of interactions built into the regular functioning of the system promotes routine, even if at times begrudging, practices of communality. In addition, the system's flexibility allows certain challenges to be overcome through communality and mutual aid, as is illustrated in the following vignettes drawn from my field research.

Traveling late one holiday night on a bus from Jerusalem to Ramallah in the summer of 2012, a driver pulled his bus onto the shoulder for a young passenger whose father was meeting him at that point in the road. It is possible that the boy's father did not have permission to enter Jerusalem and had to meet his son on the bus's path once it neared Ramallah. The driver, unbound by a tight schedule but bound to a culture of communal care, stopped the bus and got out with the boy, helping him cross the busy highway to his father's car on the other side of the road. In this case, the bus set the stage for a routine performance of communality: Palestinians coming together and maintaining meaningful connections with one another is remarkable in the context of an occupation that seeks to keep them fragmented and alienated.

Communal deliberation and problem solving are also activated in the unpleasant situations in which drivers delay departure to wait for enough passengers to fill their vehicles' seats. In May 2013, in a van headed to Bethlehem from the Jordanian border terminal in Jericho, four other passengers and I waited for more than two hours for the last two of seven passenger seats to be filled in the *Ford* transit van. An elderly passenger told me she had been waiting for two hours before I had even arrived. When a sixth person finally boarded, some of the other travelers pleaded with the driver to leave. They negotiated that we would each pay a portion of the remaining fare so we would not have to wait for a seventh person. The young man who had just joined us was reluctant to approve the deal, so another passenger agreed to cover his portion. In the end, we split the fare six ways and avoided further delay. Although the lamentably common ordeal was far from enjoyable, it created an opportunity for the practice of communal negotiation that exemplifies the system. Were it not for this passenger-brokered agreement, the departure time would have been further delayed.

Indigenous Spatial Knowledge-Power

In addition to these practices of cooperation and communal care, mundane transit engagements contribute to the process of decolonization at a different register. By communally generating and sharing knowledge about the terrain, public transit participants challenge Israeli colonial efforts to monopolize spatial knowledge. During the current period of expanding settler colonialism in the West Bank, power struggles have erupted not only over access to space, but also over how space is known.[4] In his generative concept "imaginative geographies," Edward Said (1994) emphasized the productive nature of imperial imaginations of place, through which "colonial space must be transformed sufficiently so as no longer to appear foreign to the imperial eye" (p. 226). This is especially true in the case of settler colonialism, in which imaginative geographies serve to actually produce counterfeit claims of settler indigeneity on stolen land. In other words, as Israel projects a Zionist supremacist imagination onto the West Bank, it creates spatial knowledge that is knowable only to Israelis and systematically denied to Palestinians as a way to entrench the colonial and uproot the Indigenous familiarity with the land. As Israel annexes West Bank land, it forbids Palestinians from using various routes and traversing some terrain. By restricting physical access to certain areas, Israel's policies and practices attempt to alienate Palestinians from that particular land and from the knowledge of how to traverse it. In addition, Israel imposes restrictions on Palestinian mobility with rules that constantly change and are not formally declared. Hagar Kotef (2015) has described this in the case of checkpoints, where Israel sets up an economy of knowledge about the "uninterpretable" rules of crossing them (pp. 33–36, 40–41, 46–48). In fact, this economy of knowledge is applied beyond the checkpoints, diffused throughout the territory of the West Bank. It is not only the checkpoint rules that are "unknowable" but also the knowledge of reliable timetables and routes. Again, this condition exists because rules that affect mobility constantly change and are not officially declared. So both of these tactics—making both land and movement rules inaccessible—affect the *knowability* of the means of movement. In other words, Israel claims exclusive control over the knowledge that enables mobility in the West Bank.

Given the effects of colonial imagined and imaginative geographies, Said (1994) notes the important decolonial task to "reclaim, rename, and *reinhabit* the land" (p. 226, emphasis added). In the course of routine participation in Palestinian public transportation, riders and drivers practice mobile commoning as they socially create local knowledge networks about how, where, and when to move that enable this decolonizing *reinhabitation* of the land. The significance of mobile commoning via public transit has many dimensions. Bishara (2015) has analyzed the experience of "driving while Palestinian" in various spaces in historical Palestine and notes that these experiences yield "Palestinians' systematized knowledge of closure" (p. 42). In other words, it is through driving that Palestinians develop a comprehensive understanding of Israel's restrictions on movement. Similarly, through communal negotiations and communication, Palestinian *transit* participants build an archive of local knowledge about delays, detours, and dangers on the road. This provides a valuable source of "knowledge-power" (Foucault, 1977) that challenges the settler colonial mobility regime.[5] But the significance of the knowledge derived from driving extends beyond learning about colonial restrictions. By responding to unpredictability and unreliability with resilience, mobile commoning enables Palestinian movement across and familiarity with the land and connection in the face of a fragmented landscape.

In addition to the sociality and communality that are necessary components built into the transit system, Palestinian transportation undermines the logics of Israeli settler colonialism by rejecting the attempted colonial monopoly over mobility knowledge and fostering and reasserting Indigenous social and spatial relationships. In particular, the local knowledge networks of Palestinian public transit drivers present a formidable counterforce. The power of this collective knowledge derives from intimate, in-person experiences of traveling across and interacting with the terrain.

As part of my field research, and because official route maps are not publicly available, I asked *Fordaat* drivers based at the Bethlehem Mujama' (the main transit center) to draw maps of their intercity routes for me (Figures 3.2–3.7).[6] I had intended to ask for a map from each driver I encountered sitting on the bench, waiting his turn to fill up his vehicle in the July heat of the first week of Ramadan fasting. Instead, what unfolded was an unforeseen display of mobile commoning. Once the first driver began to draw, all of the drivers who had experience with a particular route gathered around the sketchpad, yelling out landmarks that the drawer had missed or needed to include. Though moments earlier the reigning mood had been quiet exhaustion, once the map drawing commenced, the atmosphere

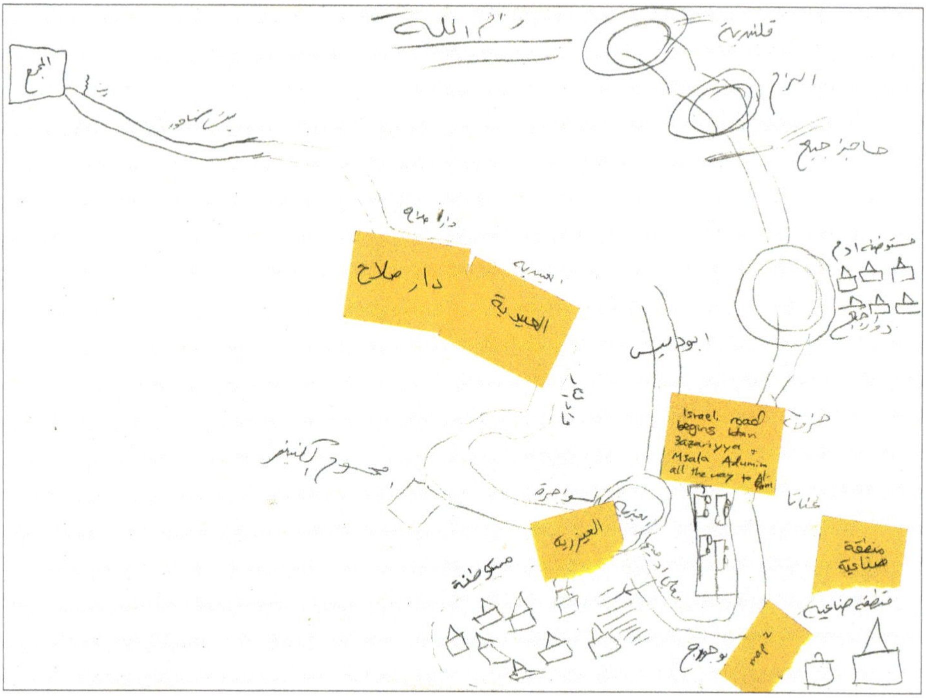

Figure 3.2 Map of the Bethlehem–Ramallah route, hand-drawn at my request
by *Fordaat* drivers based in the main transit terminal in Bethlehem, 2013.
(I added the yellow tags, after consultation with the drivers, in an attempt to
rewrite words in clearer script and append details drawn from context.)

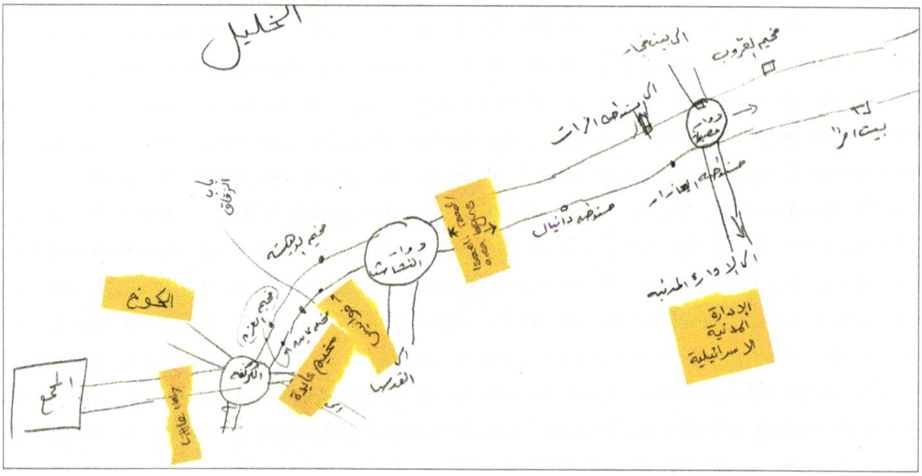

Figure 3.3 First page of the Bethlehem–Al-Khalil/Hebron route map,
hand-drawn at my request by *Fordaat* drivers based in
the main transit terminal in Bethlehem, 2013.

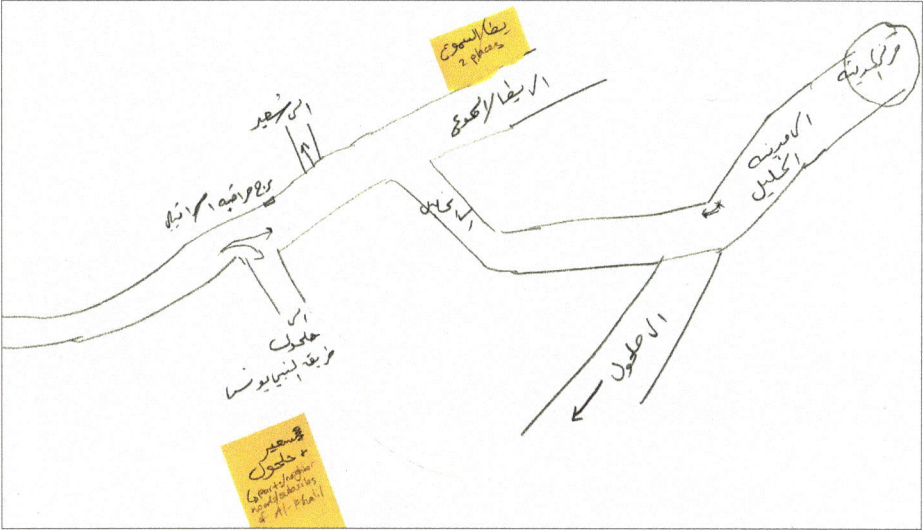

Figure 3.4 Second page of the Bethlehem–Al-Khalil/Hebron route map.

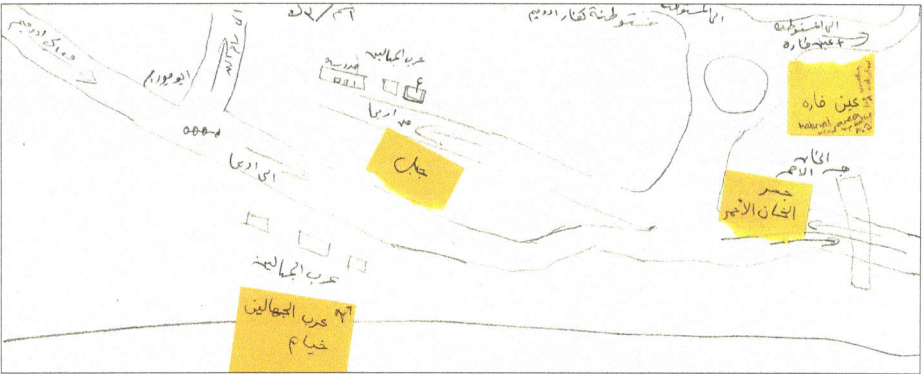

Figure 3.5 First page of the Bethlehem–Ireeha/Jericho van route, hand-drawn at my request by *Fordaat* drivers based in the main transit terminal in Bethlehem, 2013.

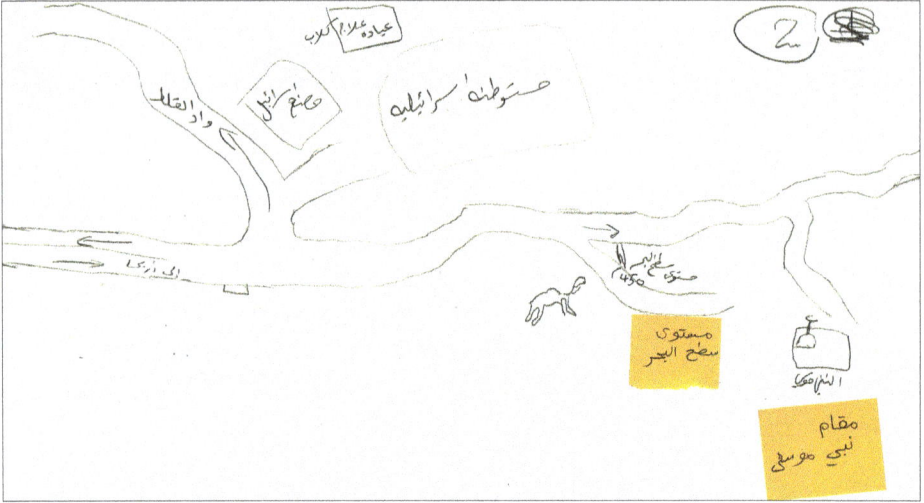

Figure 3.6 Second page of the Bethlehem–Ireeha/Jericho van route.

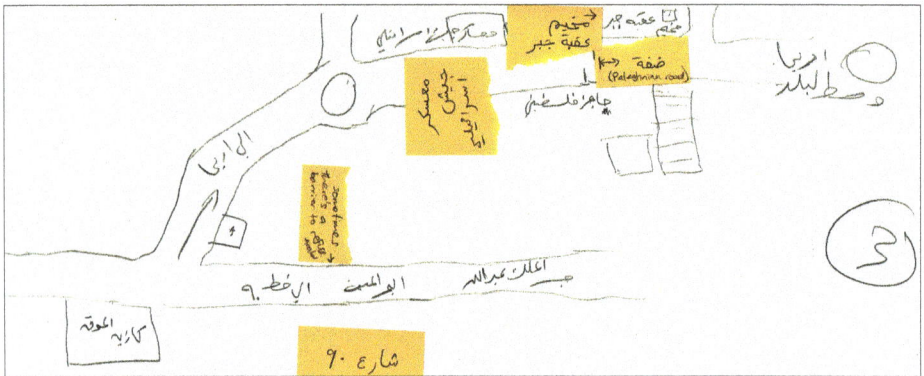

Figure 3.7 Third page of the Bethlehem–Ireeha/Jericho van route.

became jovial and boisterous; the men poked fun at one another and competed over whose suggestions would be taken by the drawer. None of these men had been driving for fewer than eight years; most had been driving for fifteen or twenty. It was clear that the exchange of knowledge—even knowledge that each of them had gained individually through vast experience—provided an opportunity to collectively craft and assert a social identity based on knowing by heart what the occupation attempts to make unknowable.

The map drawing was not only about representing familiar space in two dimensions. It also included this dynamic commoning of the spatial knowledge that enables the drivers to move around the West Bank. As they conversed, they sometimes paused to note certain features of the terrain that they all knew but suspected I did not—most notably, the places where the road passes into (and then out of) Israeli control. These points would roughly correspond with the seatbelt clicks I described in the opening to Chapter 2.

The substance of the hand-drawn maps also reveals a resilient form of knowledge-power exercised by Palestinian transit drivers. The *Fordaat* drivers drew maps without road names or numbers; they were not to scale but, instead, were characterized by the mundane and official landmarks that lay along their routes. As the driver artists sketched out the path of their routes, they would stop along the way to identify the surrounding landmarks, creating the sense that we were actually on the road as the route was being described. These landmarks are the most meaningful to those who traverse the territory regularly.

The map of the route from Bethlehem to Ramallah (see Figure 3.2) shows the terrain as it loops around the many settlements and accompanying military barracks and checkpoints that cover the landscape on the way. The tight turns of the Wadi in-Nar are only one part of the route's winding representation. The drivers drew this entire route on one page of the sketchbook, as if to mock the absurdity of Israel's attempts to both cram settler life into Palestinian land and segregate it.

The map of the route from Bethlehem to Al-Khalil/Hebron took up four pages of the sketchbook and triangulated the path with more civilian landmarks. On the first page (see Figure 3.3), the route is boisterously clustered with the Aida and Dheisheh refugee camp neighborhoods; some famous restaurants and sweet shops, including the dessert shop Fawanees (as mentioned in Chapter 2); and an elementary school. Once the drivers "arrive" at the end of the Bethlehem–Al-Khalil/Hebron route, the hand-drawn map (see Figure 3.4) focuses on marking the different offshoots that one might take to connect to the many Palestinian villages around Al-Khalil. Characterizing Al-Khalil by its connections to other places is a meaningful subversion of the intense fragmentation with which Israeli settler colonialism has targeted Hebron, for example, famously closing the once bustling central ash-Shuhada Street (along with its bus station, among other things) in the old city neighborhood.

On the second of the three pages on which the drivers drew the Bethlehem-to-Ireeha/Jericho route, the map features an Islamic center, an Israeli settlement, and a tourist attraction of a Bedouin and his decorated camel who offer tourists the opportunity to be photographed with an Orientalized caricature of the locals (see Figure 3.6).

The central feature of each map is the through line of the route, slipping around, clambering through, and moving beyond the looming symbols of settler colonial encroachment. The two-dimensional maps represent a resilient form of four-dimensional knowledge-power, based on the collective experience of driving for a public transit system, that accomplishes familiarity with a terrain that settler colonialism seeks to render unknowable. It is the creation and circulation of this knowledge, and its use in a transit system operating in the context of ongoing settler colonialization, that I characterize as mobile commoning.

The drivers' collective cognitive maps of their routes depict what Stephanie Camp (2002) terms "rival geographies" in the context of enslaved people repurposing plantation space in the United States and Audra Simpson (2014) calls "cartographies of refusal" in the context of Kahnawà:ke Mohawk movement across the colonial U.S.-Canadian border (p. 33). Both concepts describe mobile practices of redefining the meanings of different spaces, negotiating dispossessive boundaries, and refusing and recasting the limits of their mobility. By making fragmented space knowable and thus traversable, drivers' intimate, daily, and socialized experiences with the terrain of the West Bank reclaim Palestinian "use value" of the land, recovering Indigenous relationships to moving around the territory (Hammami, 2005; Handel, 2015, p. 82). In other words, this knowledge-power works, returning to Said's (1994) formulation, "to reclaim, rename, and reinhabit the land" as an everyday practice of decolonization (p. 226).

Dispatches from the Second Intifada

In early July 2013, I went to the Bethlehem Mujama', just down the street from Manger Square, to talk to drivers of shared *Fordaat* vans. I had recently developed a pilot questionnaire for transit users in which I asked about respondents' access to and reasons for using public transportation. At the end of the questionnaire I asked whether the respondents found the fares expensive, moderate, or cheap for the West Bank's three forms of shared transportation: the *Fordaat*, the *services* (pronounced *ser-vees*), and the buses.[7] Most of the pilot participants said that the *Fordaat* were too expensive, the buses were cheap, and the *services* were fairly priced.[8]

When I spoke with the *Fordaat* drivers at the Mujama' in that stifling July afternoon, I asked them about this common perception that the *Fordaat* were too expensive. Abu Omar, who at that time was driving the Bethlehem–Ramallah route but has worked on each of the main intercity lines in the southern West Bank at one point or another, quickly retorted, "Sure. All the riders think the fare is too high. And all the drivers think it's too low."[9] Beyond the sense that such opinions are to be expected from those on opposite sides of the supply-and-demand divide, Abu Omar explained that the conflict stems from a problem with the way fares are regulated by the PA Ministry of Transportation. He complained that the ministry had refused to adjust fares to reflect an increase in the cost of petroleum, a failure that led to a major workers' strike in September 2012 (Doha Institute, 2012; Ma'an News Agency, 2012).

Abu Omar also remarked offhandedly that he and the other drivers made a lot of money during the second Palestinian Intifada. Surprised, I asked for clarification, and he explained that the Israeli military imposed severe restrictions on movement during the uprising; some Palestinian transportation drivers responded by taking their services off-road, sometimes under cover of night, to transport people around roadblocks, undetected by the Israelis. If they were spotted by soldiers in jeeps, tanks, or towers, they were chased and shot at, he said, and some of his fellow drivers were arrested and imprisoned. For assuming the grave risks of making such trips, Intifada drivers were able to demand exorbitant prices from their passengers. Furthermore, because the rides were illicit, they fell outside the fledgling PA's ability to rein in prices. Other *Fordaat* drivers at the Mujama' that day confirmed Abu Omar's contention that those were the good old (price-gouging) days, as did many other taxi and *service* drivers I consulted later who had also participated in illicit transportation during the second Intifada.[10]

In what follows, I explore the history surrounding Abu Omar's account and propose that actively rebellious forms of collective movement during the Intifada are the direct antecedents to the current Palestinian public transit system in the West Bank. The refusal of im/mobilization, social problem solving, and Indigenous knowledge of terrain cultivated by the Intifada taxis together formed the roots of the current system's routine practices of mobile commoning.

By the outbreak of the second Intifada, Israel's im/mobilization regime had already crystalized into recognizable bordering processes. Israel's counterinsurgent response against the uprising was to activate all of these processes and intensify conditions of closure and containment in the Palestinian West Bank. As a result of territorial fragmentation and severe restrictions on movement, Palestinian political resistance against the colonial occupation concentrated at all of the points of encounter with these diffused Israeli borders (Baylouny, 2009; Hammami & Tamari, 2000, pp. 7–10). Responding to the shattered landscape necessitated creativity as Palestinians attempted to connect and communicate. For example, graffiti was used to communicate illicit political messages—to mobilize and memorialize—during times of prolonged curfew and when other modes of communication were cut off or rendered too risky (Rolston, 2014).[11]

Among the intensified closures of its networked borders Israel imposed hundreds of physical impediments in the West Bank and the Gaza Strip, especially at strategic locations that would completely seal off Palestinian towns (Hass, 2002). One such roadblock was installed in March 2001 at Surda, on the main route from Ramallah to the university town of Birzeit and other villages to the north. Israeli forces also erected barriers on the only two available detour routes, seriously restricting traffic between Ramallah and its northern neighbors. The particular story of the Surda roadblock—and the vibrant network of transportation that emerged to get around and even through it—exemplifies an important yet under-recognized dimension of the uprising: the popular and practical organizing undertaken to secure means of movement necessary to maintain connections across an increasingly fragmented post–Oslo Accords territory. This organizing created an overtly rebellious mobile commons—repeated activity that generated resources to enable collective movement within, against, and beyond the colonial enclosures.

The roadblock at Surda actually consisted of two separate barriers, one on each side of a 1.5 kilometer stretch of the main road between Ramallah and Birzeit. On both sides of the road at Surda, the terrain descended sharply, making off-road detours impossible. The Israeli military installed a checkpoint that would move to different places along the 1.5 kilometers of blocked-off road (Hammami, 2005). For the first fifteen months, the Surda roadblock provided a narrow lane through which vehicular traffic—coming from both directions—was allowed to pass. This partial opening generated a massive traffic jam, and many travelers opted to walk the distance of the roadblock instead of waiting (Hammami, 2005). The ubiquitous *Fordaat*, along with their predecessors (the eight-seat Mercedes stretch sedans), would congregate on each side of the blockaded area to pick up the many travelers who had just completed the crossing on foot.[12] In the summer of 2002, traffic was cut off entirely through the Surda roadblock, and the number of transit vehicles waiting on each side increased (Hammami, 2005). Most of the people who work in Ramallah come from villages outside the city, and this roadblock, in both its half-open and completely sealed iterations, vastly lengthened their commutes.

Of course, it was not just Ramallah workers who were affected by the roadblock. Schoolchildren and college students had to factor the crossing into their daily schedules. Thousands of daily commuters were subjected to the incomparable inconvenience of the roadblock. Furthermore, pregnant women, elderly and sick people seeking medical care, and even those who were dying were forced to cross the blocked area because no ambulances could pass the barriers to speed around the stopped traffic. My Ramallah-based interlocutors, educated women in their seventies who were active in community arts of different kinds, reported that such afflictions evoked no mercy from the young Israeli soldiers who staffed the checkpoint; they would check the identification of all of those crossing, adding delay to the massive detour. When I asked about transportation during the second Intifada, one of my interlocutors who was originally from Birzeit told me a story about her daily crossings at the Surda roadblock. She had witnessed a dying woman being pushed in a wheelbarrow across the 1.5 kilometer stretch. The Israelis insisted on checking the woman's papers at the checkpoint. My interlocutor protested and asked whether it was necessary to subject someone who was gravely ill to that form of humiliation. The teenage Israeli soldiers answered that they were just following orders and that the sick woman might be a terrorist.

Roadblocks such as the one at Surda deny Palestinians' right to freedom of movement and should be considered one of the many forms of collective punishment Israel imposes on the civilian Palestinian population (e.g., Falk, 2008, p. 45). Yet, as Rema Hammami (2005) observes, "Collective punishment simultaneously creates collective experience, activity and meaning" (p. 18; see also Dana, 2017). It is this collective experience that provided the basis for the vibrant scene established around the Surda roadblock. In addition to the informal assembly of public transportation vehicles waiting at each side of the blockage, local Palestinians took the opportunity to install makeshift businesses and other services at the site. In most vegetable markets in West Bank city centers, a fleet of boys from poor villages or refugee camps offer porter services, pushing around shopping carts to carry groceries for shoppers. Porters equipped with similar shopping or vegetable carts began working the Surda roadblock. Beshara Doumani (2004) adds that, at a similar roadblock on the eastern edge of Nablus around the same time, these porters had to obtain permission from the Israeli soldiers to operate their services in the space of the roadblock (p. 39).[13]

Frequently, porters filled their carts with travelers' luggage or goods to be sold at market. Sometimes they also transported children or the ill. After observing the many sick, elderly, and otherwise incapacitated travelers being pushed in vegetable carts shortly after the closure was imposed at Surda, one of my interlocutors, a prominent member of Ramallah political society, contacted Marwan Barghouti, the famed Palestinian leader centrally involved in both Intifadas who has been in Israeli prison since 2002. She suggested that he arrange to bring wheelchairs to Surda to be used to transport those who were unable to walk the length of the roadblock. Wheelbarrows were also used at times to transport the afflicted. Beyond these informal transport services, other businesses appeared in the Surda chaos, selling umbrellas to travelers baking under the sun or offering coffee, tea, cigarettes, and sandwiches to the *Fordaat* drivers, their passengers, and other travelers along the way.

Beyond the Surda microcosm, transit drivers contributed to a shared network of informal practices of "getting there" (Hammami, 2005, p. 17–19; see also Allen, 2008). Im Naser, a politically active artist and philanthropist, told me that in the early years of the second Intifada, before the Qalandiya Checkpoint became the monstrous, militarized bottleneck that so infamously frustrates traffic between Ramallah and Jerusalem today, off-road taxis would tear down rocky dirt paths or over grassy knolls to avoid the hassle, possible closure, and potential dangers of the checkpoints. In general, off-roading was common among public transit drivers on any given trip, as they were guaranteed to encounter multiple obstacles on the road (Allen, 2008, pp. 457–458). Sometimes a "taxi" would be any driver willing to fill up a regular car and embark on an illicit journey. Indeed, in the northern West Bank, "taxis" humorously named "magic carpets" were made from two-wheel mule-drawn carts (Y. Sharif, 2017, p. 54). And some journeys would take place under the cover of night, headlights extinguished, to avoid detection by the Israeli military. Of course, these risky rides were undertaken at a premium, and passengers bore the high prices. I spoke to people who paid dearly for off-road taxis to transport them to visit dying relatives in a different city, to attend important social events (e.g., weddings or funerals), or to seek medical care in hospitals. Each ride was prompted by the urgent need to connect people and places across a territory fractured by Israeli military and civilian installations.

For their part, the illicit taxi drivers were often chastised for exploiting the desperation of passengers and demanding high fares. Indeed, this ability to price-gouge was at the center of the nostalgia I heard expressed by the transit drivers with whom I spoke in Bethlehem. In her analysis of the moral economy of the Surda Checkpoint, Hammami (2005) explains that the workers who provided creative means of mobility were "victims of the same regime of sanctions that affected the people they provided services for," but they "had found a way to turn that same source of dispossession into a living[,] . . . inhabit[ing] a liminal position on the sharp line between oppressor and oppressed" (p. 26). This predation emerges out of the history of Palestinian economic dependence on Israel, from a readiness to seize any economic opportunity available in the cracks of a settler colonial project that has rendered Palestinian workers precarious.[14]

Given that conceptualizations of the commons typically describe processes that are alternative (if not outright oppositional) to capitalist relations, one might contest the characterization of the Intifada taxis as a mobile commons. Still, I do suggest that this collective cultivation of the means of autonomous mobility in contravention of colonial im/mobilization schemes laid the foundation for the kind of mobile commons that is part of the functioning of Palestinian public transit today.

The second Intifada-era operation of off-road and improvised transit presented an expression of political will with enduring relevance today. Hammami (2005) asserts that the *Ford* drivers and their informal network of elastic transportation constituted the main source of popular organizing in the otherwise more militarized second Intifada:

> The unlikely symbols of the new steadfastness [the Palestinian nationalist slogan of *sumud*] are not the "national institutions" such as the schools, but rather the sub-proletariat of Ford transit van drivers. Considered a menace on the roads and lawbreakers during normal times, now their anarchic, semi-criminal bravado subculture (exemplified by the ubiquitous Nike "No Fear" stickers they place on their back windshields) are a testament to the ethic of getting through anything, by anything, and to anywhere despite all obstacles. It is the same masculine lumpen proletariat subculture of the van drivers that has been in many ways the backbone of the informal organizing systems developed to make it possible for individuals to "get there." (p. 18)

Faced with the choice between allowing Israeli movement restrictions to destroy their livelihood and assuming risks and creating new paths to profit from the situation, public transportation drivers organized a resilient network of alternative transit that was integral to holding together separated communities. The off-road taxis generated a source of anticolonial people power rooted in self-determined mobility. The drivers explicitly refused the immobilizations that the Israeli military sought to impose by driving—and taking passengers with them—across the fragmented landscape. They also explicitly refused Israel's imposition of economic degradation. Despite the widely felt effects of unemployment that resulted from the previous thirty years of economic siege imposed by Israel's military occupation of the West Bank, the Intifada taxi drivers managed to find a situation from which they could make a living. By enabling the movement of people around the West Bank, the Intifada taxi drivers' active *sumud*, or steadfastness, contributed to the development of the "organs for the alternative," the exercise of self-determined collective mobility in a context that attempts to foreclose it. Enabling movement resulted in the maintenance of certain social ties and expectations that nurtured this assertion of autonomous mobility, even in the face of extreme im/mobilizations. In all of these ways, the operation of Intifada taxis constituted a form of rebellious mobility. Ultimately, the operation of the Intifada taxis fostered degrees of sociality, connection, access, and economic independence that are evident in the operation of Palestinian public transit today. Many of the drivers in today's public transportation system participated in the elastic transit services of the Intifada, and the resilience they cultivated during the uprising continues to influence the system through their very participation in it. Furthermore, by enabling collective movement in a time of closure, the Intifada taxis preserved the insistent expectation and exercise of self-determined mobility.

The argument that the routine functioning of Palestinian public transportation involves mobile commoning suggests deep political implications of what at first appears to be a thoroughly mundane system. Within the context of the border-enclosures that advance settler colonialism, the Palestinian mobile commons might be thought of as a vehicle of decolonization—a living institution that not only frustrates the colonial agenda of dispossession but also establishes the foundation for an alternative mode of living beyond colonialism.

Despite the thorough politicization of a colonized people, many West Bank Palestinians primarily engage public transit for quotidian reasons. Asef Bayat (2010) has theorized the "nonmovement movements" that make up the mundane activities of the noncoordinated but numerous ordinary people who most frequently engage in "active use" of public spaces, such as the street, in ways that are implicitly antagonistic to the state's claimed monopoly over spatial control and spatial knowledge (what he calls "street politics") (pp. 12–14). Nonmovements are animated by "the art of presence—the courage and creativity to assert collective will in spite of all odds, to circumvent constraints, utilizing what is available and discovering new spaces within which to make oneself heard, seen, felt, and realized" (p. 26). Palestinian public transportation in the West Bank involves more collective coordination than some of the examples from which Bayat generates his theory, but the coordination is done for the primary purpose of enabling movement that is distinct from organizing for the primary purpose of political action. Palestinian mobile commoning in conjunction with the normal course of transit operation practices the *art of presence*, according to Bayat's formulation. By enabling Palestinian mobility across a terrain of enclosures, public transit users collectively cultivate means of movement, as Bayat says, "in spite of all odds, to circumvent constrains, utilizing what is available and discovering new spaces within which to make oneself heard, seen, felt, and realized." Palestinian mobility via public transportation also refuses the chauvinistic spatial knowledge claims of Israeli colonialism, which seeks to monopolize the authority of defining space and how it is knowable. By continuing to move, and to move collectively, Palestinian transit users assert themselves as mobile agents into the intensely fragmented, colonized landscape.

Importantly, the mobile commons are more than just a source of resistance against the border-enclosure logics of Israeli settler colonialism. As with other examples of commoning, the Palestinian mobile commons are a "generative spacing that is not simply reducible to but that variously precedes, responds to, and exceeds processes of enclosure" (Jeffrey et al., 2012, p. 1249). Palestinian mobile commoning cannot be reduced to only resistance against fragmentation; rather, it must be understood as dynamic exchanges that reroot (and reroute) Palestinian life. In this way, practices of mobile commoning are an example of transformative *sumud* (Ali, 2019; Hammami, 2005), as they represent quotidian, repeated, collective practices that enable Palestinian life to remain meaningfully on Palestinian land.

The dynamic sociality and resilient reclamation of Indigenous spatial knowledge involved in the use of Palestinian transit might productively be recognized in relation to Gerald Vizenor's (2000) notion of "native transmotion": "that sense of native motion and an active presence [that] races as a horse across the page, and the action is a sense of sovereignty" (pp. 15, 179). Vizenor (1999) connects the concept of native transmotion to what he calls "survivance," or a set of active, resilient, and generative practices of Indigenous survival through and in excess of ongoing settler colonialism. Vizenor's "active presence" and Bayat's "art of presence" are both formulations meant to draw our attention to a "story of agency in the times of constraints" (Bayat, 2010, p. 26), a story that those very constraints make invisible because the story's grammar is deeply unsettling to the colonial projects built on those constraints. Furthermore, the stories that both Bayat and Vizenor feature belie colonial narratives, particularly those that represent colonialism as completed, inevitable, or unchallenged. Vizenor's (2000) is a presence in transmotion (p. 15) while Bayat's (2010) presence is the defining moment of a nonmovement (p. 26), but in both cases we find a presence animated by mobile power.

This mobile power constitutes meaningful exercises of what Avery Gordon (2004) drawing from Herbert Marcuse (1964) calls the "organs for the alternative," an unauthorized practice that effects the deep embedding of the instinct for freedom (p. 124). In the case of Palestinian public transit, the persistence of engaging a system of collective mobility and the social relations and spatial knowledge it both necessitates and generates results in the repeated practices of self-determined mobility and the cultivation of an expectation for "freedom without exploitation and misery" that drives these practices (Gordon, 2004, p. 124). Both nurturing and fulfilling this collective imperative of self-determined mobility constitutes a powerful and, most important, enduring alternative to the shattering dispossession of settler colonial enclosures.

The mobile commons allow system users to deal with constant disruptions, in effect holding together the system by offsetting the unpredictability that would otherwise jeopardize its functioning. Through a combination of bureaucratic strangulation and arbitrary disruption and destruction, Israel's im/mobilization regime makes movement by public transit difficult, dangerous, unpredictable, and thus unreliable in an attempt to thwart connection and intensify separation for Palestinians living in the West Bank. Yet in continuing to use public transportation, Palestinian passengers build and strengthen knowledge networks that caulk the resulting service gaps. Through their adaptable, communal knowledge networks Palestinian transit riders and drivers engage in mobile commoning—the repeated practices of sociality that generate resources for getting around. They take quick measure of daily, shifting, structural limitations and disruptions; disseminate the information; and create ad hoc solutions together.

While conditioned by the danger and inconveniences of a terrain marked by diffused bordering processes, the flexibility, negotiability, and communality of transit ridership in the West Bank present opportunities for mobile commoning. Through mundane engagements with the public transit system participants cultivate and maintain connections with one another in the face of widespread spatial divisions. Insofar as it enables mobility via transit across a fractured landscape and preserves practices of sharing Indigenous spatial knowledge, this commoning restores to Palestinian society some degree of freedom—here, not merely the ability to choose between the given alternatives, but also the power to determine what choices are available (Mills, [1959] 2000, p. 174). In this way, West Bank transit is a terrain on which ordinary Palestinians cultivate the connection and coherence that Israeli settler colonialism is targeting with fragmentation, thereby preserving a potent source for Indigenous power that exceeds its domination.

The mobile commoning described in this chapter is one of the ways that Palestinians contest and shape the borderscape of the West Bank as discussed in Chapter 2. As Israel develops its mechanisms for im/mobilizing Palestinians, collective Palestinian mobility functions in ways that oppose the logics and effects of those mechanisms while cultivating alternative social and spatial relations. Yet, of course, this is not the only way that Palestinians attempt to transcend the confines of a settler colonial regime that relies on denying their self-determined mobility. A broad repertoire of Palestinian political actions challenges Israeli settler colonialism, and specifically its im/mobilization regime.

As the spatial reconfigurations of the post-Oslo period have reshaped the opportunities for and spaces of Palestinian resistance, several scholars have addressed the many forms of politics that emerge (see, e.g., Baylouny, 2009; Handel, 2015; Peteet, 2017; Tartir & Seidel, 2019). The effects of im/mobilization have also amplified Palestinians' thorough disappointment with the duplicitous state actors responsible for the Oslo Accords and the so-called peace process, which brokered only a deceptive pseudo-sovereignty for Palestinians that gave cover to Israeli settler colonial expansion. With these betrayals in mind, Palestinians have revived political strategies that focus on communicating with civil society audiences, internationally and domestically, of which the BDS Movement is the best-known example (see, e.g., Barghouti, 2011; Erakat, 2019; Falk, 2014, 2017; Maira, 2013; Said, 2001a). This turn to local and global civil society has interacted with the im/mobilization regime to produce particular Palestinian political actions that engage public transportation as both vehicle and symbol. In the next chapter, I examine three transit-focused political actions that use the bus to undermine the colonial mobility regime and cultivate informed solidarity for Palestinian decolonization.

4

Public Transit Protests
Traversing the Enclosures

I began Chapter 1 with a description of a typical morning commute for Jameel in 2013–2014, during which he would cross through the imposing structure of Checkpoint 300, the only nearby crossing point to Jerusalem accessible to him as a permit-holding Palestinian West Bank resident. But there is another opening in the Apartheid Wall just a stone's throw from Checkpoint 300: a gate seamlessly tucked into the Wall's façade that periodically opens to allow Israeli settler buses to pass through from the settlements to Jerusalem and back. The settler gate is visible from inside the checkpoint. Crossing Checkpoint 300 involves passing through two different structures separated by a fenced-in open-air lot. After passing through the first structure, the part of the checkpoint that is actually embedded in the Wall and that involves the lanes and lines I previously described, travelers walk across the open lot. On the other side of the lot, they reach the building containing the bulk of the security machinery of the checkpoint: metal detectors, booths with soldiers ordering travelers through the metal detectors, more booths with soldiers collecting identity documents, travel permits, and fingerprint scanners. It is while walking through the lot between these two buildings that one can see the settler gate on the other side of the razor-wire fence, slowly opening to allow the settler buses uninterrupted passage through the Wall. The Wall sharply pierces the Palestinian landscape and causes endless delays and disruptions to Palestinian life, but it is no match for the settler buses, which seem to barely stop for the gate to open.[1]

This juxtaposition between the operation of the settler buses—easy, direct, and uninterrupted—and the jarring stops and starts of Palestinian collective mobility has driven a set of Palestinian political actions that take place on buses. In this chapter I examine three Palestinian political protests that occurred in the past decade and involved the bus as a vehicle and symbol. The actions on which I focus are the Palestinian Freedom Rides of 2011, the Freedom Bus of 2011–2016 (and specifically the 2014 ride), and the bus sabotage of 2013. I discuss them in a particular, nonchronological sequence to scaffold my analysis: while the first two actions involved rhetorical interventions based on nonviolent acts of movement, the third action generated rhetorical interventions out of the violent destruction of a means of segregated movement. The bus as a vehicle and symbol for protest actions enabled Palestinian activists to achieve the dual goals of, first, reaching global audiences by connecting to transnational solidarity networks; and second, educating their audiences about their particular experiences of Israeli im/mobilization. In using this symbol of collective mobility to navigate the restrictions of the post–Oslo Accords landscape, Palestinian activists also moved among a collection of terms to describe the many faces of a racially organized settler colonial occupation. Through their focus on transit, Palestinian activists tapped into a legacy of revolutionary transnationalism, advancing decolonizing visions and practices of self-determined mobility on their land.

I have discussed the consequences of Israel's im/mobilization regime on Palestinian life in the West Bank, among which is the attempted control of Palestinian movement out of the territory that denies self-determination. In addition to physical im/mobilizations, Palestinian freedom of expression and, in particular, the mobility and circulation of Palestinian political thought are special targets of the Israeli government.

The ways that Israel has attempted to suppress Palestinian ideas and perspectives are myriad and include, but are far from limited to, the intentional shooting of Palestinian journalists (Human Rights Council, 2019); the confiscation and restriction of Palestinian archives (see, e.g., Sela, 2017); the censorship of Palestinian textbooks (see, e.g., Alayan, 2017); the surveillance and censorship of media, including news media, social media, and Israeli news reporting addressing anything about Palestinians (see, e.g., Kuntsman & Stein, 2015; Matar, 2019); and even the attempted erosion of the Palestinian imagination (e.g., Burris, 2019, pp. 1–4). The public communication of Palestinian political beliefs, especially in formats available to global audiences, are of special concern to Israel, as they challenge Israel's global legitimacy (Falk, 2010, 2014). For example, from October 2015 to November 2017, Israel arrested 280 Palestinians for political expression via social media, including writing posts with political messages but also simply "liking" posts written by others with such content (*Middle East Monitor*, 2017).

Physical im/mobilization has also directly hindered Palestinian politics. Anne Marie Baylouny (2009) argues that the fragmentation of Palestinian territory resulting from the Oslo Accords reduced the spaces available for the kinds of collective and public protests characteristic of the first Palestinian Intifada. As a result, no longer able to rely on the undeniable power of the collective presence of large numbers of demonstrators that drove the first uprising, the protesters of the second Intifada turned to violence to register their message (Baylouny, 2009). Israel's anti-Indigenous program of political repression also includes systematic political imprisonment, the total denial of freedom as a form of immobilization. According to the Addameer Prisoner Support and Human Rights Association, in December 2018, Israel was holding 5,500 Palestinians in prison because of their political beliefs. Furthermore, Israel (sometimes working with the United States) has denied both entry and exit to various prominent figures involved in or supportive of the Palestinian struggle, such as the Gazan football club Khadamat Rafah (*Al Jazeera*, 2019); the Palestinian artist Khaled Jarrar (Vanneschi, 2014); the cofounder of the Boycott, Divestment, and Sanctions Movement, Omar Barghouti (Allam, 2019; Barghouti, 2019); and the U.S. Congresswomen Rashida Tlaib and Ilhan Omar (Hudson et al., 2019). At the level of quotidian movement via public transportation, Israeli forces at checkpoints use these encounter points to target and detain not only known political activists but also residents of refugee camps (information visible on the identity card), particularly in the wake of political demonstrations in their camp, as soldiers may impute subversive politics to all camp residents.

In order to combat the professionalized Israeli im/mobilizations of the post-Oslo era, grassroots Palestinian activists have organized a variety of actions that involve forms of mobility and that target local and global audiences.[2] For example, the Bethlehem-based Right to Movement (RTM), the name given to the Palestine marathon, has sparked a number of RTM running groups in other Palestinian cities. Scholars have recently begun to analyze the significance of these running collectives. Una McGahern (2019) argues that they simultaneously demand and exercise the right to move and the right to recreation as part of a broader claim on the right to fully access their cities, while Joshua Stacher (2018) and Anne Paq (2018) note that the runs are opportunities to educate foreign fellow runners (and remote foreign audiences) about the barriers to movement Palestinians experience. Walking is also an arena for resilience and resistance to im/mobilization, crystalized potently as an indigenous form of territorial and temporal reclamation, as per Raja Shehadeh's (2007) canonical formulation of *sarha*, the unfettered, roaming form of walking Palestine's natural landscape (see also Anne Meneley's [2019] discussion of different forms of walking in Palestine, many both restricted and resilient). Relatedly, Jennifer Kelly (2016) focuses on Palestinian political tours to argue that Palestinian "tour guides use the expansive mobility of tourists to underscore the restricted mobility of Palestinians [and] . . . frame this contingency and racialized precarity of movement as a constitutive part of the regime of military occupation" (p. 735).

I situate within this emerging tradition of mobility-related political actions the three cases I analyze here. All three involved buses, literally and figuratively, to communicate to broad international and domestic audiences about the racially differentiated mobility regime that accomplishes Israel's colonial occupation. The imagined audiences for these actions are multiple and open. The actions attempt to use buses to engage media and then offer rhetorical framings of the actions that communicate insights about the Palestinian struggle to multiple global audiences. The framings—combining racial segregation, apartheid, occupation, and colonization—appear aimed at potentially sympathetic civil society audiences who oppose similar systems in other contexts. But the audiences are not clearly defined because of the activists' aim to reach as broad a solidarity audience as possible.

Among symbols of collective mobility, the bus is a particularly generative site for four reasons. First, as a vehicle used by an earlier generation of civil rights activists in the United States, the bus carries powerful symbolism, wordlessly evoking the triumphs of a collective, grassroots movement against racial segregation. Second, because the bus is a recognizable form of public transportation and mobility, its use allows Palestinian activists to focus international attention on one of the central hardships of occupied life: Israel's heavy controls over movement that entrench the ongoing separation of Palestinians across Palestine. Third, and in light of these controls, the bus provides organizers with the physical mobility and connection that help to transmit their stories to other Palestinians and to foreign visitors and audiences. By harnessing the multiple, cross-contextual resonances of the bus as a motif and a vehicle for collective mobility, Palestinian activists make their collective *im/mobilization* legible to an international community and cultivate an informed solidarity among international allies. Finally, with its connotations of mobility, the bus becomes a platform to engage in *terminological* mobility, moving among language connoting racial segregation, occupation, and colonialism to describe contemporary Israeli rule that involves all three of these systems.

In the protest actions analyzed in this chapter, Palestinian activists pair a focus on collective mobility via the bus with a terminological mobility among different frames to describe Israeli rule in the West Bank. In doing so, Palestinian activists employ what Loubna Qutami (2014) has termed "a Palestinian analytic," or a lens for situating the Palestinian struggle against Zionism in relation to other global struggles against settler colonialism and related or intertwined injustices. Scholars of social movements who use frame theory have centered the agency of social movement actors "as signifying agents actively engaged in the production and maintenance of meaning for constituents, antagonists, and bystanders or observers" (Snow & Benford, 2000, p. 613; see also, e.g., Oliver & Johnston, 2000; Snow et al., 1986). Pamela Oliver and Hank Johnston (2000) warn that frames and ideologies are not synonyms and that ideologies cannot always be extrapolated from frames, as indicated by the fact that sometimes movement actors from opposing ideologies vie over the same frame (pp. 39, 45–49; see also, e.g., Thomsen, 2015). When activists infuse widely circulating frames with localized meaning, they can disrupt dominant discursive conventions, as Carly Thomsen has demonstrated in the case of Native women activists in South Dakota whose reconceptualization of terms such as "privacy" and "freedom" challenge the troublesome binary between reproductive "rights" and reproductive "justice." Similarly, the Palestinian political actions discussed in this chapter disrupt common conceptions of the distinctness of "occupation," "settler colonialism," and "apartheid." In my analysis, I focus on assessing the compound frames that the Palestinian activists have used in their bus-centered protests in terms of how they work to communicate the complex realities of their political context to potentially sympathetic audiences.

Until now, this book has focused on West Bank public transit that is organized, owned, and operated by Palestinians. But there is another public transportation system that runs in the West Bank: the busy system of Israeli buses belonging to companies such as Afikim and the transportation giant Egged.[3] These buses are designed to serve the Jewish-only Israeli settler population, connecting the settlements in the West Bank to one another, to Jerusalem, and to cities inside 1948 Palestine (Figure 4.1). The connections enabled by these buses support the social reproduction of the colonial settlement communities, allowing settlers to commute efficiently to their jobs and other opportunities in Jerusalem and areas beyond the Green Line. Thus, the settler buses may be thought of as a component of the Israeli enclosures because their operation is an integral part of the settler project that divides and displaces Palestinian communities from one another and their land. Yet the ridership of the settler buses is not entirely Jewish Israeli. West Bank Palestinian workers also sometimes ride the settler buses in particular circumstances and directions.

West Bank Palestinians who have managed to obtain travel permits to cross into Jerusalem or 1948 Palestine must cross the Wall through a designated checkpoint. Of the roughly one hundred Israeli checkpoints that have

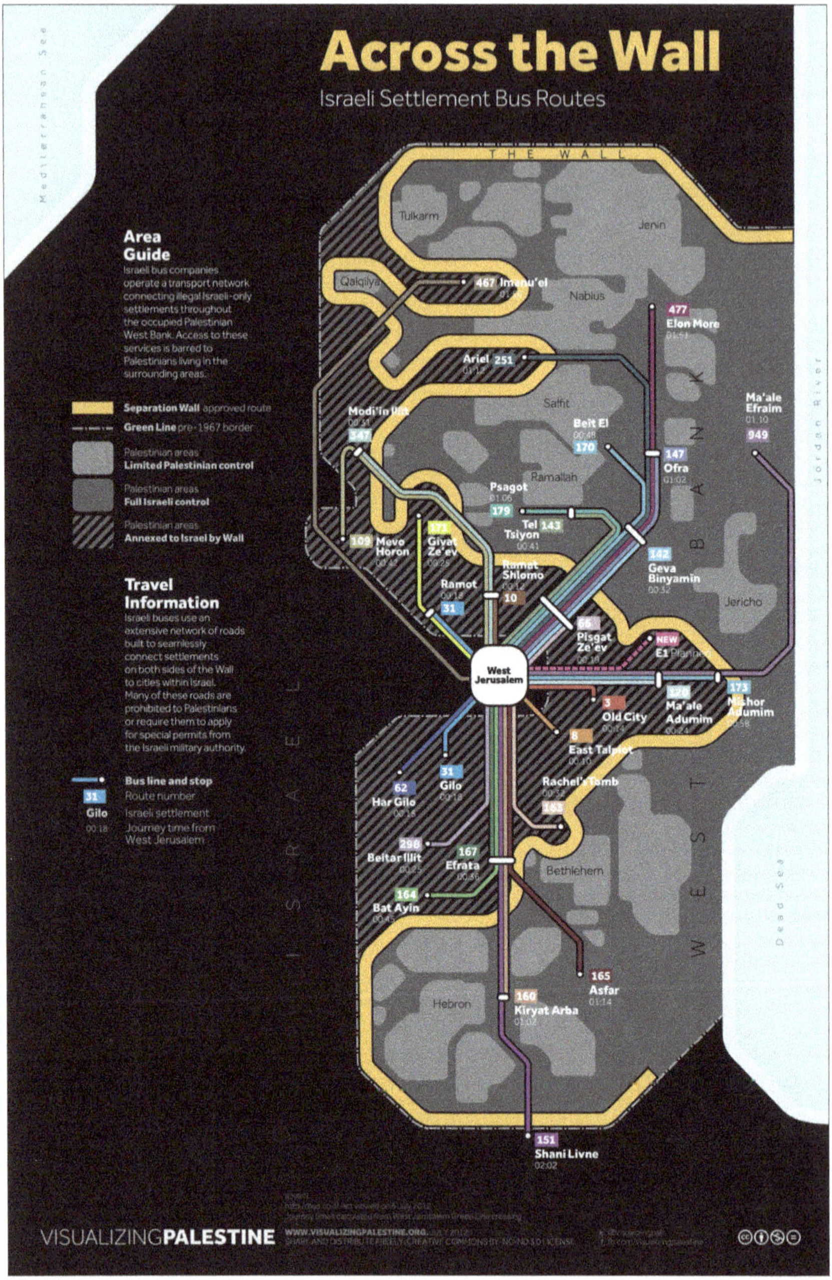

Figure 4.1 Subway-style map of Israeli settler bus routes connecting West Bank settlements to Jerusalem across the Wall. *(Source: Visualizing Palestine.)*

Figure 4.2 Afikim bus at the Ariel settlement. *(Photograph by "Ori~.")*

operated inside the West Bank over the past decade, approximately 60 percent have been located deep inside West Bank territory.[4] The other 40 percent serve as "last inspection points" or "points of entry to Israel." They can be considered Israeli "border" checkpoints, even though most of them are located along the Wall that runs well into the territories east of the Green Line. In other words, they present themselves as traditional border terminals even while they also perform the other functions of bordering processes—fragmentation, annexation, dispossession—that I discuss in Chapter 2.

Even among this subset of "border" checkpoints, permitted West Bank Palestinians are severely restricted in terms of where and how they may cross. First, with very few exceptions, West Bank Palestinians, even those who hold permits, are not allowed to drive cars through checkpoints into Jerusalem or 1948 Palestine.[5] Second, Palestinians who hold nonresidence-related entry permits can cross through less than a third of the approximately forty "border" checkpoints.[6] Importantly, these are *entry* rules, strictly applied on the way into what Israel considers its uncontested territory, but rarely on the way into the West Bank. At the time of my research, the Tunnel (an-Nufuq) Checkpoint on the edge of the Bethlehem suburb of Beit Jala was accessible only to East Jerusalem residents; it was not accessible to West Bank permit holders (except, at times, to those who held medical permits). Yet it was common to see buses crammed with West Bank workers crossing back through the Tunnel Checkpoint into Bethlehem at the end of each workday.

Israeli settler buses (Figure 4.2), by contrast, do not usually pass through the border checkpoints accessible by West Bank permit holders. It is well-known among the Palestinian West Bank population that those Palestinians who ride Israeli settler buses usually work in 1948 Palestine, Jerusalem, or Israeli settlements. Those who must cross the Apartheid Wall to get to work are unlikely to ride the settler buses because, once the bus reaches its entry point at the Wall, the permit holders will be turned away. It is much more common for those workers to take the Israeli buses home because of the lax enforcement of crossing rules in that direction. Typically, a West Bank Palestinian who works in 1948 Palestine might take a settler bus home because its route runs closer to his home. He will get off the bus on the highway before it reaches the settlement to which it is heading.[7]

One such commute home made the news in August 2012, when an Israeli bus driver leaving Tel Aviv on his route to the West Bank refused to allow Palestinian riders to board. The Palestinians had legal work permits to be present there and were trying to get home to the West Bank, an urgent matter on what was a hot and exhausting day of Ramadan. The driver denied them entrance and delayed the bus until an Israeli police officer arrived and forced him to let the Palestinians ride. However, once the bus had entered the West Bank and arrived at the first settlement of Barkan, the driver called over a guard at the gate to force the Palestinians off the bus. According to one of the witnesses on the bus, "All this time one of the passengers was encouraging the driver to do this 'cleansing,' and once the deed was done the driver told him: 'That's the only way they're going to learn. Anyone who boarded the bus today won't dare to do it again'" (Matar, 2012).

The chief executive of the bus company, Afikim, defended the driver, stating that he did exactly as is expected of him:

The official policy is simple: anyone who can pay the fare can go on the bus. This means we have no choice but to also take Palestinians on board in Israel and drive them to Judea and Samaria [meaning the West Bank], even though it always causes problems with the Israeli passengers, and both sides start verbal and physical slights with the other. Inside Judea and Samaria the case is different, as Palestinians are not allowed inside the Israeli settlements without a permit by local security and an armed guard even if they do have an entrance permit to Israel, so the driver did the right thing in forcing them off. Every now and then Palestinians fall asleep on the bus and get unnoticed, and when they wake up at the last stop inside Ariel [an Israeli settlement] we have to call the police to show them the way out. (Matar, 2012)

But the driver's decision struck at least one eyewitness as involving more than a simple enforcement of the complex Israeli permit system that governs Palestinian mobility. The same person who testified to the collusion between the driver and another passenger later reported the incident to the Israeli Ministry of Transportation: "The driver's behavior was racist and in violation of the policewoman's orders. He humiliated people just in order to teach them a lesson" (Matar, 2012).

The Palestinian Freedom Ride

In light of the role settler buses have played in Israel's settler colonial enclosures, it is unsurprising to find the Israeli settler buses at the center of one high-profile Palestinian protest action: the Palestinian Freedom Rides of 2011. In what follows, I offer an analysis based on journalistic and participant accounts of the rides (which took place before I began my field research in the West Bank but motivated my research into the politics of Palestinian public transit). The rider-activists set out to cause a "spectacle," an event in which rules are temporarily suspended and the powerful are subjected to critique and exposure that would otherwise be risky in a context of wildly asymmetrical power relations (Bakhtin, 1968). The Freedom Rides exposed Israeli segregation of mobility for an international civil society audience, and they used the bus as both motif and physical vehicle to transport the activists' message. Their multiregister use of the bus set the stage for using terminological mobility, moving among several terms, to describe the grammars of Israeli rule that condition life in the West Bank. This strategy enabled them to simultaneously cultivate solidarity among and educate an international audience about the details of Israeli control over mobility and space.

On November 15, 2011, fifty years after the iconic Freedom Rides of the U.S. Civil Rights Movement began, a group of six Palestinian activists mounted their own antisegregation protest using the same name. They set out to board segregated "Jewish-only" buses that connect Israeli settlements in the West Bank to occupied East Jerusalem. At 3:30 P.M., the activists boarded Jerusalem-bound bus 148 at a stop near the Psagot settlement, just east of Ramallah. The riders made it to the Hizma Checkpoint, about 16 kilometers away—an opening in the Wall that allows access between the Hizma area in the West Bank and the Beit Hanina and Shu'fat neighborhoods of East Jerusalem (BBC News, 2011; Horowitz, 2011).

At the checkpoint, and as in so many other antisegregation protests, the riders were met by police—a swarm of Israeli military and border control agents, perhaps alerted in advance by the Israeli bus driver. Palestinians are not allowed to cross the checkpoints into Jerusalem unless they have a difficult-to-obtain travel permit, which can take months to process (see Berda, 2018; Kay & Abu-Zahra, 2012). The six Palestinian Freedom Riders, plus a seventh passenger, had not obtained permits but nonetheless refused to get off the bus. The ensuing arrests by military police highlighted the fact of the permits, required only for Palestinians, and the existence of the de facto Jewish-only settler bus line for the audience of international reporters looking on. In this way, the bus provided the stage for a discursive battle in which the rider-activists would need to use terminological mobility—to move among frames—to maximize the impact and nuance of their message.

According to the activists' first press release, "Palestinian Freedom Riders [were] asserting their right for liberty and dignity by disrupting the military regime of the Occupation through peaceful civil disobedience." The Palestinian Freedom Riders were very explicit in their use of analogies to the U.S. Civil Rights Movement, as is apparent from the first paragraph of the initial press release: "On Tuesday, November 15th, 2011, Palestinian activists will reenact the U.S. Civil Rights Movement's Freedom Rides to the American South by boarding segregated Israeli public transportation in the West Bank to travel to occupied East Jerusalem" (Alsaafin, 2011a).

Importantly, and unlike the original movement on which they modeled themselves, the Palestinian Freedom Riders were not seeking desegregation of or equal access to the settler buses. They were so concerned their action might be read this way that they issued a second press release, stating, "Palestinians do not seek the desegregation of settler buses, as the presence of these colonizers and the infrastructure that serves them is illegal and must be dismantled. As part of their struggle for freedom, justice, and dignity, Palestinians demand the ability to be able to travel freely on their own roads, on their own land, including the right to travel to Jerusalem" (Alsaafin, 2011b). They further clarified important differences in their international message from that of their political forebears:

> While parallels exist between occupied Palestine and the segregated U.S. South in terms of the underlying racism and the humiliating treatment suffered then by blacks and now by Palestinians, there are also significant differences. In the 1960s U.S. South, black people had to sit in the back of the bus; in occupied Palestine, Palestinians are not even allowed ON the bus nor on the roads that the buses travel on, which are built on stolen Palestinian land. (Alsaafin, 2011b)

Critically, the organizers used the words "occupied Palestine," "racism," and "stolen Palestinian land" alongside their attempt to analogize (and carefully distinguish) their experiences of the Israeli occupation to that of Black Americans in the de jure segregated United States. This movement among multiple terms animated their desire to clarify the reading of their first press release by issuing the second—to ensure that their readers understood that Israel's occupation is organized through racial supremacy logics and oriented toward the ultimate confiscation (rather than temporary occupation) of Palestinian territory. Furthermore, through the use of the bus and its symbolism of the importance of mobility to everyday life, the protest organizers were able to educate solidarity networks about the central im/mobilization features of the occupation.

The Freedom Bus

In addition to the 2011 rides aimed at drawing attention to the spatial segregation and territorial annexation of the Israeli occupation, another group of Palestinian activists used the bus as vehicle and symbol to organize the Palestinian Freedom Bus. The Freedom Bus organizers, members of the famed Freedom Theater in Jenin, coordinated an annual tour each year from 2011 to 2016,[6] which was oriented toward both international and domestic audiences. While the Freedom Riders were primarily protesting for an audience of international journalists who would carry evocative soundbites to their readers, the Freedom Bus organizers invited international solidarity activists to ride alongside Palestinian activists between Palestinian-inhabited cities and villages in the West Bank, listening to local testimonies about specific horrors that the occupation inflicts on residents' lives.

The 2014 tour of the Freedom Bus aimed to expose its international and Palestinian riders to the particularities of life in small West Bank towns, particularly those rural villages located in Area C, the territory under Israeli civil and security control. During that year, the organizers used explicit analogies to South African apartheid while simultaneously pursuing a campaign to educate locals and foreign visitors about the conditions of life under Israeli settler colonialism. The Freedom Bus passengers visited each destination for a few days, contributing to local community improvement projects by day, as well as making observations about settler violence. At night, they participated in the Freedom Theater's signature "playback" performance art, in which Palestinian audience members are invited to share their experiences of occupation while trained actors improvise onstage interpretations of the stories as they unfold.

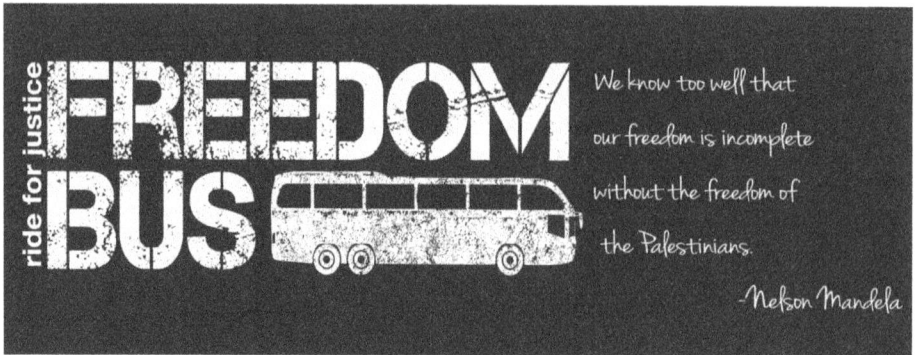

Figure 4.3 Image of a bus with a quotation from Nelson Mandela used on the Freedom Bus blog site. *(Source: The Freedom Theatre.)*

In an interview I conducted in late March 2014, one of the organizers, Khalil, whose name I have changed to protect his identity, explained that the goals of the Freedom Bus are, first, to build awareness among internationals by exposing them to the up-close realities of life under occupation; and second, to "rebuild the connections" among Palestinians from different parts of the West Bank to resist the social effects of cantonization. These goals are interrelated, as the group's signature "playback theater" performances are the means by which an array of stories from across Palestine are shared with both internationals and other Palestinians. The online publicity for the Freedom Bus most directly targeted internationals; it was written in English and featured a quotation from Nelson Mandela (Figure 4.3), a hallmark of the strategy to draw an analogy between Palestine and apartheid South Africa. But on the ground, the organizers seemed most concerned with exposing and remedying the threat to Palestinian social and territorial unity. Khalil commented that the Freedom Bus ride "keeps Palestinians from forgetting one another" by providing opportunities to share with stories about "the many tools used by the occupation."

When asked what the "freedom" in the Freedom Bus's name represents, Khalil responded that it reflects "many faces of freedom." By transporting a mixed group of witnesses to hear testimonies about Palestinian life, the Freedom Bus provides "an opportunity to test freedom: the freedom to tell the truth and the freedom of movement." This mixture of mobility and testimony not only invites solidarity with the Palestinian struggle from outsiders; it also purports to counter the social isolation that results from geographic fragmentation. Khalil noted:

Palestinian people are bored from help like flour, aid, food, money. . . . People don't want this. People need somebody to listen to them, to ask them how [they] feel, to ask their story. Because usually everybody that represents Palestine is talking about all of Palestine. . . . But through the arts, we want to hear the individual people, and this is important. . . . And through this we support the community and tell them, "You are not alone."

He added that even he, someone who has lived in the West Bank his entire life, has heard stories that are completely new to him, revealing the nuanced varieties of hardship under occupation. The Freedom Bus, then, transports West Bank residents and international allies together to places where they can get a clearer understanding of occupied life and begin to practice the many faces of freedom.

Transit Segregation, Sabotage, and Exposure

The nonviolent use of buses in protest actions has been accompanied by more pointed tactics, which, in turn, also present an opportunity for the use of multiple terms to frame the conditions of Palestinian life under Israeli occupation. In early 2013, the Israeli government announced the opening of a new Palestinian-only bus line to run from the West Bank into 1948 Palestine, across the Green Line that divides them, in order to transport Palestinians with Israeli work permits. The new line was criticized by some who considered it de facto racial segregation, following Israeli media reports that it was created at the behest of Jewish West Bank settlers who wanted to avoid the "security risk" of riding in buses with Palestinians. Just hours after the buses began to run, two were torched in the Palestinian town of Kafr Qasim, signaling a rejection of systematized segregation in transportation. The bus, originally intended as a state-imposed separation of Jewish and Palestinian riders, became a locus for rebellion against the racial segregation it represented.

The Israeli Ministry of Transportation's original announcement of the separate Palestinian bus line came cloaked in a collection of euphemistic rationales. The more elaborately costumed version asserted that the new line would be more convenient and comfortable for Palestinian workers, while the more thinly veiled justification cited "security," the go-to reason for so many of the oppressive policies Israel imposes on Palestinian life. It was these façades that the bus burning, as a violent and highly visible attack on a nascent transit line, destroyed, revealing the powerful truth that the line actually represented another instance of de facto racial segregation.

Indeed, the exposure of the racial segregation as de facto, meaning that it appears in fact as opposed to the de jure alternative that is enshrined in law, illuminates one of the features of the Israeli occupation as it functions in the West Bank. Israeli military rule relies on the unpredictable domination of ad hoc discretion and discriminatory policies that are not officially recorded. This is the case, for example, with the Israeli system of segregated roads in the West Bank. While it is popularly known which roads are designated for Israelis only, this information is not posted anywhere or documented publicly; instead, it is based on "the state's whims, the instructions given to soldiers at the local [District Coordination Office], and the way in which they implement them" (B'Tselem, 2017b). Racial segregation of a de facto nature is particularly well insulated from criticism because its source is obscured.

In 2014, Defense Minister Moshe Ya'alon proposed to formalize transit segregation by decree, attracting precisely the negative publicity that less explicit policies might avoid. Subtly evoking the same analogy as the Palestinian Freedom Riders, the Israeli human rights group B'Tselem reported the development with the headline, "Minister of Defense Not Content with Moving Palestinians to the Back of the Bus, Means to Keep Them off Entirely" (B'Tselem, 2014). In response to Ya'alon's announcement, the Palestinian General Federation of Trade Unions, Workers, and Laborers said the decision sheds light on "Israeli racism and the brutality of the occupation" (Khan, 2014).

The January 2013 sabotage actions against the new segregated bus line were not obviously directed toward any particular audience, let alone international civil society. Yet a message characterizing Israeli transportation segregation as racism reached foreign audiences through the media. Palestinian officials asked for comment by international press agencies did not mince words in explaining the bus burning as a rejection of institutionalized racial segregation. The Palestinian Authority's Deputy Labor Minister Assef Said told Agence France-Presse reporters that the opening of the bus line was "a racist policy of segregation." The Palestinian Workers' Union also called it "a racist measure" (Agence France-Presse, 2013). In addition to Agence France-Presse, Reuters, *Al Jazeera*, and the *Palestine Monitor* covered the incident as a thinly veiled effort to racially segregate transportation (*Al Jazeera*, 2013; Black, 2013; Reuters, 2013). Although they all presented the official Israeli Transportation Ministry's justification for the line as a service to commuting Palestinian laborers "to replace the pirate operators who transport the workers at inflated rates," *Al Jazeera* exposed this as prejudice masquerading as paternalism. *Al Jazeera* quoted the Facebook page of the mayor of the Ariel settlement as announcing that the Transportation Ministry was working on ways of "stopping Palestinians from boarding buses that go to Ariel," further stating, "We hope they will soon find a solution to the reality that is bothering our people" (*Al Jazeera*, 2013). In an op-ed for the *Palestine Monitor*, Felix Black (2013) stated directly: "There is little doubt that the new bus service and the South African apartheid or civil rights movement in the United States bear several resemblances."

The act of sabotage itself opened up these opportunities to expose transportation segregation to an international audience and cultivate solidarity by using the evocative and resonant vocabulary of racism, but there are subtler invocations of other terms at play. In this case, while the terms used to describe the sabotaged bus line mainly focused on characterizations of the racist logics of its creation, the site of the sabotage—an Israeli-run bus for West Bank Palestinians who work in 1948 Palestine—connected this racism to the larger project of settler colonialism advanced by the occupation. For example, in *Al Jazeera* (2013), as mentioned earlier, the justification for the line was attributed to the community of Israeli settlers, highlighting the fact that the racism of the separate bus logic is important for the advancement of settler life on occupied Palestinian land. Black (2013) also identified settlers' anxieties as the driving force behind the proposal, adding that, at best, the line would provide a slightly more comfortable transit service to normalize the condition of Palestinians crossing the Green Line for work, conditions that result from Israel's occupation and economic strangulation of the West Bank.

Framing a Multimodal Occupation

Across the three actions discussed in this chapter—the Palestinian Freedom Rides of 2011, the Freedom Bus of 2014, and the bus sabotage of 2013—a tactical focus on transportation provides a literal and symbolic vehicle to move among descriptive terms to transmit accounts of the Palestinian struggle beyond the Israeli border-enclosures. Paralleling their focus on the bus as a symbol of mobility, the actions also feature movement between multiple frames, including terms connoting racial segregation, but also invocations of occupation and settler colonialism. This frame mobility reflects the challenges of communicating about a multimodal occupation. Drawing from the work of Derek Gregory (2004) and Thomas Blom Hansen and Finn Stepputat (2005), Haley Duschinski and Mona Bhan (2017) note that "in practice, occupation as an exercise of sovereign control draws from and aligns with other patterns of authoritarian power such as colonialism and settler colonialism, apartheid regimes, states of emergency, militarization, and counterinsurgency warfare" (p. 5). In the case of Israel, Honaida Ghanim (2018) has argued, settler colonialism has become "intertwined with military occupation and apartheid-like practices" (p. 23).[8]

In addition to the deployment of these multiple, intertwined modalities of power, "late-modern colonial occupations," as Achille Mbembe (2003) calls them, also have the frustrating "tendency . . . to deny their legal status as occupying powers on foreign soil" (Duschinski & Bhan, 2017, p. 4, citing Benvenisti, 2013), if only to avoid the responsibilities that such a label would impose under international law.[9] While, as Duschinski and Bhan (2017, p. 4) point out, this refusal to acknowledge their occupier status can frustrate determinations about whether or not to apply occupation law to such regimes, it also creates a challenge for anti-occupation activists, who must wage a terminological battle while simultaneously organizing for change. This is precisely the case for Palestinian activists, who must develop rhetorical strategies to transcend the peculiar experience of living under an Israeli regime that at once resists all of the labels—occupation, apartheid, and colonialism—while simultaneously incorporating strategies from each of them. In light of these discursive conditions, I contend that Palestinian activists move among these various frames to maximize the number of dimensions of Israeli rule that they can expose, thereby connecting with and educating multiple global audiences at multiple registers.

While the activists move among frames, the leading frame—the one that directly draws its power in each case from the site selection of the bus—is that of racial segregation and related terms. This frame operates through the deployment of analogy, specifically analogizing Israeli rule to the apartheid South African and segregated U.S. American regimes and analogizing the Palestinian activists as counterparts to Black American and Black South African activists. We might understand analogy as the provocation of comparisons for rhetorical purposes; as such, the deployment of analogies typically surfaces questions about the accuracy of the comparisons.

There are clear resonances that bolster the activists' use of a racial discrimination frame. John Reynolds (2017) has argued that the Israeli occupation uses "a pervasive patchwork of emergency modalities" that are "marked by . . . racialisation" (p. 269) to justify authoritarian policies and practices that advance settler colonialism. Furthermore, in terms of historical comparisons, similarities abound among the racially segregated terms of occupied life, Jim Crow segregation, and South African apartheid. In each case, Black Americans/South Africans or (West Bank) Palestinians are confined to separate vehicles, structures, and spaces, and government officials justify the separation with racially coded concerns. One such parallel appears in the marshaling of racialized anxieties about sexual assault. In the United States, the trope of the Black sexual predator victimizing white women was so powerful that it led to lynching and wrongful legal convictions (see, e.g., Dorr, 2004). The same trope was marshaled by settlers lobbying to ban Palestinians from riding settler buses. In November 2013, a Knesset subcommittee on "Judea and Samaria" held a hearing on the settler buses, at which settlers testified to the horrors of riding in buses with Palestinians. As reported by the Israeli newspaper *Ha'aretz*, a twenty-three-year-old settler woman spoke to the subcommittee about being groped by a Palestinian worker and being powerless to do anything "because the bus was filled with

Arabs" (Levinson, 2014b). Knesset Minister Moti Yogev (of the pro-settler Jewish Home Party) echoed these concerns in support of bus segregation: "We have heard disturbing testimonies from girls who were harassed by Arabs during the bus rides" (Levinson, 2014a).[10] Not only are the policies of segregation across contexts similar; so are their rationalizations.[11]

Several scholars have sought to assess the factual basis for the comparison of Israel's treatment of Palestinians to other examples of racial discrimination. Embarking on the comparative method to refute the exceptionalism that Israel invokes to exempt itself from critique, Julie Peteet (2017) focused on the comparison between South African apartheid and Israeli *hafrada*, or the explicit policy of separation that has animated Israeli policies toward Palestinians across historical Palestine since at least the 1990s (with resonances in antecedent policies). Peteet (2017) analyzed the commonalities in experiences of separation and spatial containment, segregationist ideologies, and programs of mobility control (pp. 262–272) while also noting distinctions in the areas of demographics (whites in South Africa were a small ruling minority, while Jewish Israelis are a majority, the size of which depends on the territory included in the calculus) and the role of Indigenous labor in the settler economies (pp. 272–274). Andy Clarno (2017) explains that, because Israel has tried to replace Palestinian labor in the Israeli economy, Palestinian political power is also undermined, which, in turn, requires the involvement of Israeli dissident and international advocates. The factual commonalities and distinctions are important to assess because, as Peteet (2017) and others have highlighted, they challenge Israel's self-proclaimed exceptionalism while also situating contemporary Israel and apartheid-era South Africa as examples in "a panoply of settler colonial societies . . . that are both conceptually and operationally embedded in a global system of domination" (p. 254). Even where the comparisons are not perfect, or do not produce a perfect identity, their power is not diminished. As Keith Feldman (2009) argues, "Analogies have extraordinary rhetorical force precisely because their form keeps these limitations in full view" (p. 87; see also Peteet, 2017, p. 255, citing Nader, 1994, p. 92).

Despite some scholarly contentions that analogies do not pave over important differences, others contend that analogies may in fact obscure differences in ways that counterproductively trivialize them. In his powerful testimony at the Russell Tribunal on Palestine in New York, Saleh Abdel Jawad (2013) argued that the use of the term "apartheid" alone is inadequate to capture the full breadth of the Israeli occupation's technologies or the full depth of their purpose. He has proposed a more expansive term, "sociocide," to encapsulate the depopulation, destruction of culture, neutralizing of national leaders, fragmentation of communities, and enclosure—in addition to segregation or apartheid—that Israel has imposed on Palestinians since 1948 (Abdel Jawad, 2013).[12] Abdel Jawad's intervention does not necessarily disregard the strategic use of the racial segregation frame to connect with potentially sympathetic global audiences; instead, he challenges its strategic value when it risks attracting an incomplete or misinformed solidarity.[13] His intervention underscores the importance for an international solidarity audience to appreciate the frame mobility that Palestinian activists are practicing—moving among "racial segregation," "occupation," and "settler colonialism"—and to appreciate that it is a strategy meant to capture as many facets of life under Israeli domination as possible.

In addition to questions about the accuracy of comparison, analogies expose the limitations of efforts to combat analogous cases of racial segregation. In this case, the Palestinian actions' use of racial frames risks suggesting the solution of desegregation by law, the betrayals of which have become evident in our own racial context in the United States. Here, as Kimberlé Crenshaw (1988) has famously argued, the organizing force of white supremacy retrenched its power in the face of a successful civil rights uprising by insisting that it was de jure, or legally enshrined, segregation that was corrupting the country. By that logic, which eventually became hegemonic, de facto segregation, insofar as it was not the result of demonstrably intentional discrimination on the part of any actors tied to the state, could not be targeted for state-sponsored remedy. Indeed, de jure segregation was successfully outlawed, which, among other results, has allowed for many important civil rights wins through the courts. Yet material segregation has not been defeated, and, in fact, many social spaces and institutions have resegregated (see, e.g., Branton, 1983; Chemerensky, 2002–2003; Reardon et al., 2012).

In the case of the bus sabotage, Israeli officials attempted to control the application of the racial segregation frame in ways that resembled the retrenchment of white supremacy in the United States. The fact that Israeli officials attempted to engage this frame, despite espousing and advancing a radically different ideology from that of the Palestinian saboteurs and their interlocutors, adds emphasis to the aforementioned insights of Oliver and Johnston (2000) about the distinction between frames and ideology. In response to the controversy surrounding Israeli Defense Minister Ya'alon's 2014 directive to ban Palestinians from the Israeli settler buses, discussed in the previous section, Justice Minister Tzipi Livni raised concerns about how the directive's racially discriminatory purpose was presented rather than its effect. Noting that Ya'alon's plan was meant to cater to the prejudices of the settlers, Livni called it "apartheid" and "discrimination that is forbidden by Israeli law." But Livni also commented, "If [the plan] is due to security considerations, that's something I cannot only live with, but I'll even support" (*Ha'aretz*, 2014). Moreover, at the request of Israeli Attorney

General Yehuda Weinstein, the Defense Ministry clarified that there would not be a blanket ban on Palestinians riding the buses; rather, on their way back into the West Bank, Palestinians would be required to return via the same checkpoint through which they had come. This formulation of the directive would have the same racially discriminatory result of eliminating Palestinian ridership on the Israeli settler buses without an explicit rule banning them. In May 2015, Ya'alon's plan was publicly shelved once and for all, with reports that it was "unacceptable" emanating from Prime Minister Benjamin Netanyahu's office (Miller, 2015). The cancelation came on the heels of Livni's statement characterizing the plan as apartheid, perhaps in an attempt to rein in the negative publicity that might compromise the image of Israel as a liberal democracy that politicians such as Livni and Netanyahu are invested in projecting. Yet their hollow protests left untouched all of the other structures that impose racially differentiated mistreatment of Palestinians, including the requirements that West Bank Palestinians pass through specific checkpoints on their way into 1948 Palestine, which the Ya'alon plan would have simply mirrored on their way out.

The tendency for the racial segregation frame to invoke de jure desegregation and its historical baggage is, of course, also troubling because, as mentioned in the earlier discussion of the Freedom Rides, Palestinian activists have taken pains to clarify explicitly that desegregation was not what they were demanding. For the Palestinian workers traveling with Israeli permits, the bus segregation issue would have been much more urgent than it was for the Freedom Rider activists. They ride the settler buses because their direct route gets them home more quickly, an important matter at the end of a grueling workday. To be sure, Ya'alon's plan to forcibly reroute them through the Eyal Checkpoint would have doubled their commuting time, to say nothing of the added wait that would surely ensue if inspections were imposed on the way out, just as they are on the way into work. Yet here, too, desegregation would be a deeply insufficient solution, as the workers would benefit much more from being allowed to cross into 1948 Palestine from the border points closest to their homes, or, more to the point, they would benefit most from a reversal of the de-development of the Palestinian economy so they would not have to work in the Israeli market to find higher wages at all. As Noura Erakat (2019) argued in a stirring discussion of the limitations of a rights-based approach to the Palestinian struggle, of which desegregation by law would be one example, "Striving to dismantle the legal barriers to inequality without addressing the territorial dimensions of the Palestinian struggle . . . has the potential to democratize the settler-colony without upending the 'elementary terms of cohabitation' structuring the relationship between Jewish settlers and Palestinian natives" (pp. 231–232). These concerns represent the potential pitfalls of analogy, a warning for both its proponents and its audience. Yet the power of these multiple frames and their implied analogies appears when examined through the lens of decolonization, which centers the issue of meaningful repatriation of Palestinian land to the Palestinians.

The activists' strategic adoption of frames that connect racism, settler colonialism, and occupation manages to represent and connect repertoires of power *and* freedom struggles in ways that draw from revolutionary transnationalism. It is a paradigmatic practice of Qutami's (2014) notion of the "Palestine analytic," which seeks to highlight the substantive connections, without sacrificing particularity, among different but interrelated constellations of oppression and modalities of resistance and decolonization. In the specific cases I have considered, the frames of *apartheid* and *racial segregation* that the Palestinian activists selected were most likely to resonate with international civil society audiences who share their goals to end such unjust practices that advance exploitation, dispossession, and repression in other contexts. By adopting this frame, the Palestinian activists contribute to what Erakat and Hill (2019) have identified as a "renewal of Black internationalism" through the framework of Black-Palestinian transnational solidarity (BPTS) (pp. 8–9). In his contribution to Erakat and Marc Lamont Hill's special issue of the *Journal of Palestine Studies*, Robin D. G. Kelley (2019) argues that, rather than a politics of analogy between similar experiences of racial and colonial oppression, it is instead "a vision of worldmaking . . . [that] has been the real cement for BPTS" (p. 73). He explains that world-making can be detected in "the *critique* of captivity from a place of confinement, the shared dreams of liberation, and the mobilizing and planning to fulfill that dream" (p. 85, emphasis in the original).

Such a transnationally collaborative vision revives earlier histories of revolutionary politics. In the 1960s and 1970s, the cause of Palestinian liberation was woven into a tapestry of Third World revolutionary struggle (Chamberlin, 2012; Feldman, 2009; Lubin, 2014).[14] During this era, the Palestine Liberation Organization took its liberation struggle, with both its diplomatic and guerrilla fronts, to the international arena, which had significant effects on the Cold War policies of the United States (Chamberlin, 2012). In addition, this globalization of the anticolonial struggle mutually influenced its participants. For example, out of such transnational exchanges Black intellectuals developed "geographies of liberation"—radical notions of freedom from injustice—by drawing connections among the United States, Palestine, and Israel (Lubin, 2014, p. 7). Similarly, Steven Salaita (2016) has traced a repertoire of "inter/nationalism" in the decolonial practices that demonstrate solidarity, intellectual exchange, and mutual support among American Indian and Palestinian communities.

By invoking a variety of terms and frames, and by using the meaningful symbol of the bus, the current-day transit-themed Palestinian protests I discuss here connected to this global revolutionary tradition. Thus, we might consider this another kind of *mobile commoning*, following Dimitris Papadopoulos and Vassilis Tsianos (2013, p. 191) and Mimi Sheller (2019, pp. 168–171), who identify solidaristic engagements among transnational movements for justice as part of the mobile commons. These Palestinian activists engaged in a transnational exchange of concepts, visions, and strategies for developing ways of communicating, moving, and living that exceed the bounds of their oppression. Kelley's *world-making impulses* are indeed present here. The protest actions conjured a world in which the global audience is able to see the typically obscured, de facto injustices of a racially organized settler colonial occupation. By moving among frames, the bus-centered Palestinian protest actions modeled for their multiple global audiences the kind of meaning making that connects racial segregation, military occupation, and settler colonialism and identifies them as, in the Freedom Bus organizer Khalil's words, "the many tools used by the occupation." The specifics of that story are as important as the connections and comparisons to other stories, and the Palestinian activists attached frame mobility to the means of collective mobility (public transit) to highlight both the specifics and the commonalities in order to connect with and educate their global comrades.

Moreover, in doing so they simultaneously practiced precisely the kinds of freedom that Khalil emphasized: "the freedom to tell the truth and the freedom of movement." By inviting global audiences to engage on their shifting terrain of mobile frames and mobility-themed protests, the Palestinian activists collaborated with a rich revolutionary legacy of both claiming and exercising freedoms. They activated Palestinian self-determination through their transit-focused interventions: to place their bodies in implicitly forbidden, segregated spaces; to repair and rejuvenate connections across fragmented territory; and to recenter—for local and global audiences—their right to movement on their land.

This chapter and Chapter 3 show that Palestinian public transportation in the West Bank is a site where Indigenous power is cultivated in both mundane and spectacular ways to transcend the limits of Israel's im/mobilization regime and the settler colonial project it advances. The quotidian engagements with transit discussed in Chapter 3 are driven by a collective pragmatism: communal networks of knowledge and care work to help riders and drivers accomplish meaningful movement across territorial and social fragmentations. The activist engagements with transit featured in this chapter's analysis were also developing their strategies with pragmatism in mind.

Their actions featured terminological dexterity meant to maximize their effect on local and global audiences. In addition to these mundane and spectacular formats, public transit engagements have appeared in the artistic realm. Palestinian artists use representations of transit to challenge the spatial and temporal chauvinism of settler colonialism and to exercise self-determined movement across space and time. In the next chapter, I present a discussion of three such Palestinian artworks.

5

Speculative Art and the Ghosts
of Palestinian Transit

Past-Present-Future

In this chapter, I argue that Palestinian artwork featuring representations of public transportation palpably invokes Palestinian self-determined mobility and temporal autonomy, linking decolonization to a collective freedom of movement across time and space. I consider the imaginative power of art against a sharply constrained political backdrop. In her article analyzing Israel's weaponization of time and waiting against the Palestinians, Julie Peteet (2018) notes a lingering question: "What sort of temporal order do Palestinians envision, or are they even able to conceptualize a future when the present is so profoundly restricted?" (p. 44). Peteet, a dedicated anthropologist of the Palestinian struggle, may have formulated this question in light of an often expressed Palestinian frustration that Nasser Abourahme (2011) traces to "a generalized feeling of political impotence" that congeals in the "common rhetorical refrain . . . '*shou nisawee . . . ma fee hal*' ('What can we do? . . . There is no solution')" (p. 456).[1] These analyses identify the undue hardship of imagining liberated futures from within "a colonial present" (Peteet, 2018).[2] Yet formulated alternatives to the ravages of settler colonialism—including alternative temporal orders—abound, and part of my task in this book is to underscore their omnipresence, even in mundane sites such as public transit.

In what follows, I examine works by Larissa Sansour, Mohamed Abusal, and the collective known as the Decolonizing Architecture Art Residency (DAAR), in which each of the artists uses vehicles of collective movement to haunt settler colonial landscapes with specters of quotidian Palestinian self-determination.[3] These imagination workers see openings, contradictions, and provocations that others might overlook because their creativity is not constrained by the counterfeit boundaries of political realism. Robin D. G. Kelley (2002) explains that "the conditions of daily life, of everyday oppressions, of survival . . . render much of our imagination inert" (p. 11) and argues that the power of both radical art and social movements emerges from their ability to "transport us to another place, compel us to relive horrors and, more importantly, enable us to imagine a new society" (p. 9). Lila Sharif (2016) poignantly notes that, particularly "in the context of settler colonialism, new sites of knowledge necessarily emerge from the realm of the imagination where disappearances haunt through the most seemingly benign sites" (p. 19). In the context of Palestine, as Sophia Azeb (2014) demonstrates, imagination work makes incomparable contributions to "creating and sustaining a truly autonomous Palestinian nation . . . a nation that is lived without restrictions through the innovative and agile practice of imagining *otherwise*" (p. 31). The artworks I examine in this chapter transport their audiences (and sometimes the artists themselves) through past, present, and future horrors and liberated alternatives. These journeys are advanced by representations of public transit that are used to signify the traversing of both fragmented space and time in contravention of settler colonial logics. Renderings of transit vehicles—the means of collective mobility—provide an opportunity for Palestinian artists to enact self-determination by reclaiming collective relationships to space and time that have been subject to Israeli colonization.

While this book has until now focused on public transit in the West Bank, the Palestinian artwork that I consider in this chapter involves representations of territory across historical Palestine, including Gaza, coastal cities, and Jerusalem, in addition to the West Bank. In the Introduction I discussed how Israeli *im/mobilization*—the exertion of control over Palestinian movement in ways that variously force, forbid, or otherwise influence it—has generated increasingly differentiated experiences for Palestinian communities relative to which part of historical Palestine they have been confined. I noted that this differentiation, which stems from spatial fragmentation, means that there is no common transit system shared by all Palestinians; thus, it is not possible to extrapolate the mobility concerns of the West Bank onto the Palestinian communities of other parts of historical Palestine. While that remains true in terms of day-to-day travel, the Palestine-based works I discuss in this chapter provide an opportunity to examine overarching mobility concerns that transcend the fragmenting effects of the Israeli border-enclosures that have imposed im/mobilization, in some form, on all Palestinians. I argue that considering this artwork illuminates the ways that representations of public transit serve as a vehicle for conjuring a unifying vision of self-determined mobility across historical Palestine.

Settler Colonial Confiscations of Time

The Israeli border-enclosures impose control over mobility in a way that accomplishes the dispossession of Palestinian time, as well as land. In Chapters 1 and 2, I discussed the Israeli confiscation of land through the multiple components of the border-enclosures strategy. Here I return to the point from that earlier discussion that, by impeding and disrupting the means of mobility, Israel also accomplishes the permanent confiscation of Palestinian time and denies Palestinian temporal self-determination. The Israeli border-enclosures elongate Palestinian routes by forcing them to wind around the physical structures of colonialism (see, e.g., Allen, 2008; Kotef, 2015; Makdisi, 2008); impose unpredictable waiting times and harassment en route at the various border encounter points that can lead to death, danger, inconvenience, missed opportunities, and boredom (see, e.g., Peteet, 2018; Qato, 2004; R. Sharif, 2014; Tawil-Souri, 2017); and suspend Palestinians in different social relationships that cannot progress due to a lack of mobility (on this latter point, see, e.g., the general discussion of "the temporality of the border" in Anderson et al. [2009, p. 7] and Makdisi [2008], which addresses this phenomenon in the Palestinian context [e.g., p. 43]).

As discussed in Chapter 2, Israel uses its diffused bordering processes to subject Palestinians to colonial manipulations of time. Helga Tawil-Souri (2017) explores the particular form of time that emerges in the space of the checkpoint, a kind of zero-sum temporal relationship in which Israel conditions the speed of Israeli movement on the confiscation of Palestinian time. Amira Hass (2005) has noted that this confiscation of Palestinian time, different from land, is an irreversible loss to settler colonialism that cannot be repatriated. Peteet (2017, 2018) writes about Israel's weaponization of waiting, in which the Palestinian body is held in stasis to enact and display colonial dispossession and domination (2018, p. 45). And John Collins (2011) uses Paul Virilio's (2006) work on chronopolitics to analyze Israeli "dromocracy," which he defines as the harnessing of a politics of speed (and control over it) and the acceleration of violence. In each of these theorizations, Israel asserts a monopoly over the control of time, denying Palestinians what Peteet (2018) calls "temporal autonomy."

While the mundane dispossessions of Palestinian time—hours literally lost forever—are an integral element of the Israeli im/mobilization regime that advances settler colonialism, it is typical of settler colonial projects to be deeply invested in confiscating a different kind of time: the control of both history and future. Many scholars have examined Israeli colonization of Palestinian history and narrative and have generated research that presents an anticolonial version of history (e.g., Batarseh, 2019; Doumani, 1995, 2009; Khalidi, 1997; Masalha, 2012; Sa'di, 2002; Seikaly, 2015). Drawing from Walter Benjamin, Nasser Abourahme (2011) has argued that Israeli constrictions and the disfigured Palestinian statehood project that attempts to proceed in the shadow of colonialism have "produced a perpetual, suspended present marked by a paradoxical mixture of transience and stasis" (pp. 455–456). It is a present constructed to be devoid of past and future yet is also fleeting in its own moment.

In the context of being stuck in time, the future as much as the past becomes dangerous, precious terrain that settler colonialism necessarily seeks to foreclose, and where Indigenous imagination can thrive. In other words, the terrain of time is a contested one. One pillar of many decolonial projects is an Indigenous reclamation of collective control over time in open opposition to its colonization. Mark Rifkin (2017) highlights the concept of "temporal sovereignty," offering a discussion of "Native time" that centers "Indigenous temporal frames of reference" (p. x) and rejects the monopoly over legitimate narrations of time often claimed by settler colonial frameworks. Relatedly, la paperson (2010) recognizes that "the postcolonial sense of time emerges from a specific set of disruptions, so that we can see the time now (colonization), the time before that (precolonial), and the time outside of all of that (postcolonial)." Bill Ashcroft (2016) surveys utopian postcolonial literature and identifies therein "a transformed conception of time that sees it as layered and interpenetrating, spiraling rather than linear" and "conjoining [the] past, present and future" (pp. 52, 57). This layered approach to portraying time "affirm[s] that a different world is possible" and that "home" is still achievable for those who have been displaced by colonialism (p. 62). Such conceptions resonate with Greg Burris's (2019) analysis of Palestinian documentary film, with a focus on *My Love Awaits Me by the Sea* (2013), by Mais Darwazah. Burris argues, "Like space, time can be insubordinate, and if some modes of time are susceptible to colonization, there are other modes that resist it" (p. 85). Burris conceives of "Palestinian Time" as an example of "the utopian future . . . in the here and now" (p. 88), arguing that this "Palestinian future [that] is already here" (p. 100) not only resists Israeli colonialism but, in fact, exceeds colonial comprehension (p. 85).

Indigenous temporal frames are more than alternatives to settler time; they are exercised agentically (Goeman, 2014; Peteet, 2017; Rifkin, 2017). Rifkin's notion of "temporal sovereignty" posits that Native autonomy depends on the recognition of distinct Native experiences of time—"ways of inhabiting time that shape how the past moves toward the present and future" (p. 2). Peteet's "temporal autonomy" describes the assertion of Indigenous control over quotidian experiences of time, as in negotiations of waiting at checkpoints or taking traffic detours. Both scholars can be understood as addressing both valences of time—that is, epochal and quotidian—though each seems to focus on one or the other. In this chapter, I use the term "temporal self-determination" to encapsulate both the quotidian and the historical meanings of time and to flag autonomous collective decisions about moving across time and space.

To the bodies of rich scholarship that explore the struggle over different dimensions of Palestinian time in relation to mobility I add my engagement with Palestinian art that features representations of public transit. I note that these representations and reimaginings of transit conjure the specter of self-determined mobility of Palestinians across Palestinian territory and time.[4] These transit symbols deliver the artists' critiques of settler colonialism—particularly, Israel's use of im/mobilization to dispossess Palestinians—and simultaneously assert and enact Indigenous self-determination in multiple dimensions.

Furthermore, I posit that, in their representations of public transit as a means of self-determined, collective movement across space and time, the artists use the method of *haunting* (A. Gordon, 2008, 2018; Morrill et al., 2016; Tuck & Ree, 2013). In her radical conception of the social struggles that sociology, among other disciplines, tends to miss (or ignore or, worse yet, obscure), Avery Gordon (2008) urges scholars to attend to "haunting" as "an animated state in which a repressed or unresolved social violence is making itself known" (p. xvi). These disquieting spectral presences signal the residues of systemic violence, as well as the resilience and refusal that evince the limits of that violence's power. In a series of writings and performances that constitute an ongoing conversation, Eve Tuck, K. Wayne Yang, Angie Morrill, C. Ree, and F. Sam Jung (the latter three sometimes appearing and writing together as the Super Futures Haunt Qollective [SFHQ]) evoke the notion of haunting as method.[5] Against the backdrop of halting, multidimensional dispossessions, "Haunting lies precisely in its refusal to stop" (Tuck & Ree, 2013, p. 642). In one sense, this refusal is a begrudging opposition to the relentlessness of colonial dispossession—"I'll do it if I have to"—and begrudging not because it is half-hearted, but because it refuses to be defined against dispossession as its opposite (Morrill et al., 2016, p. 5). In another sense—or perhaps they are facets of the same sense—it is a "refusal to stay gone" (Quiray Tagle, 2018), an Indigenous affirmation. "Haunting is a materializing. Haunting is a mattering" (Morrill et al., 2016, p. 3), a mattering on its own terms, because to matter is the opposite of being dispossessed in that it thoroughly exceeds dispossession (pp. 2, 5).

One constitutive feature of haunting as method is an Indigenous reclamation of temporal self-determination, which sometimes looks like a disruption of the rigid colonial segregation of past, present, and future. Gordon (2018) explains that the ghosts do their disorienting work with time as their medium: "Haunting alters the experience of being in linear time (past present future) . . . [and it] always registers the harm inflicted or the losses sustained by the past or present social violence . . . [while it simultaneously] produces a something to be done" (p. 209). Native haunting necessarily inflicts temporal disruptions to settler colonial logics, such as temporal chauvinism (Rifkin, 2017). While this disturbance is the methodology of haunting, the goal is the imperative of decolonization. Tuck and Ree (2013) assert, "For ghosts, the haunting is the resolving, it is not what needs to be resolved" (p. 642). In other words, in the context of ongoing settler colonialism, the "active presence" (Vizenor, 2000, p. 179) of the ghosts on their land and in their time is both Gordon's "something to be done" and the doing.

In the projects I discuss in this chapter, the artists use public transit to represent Palestinian modes of living on their land that involve autonomous decisions about movement—whether to move, as well as how. They also represent Palestinian modes of living in relation to time, reclaiming autonomous relationships to the past, present, and future, as well as reclaiming time through less burdened means of mobility. These "modes of living" are properly understood as part of the "utopian margins"—practices and evidence, both already concrete and still anticipated—of social relations and ways of life that exceed conditions of domination (Gordon, 2018, pp. xi, 284). It is the specter of these utopian margins that the artists invoke to accomplish their haunting in the service of decolonization, and they "install" these specters through layered temporal frames and actual infrastructures of movement. Depictions of Indigenous Palestinian self-determined movement across space and time generate critiques, confronting their audiences with the "losses sustained" (Gordon, 2018, p. 209) as a result of ongoing settler colonial dispossession, among them the continued denial of the Palestinian right of return and the irreversible confiscations of Palestinian time in its many meanings.[6] Simultaneously, and perhaps more important, they illuminate modes of living that exceed dispossession, presenting the "once and future ghosts" (Tuck & Ree, 2013, p. 642) of mobile Palestinians exercising self-determined, collective movement via public transit vehicles across *once and future* Palestine.

The Right of Return by Train

The work of the radical architecture group Decolonizing Architecture Art Residency frequently explores the "ghostly matters" of settler colonial infrastructures and the alchemy that occurs when they are repurposed for decolonization. Established by Sandi Hilal and Alessandro Petti in collaboration with Eyal Weizman, DAAR is based in the Palestinian West Bank city Beit Sahour, a suburb of greater Bethlehem. According to the website (www .decolonizing.ps), DAAR's work "explores possibilities for the reuse, subversion and profanation of actual structure [*sic*] of domination."[7]

One characteristic DAAR project is the Palestinian civilian reclamation of the former Israeli military base, abandoned in 2006, known as Oush Ghrab (Crow's Nest) in Beit Sahour. Immediately following the base's evacuation, in acts characterized by DAAR as "spontaneous architectural moments of reappropriation," locals dismantled the structures and took any and all usable materials, which are usually costly and somewhat difficult to access under occupation (*Military Bases*, "Project: Return to Nature," www .decolonizing.ps/site/texts). DAAR reports that these materials have been reused in many West Bank cities beyond Bethlehem: in Jenin, Nablus, Ramallah, and East Jerusalem to the north; Jericho to the northeast; and Hebron to the southwest. DAAR originally envisioned an architectural intervention into the evacuated base that would "accelerate the processes of destruction and disintegration" by repurposing the buildings of the base as structures that would host the many migratory birds that stop in the area each year. The spirit of this proposal exemplifies DAAR's approach even while the area was eventually repurposed differently.

The area where the Israeli military used to park its tanks was converted in 2008 into a family recreation area, the "Peace Park," which includes a restaurant and snack shop to serve patrons seated at picnic tables arranged across a large, outdoor, concrete area.[8] The park is closed for three months in the winter, but during the warmer seasons it fills up with families barbecuing on long rectangular charcoal grills, groups of friends watching back-to-back World Cup matches projected onto one of two big screens, and local residents who just want to get out of the house and enjoy the fresh air. Down a set of stairs on the side of the restaurant, the Beit Sahour municipality constructed a small theme park with rides and carnival games for children and adults. One can see, perched above the park, an Israeli military tower, which was evacuated for a time but seems to have been returned to use. The army maintains control over the peak even when it is not using it (*Military Bases*, "Introduction," www.decolonizing.ps/site/introduction-2/)—just another site in its decades-long "battle for the hilltops" around the West Bank (Weizman, 2007).

I describe the Oush Ghrab reclamation project—both DAAR's initial proposal and the actual Peace Park, which DAAR did not create—because it reflects many of the central logics of DAAR's approach to decolonization, which apply the structures and raw materials of the current Israeli occupation to new uses that reconnect fragmented Palestinian communities and revive meaningful Palestinian relationships among one another and with and on their land. DAAR's work recognizes, in Gordon's (2008) terms, "the shadowy grip of ghostly matters" (p. 165) that haunt the defunct remnants of repression and rule to excavate "the memory and possibility of connection" embedded within them (DAAR, 2011).

DAAR developed another project, *Right to Mobility* (2011), that centers directly on public transportation and the collective movement it can enable. *Right to Mobility* was developed in collaboration with the Belgian writer and activist Lieven De Cauter as part of the Design Studio at the Berlage Institute in the Netherlands. In its current form as featured on the DAAR website, *Right to Mobility* includes narrative text describing relevant contextual information and the current social, political, and economic significance of their proposal; images of Palestinian landscapes sometimes overlaid with architectural modifications that illustrate the project's ideas; and reference maps that connect their proposed interventions to older cartographic configurations. In *Right to Mobility*, DAAR focuses on the old Ottoman-turned-British train system as a site for the radical repurposing that animates many of their projects. DAAR traces the lines of the original Ottoman plan and proposes a resuscitated train system along the same routes to (re)establish connections among Palestine and other parts of the Middle East region. But DAAR's revival starts first with the restoration of key Palestinian nodes of the railway, repurposing the sites of the old train stations as hubs for social bonding and exchange. Notably, DAAR's proposal interweaves with other ongoing Palestinian reclamation projects. For example, *Right to Mobility* incorporates local plans to establish a library or museum in the Jenin train station that would augment its current commercial use with a memorialization of its former function. With the train stations revived in ways that reanimate memories of connection across Palestine, ground would be laid for DAAR's proposed transit lines in a "future reopened geography" ("Reactivating the Network," www.decolonizing.ps/site/return-to-the-camp). DAAR moves among historical memories, present-day material structures, and speculative proposals, highlighting the ways that current infrastructural use and design might form the basis for a broader program of self-determined Palestinian mobility.

Right to Mobility includes descriptions of several once busy West Bank train stations that now lie in ruins (Massoudieh [Figure 5.1]), are totally destroyed (Battir), or have been used for private purposes (Jenin). These stations and other portions of the railroads in the West Bank and Gaza were once bustling hubs of rail transportation, but they became defunct in 1948 with the creation of the State of Israel. As I noted previously, railways provided an unparalleled level of connection and access across Syria, Jordan, Egypt, Saudi Arabia, and beyond, despite being constructed in pursuit of colonial ambitions (Mansour, 2006). After this system was dismantled (and some parts were repurposed for an Israeli train system), Palestinian communities were

Figure 5.1 Ruins of the Massoudieh train station.
(Source: Decolonizing Architecture Art Residency.)

cut off not only from one another but also from the wider region. DAAR focuses on the historical railways and their stations to critique Israeli settler
colonialism. In particular, their transit proposal underscores how Israel has
used im/mobilization to effect Palestinian dispossession. With the establishment of the Israeli state on Palestinian land, Palestinians in the West Bank
and Gaza were no longer able to access travel or shipment via train, a restriction that continues to this day. In addition to the denial of a form of collective
movement across Palestinian territory, DAAR's train proposal highlights that
this early example of Israeli im/mobilization dispossessed Palestinians of
their connection to the rest of the region and continues to do so.

DAAR's *Right to Mobility* proposal uses a transit vehicle—namely, the
train—to accomplish a decolonial engagement with time (Figure 5.2). The
collective draws the foreclosed avenues of interregional connection from
Palestinian history into a future-oriented proposal that anchors itself in
mundane artifacts of the present. Through this decolonial reorganization of
time, DAAR uses haunting as method (Gordon, 2008, 2018; Morrill et al.,
2016; Tuck & Ree, 2013), generating visions of an active, connected, and
mobile Palestinian presence on Palestinian land. Haunting highlights the
ongoing confiscations caused by Israeli settler colonialism, including the
destruction of interregional connection, while recovering and proposing a

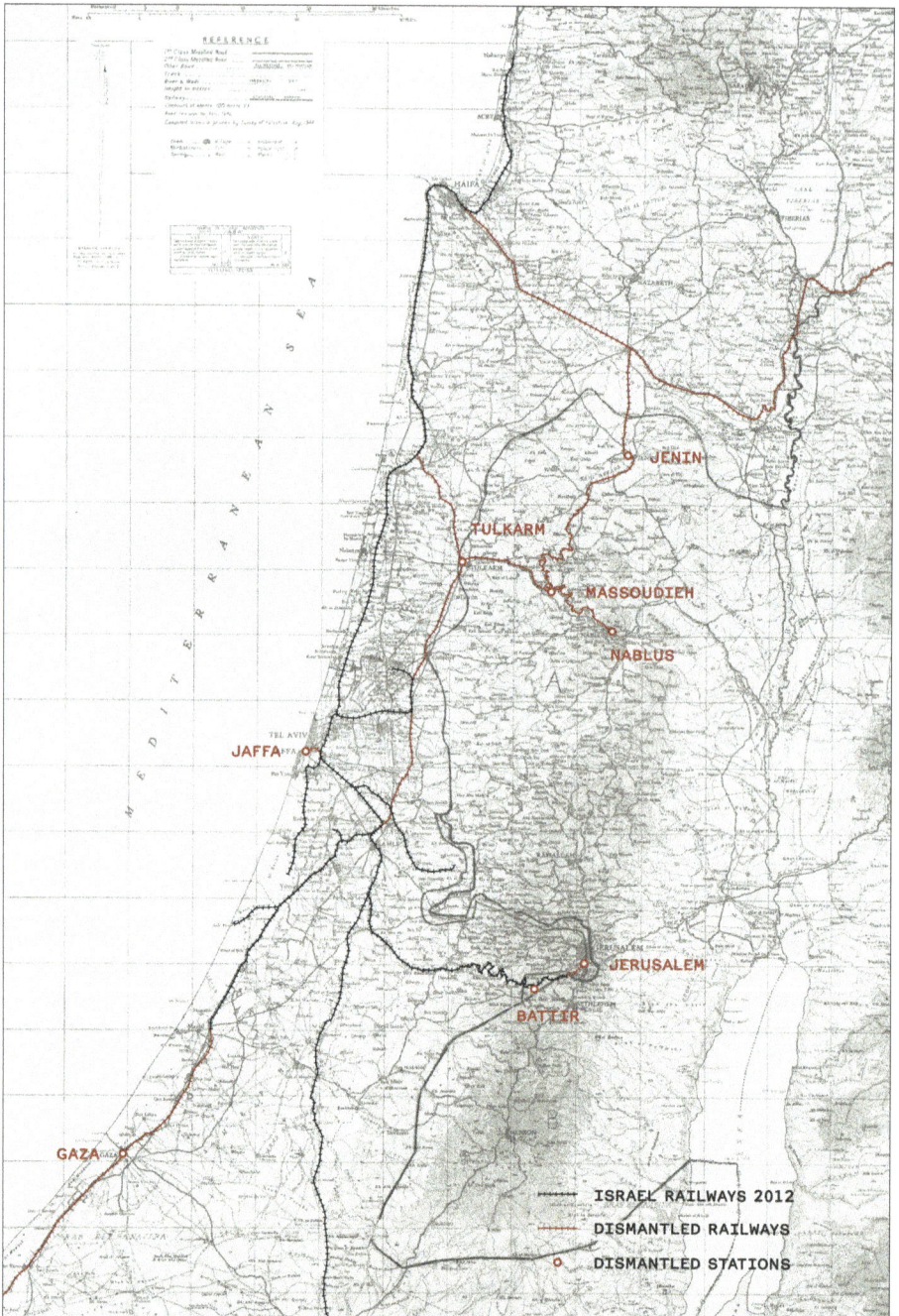

Figure 5.2 Map of a revived railway network across Palestine.
(Source: Decolonizing Architecture Art Residency.)

historically inflected alternative future, anchored in present-day infrastructure, of Palestinian self-determined movement. On the DAAR website, the architects explain the critical function of centering their project on the rail lines of the historic system: "The sites of the remains of this infrastructure tell the story of transformation resulting from the Nakba and ongoing occupation" (*Right to Mobility*, "Ottoman Railway," www.decolonizing.ps/site /return-to-the-sea). These ghostly residues haunt the present with loss and possibility, but their materiality can also, as DAAR demonstrates, provide the basis for a resuscitated system of collective movement.

Moreover, the *Right to Mobility* project connects Palestinian travel to the internationally recognized Palestinian right of return—a right that emerged to counter the effects of the 1948 establishment of the Israeli state that displaced three quarters of the Palestinian population at the time. DAAR proposes the railway reclamation to materialize the Palestinian right of return as a broader right to freedom of movement, such that, "[it would] not mean the migration from the [refugee] camp to the ancestral village, but the possibility of being able to travel between the two and throughout the whole region" ("Reactivating the Network"). This idea conjures self-determined Palestinian mobility across both the territory of historical Palestine and the meaningful lives that have been lived over seventy years of displacement and dispossession. In a way, DAAR's decolonial intervention appears to anticipate the problem that, without meaningful freedom of movement across Palestinian land, Palestinian return would have only a kind of prison as its arrival point. Instead, *Right to Mobility* envisions the act of return in and through the exercise of self-determined movement, which includes staying, traveling, wandering, and returning, across space and time.

A Metro Map for Palestine

The spirit of infrastructural repurposing evident in DAAR's work animates another creative reimagining of Palestinian transit, this time situated in the tunnels of Gaza. The interdisciplinary Gazan artist Mohamed Abusal introduced an installation meant to conjure a vision of rapid underground subway travel in the Gaza Strip. For *A Metro in Gaza* (2011), Abusal meticulously mapped out an underground subway system composed of seven lines that connect two hundred metro stations in all of the cities in the Gaza Strip and at important points along and beyond its edges (Figures 5.3–5.4). In addition to the precise metro map, the heart of the installation involved physical interventions in space. He erected poles with a big, red encircled "M," resembling the classic Parisian metro marker, and a smaller sign underneath bearing the words "metro station" in Arabic, at various sites all over the Gaza Strip (Abusal, 2011). He also observed and photo-

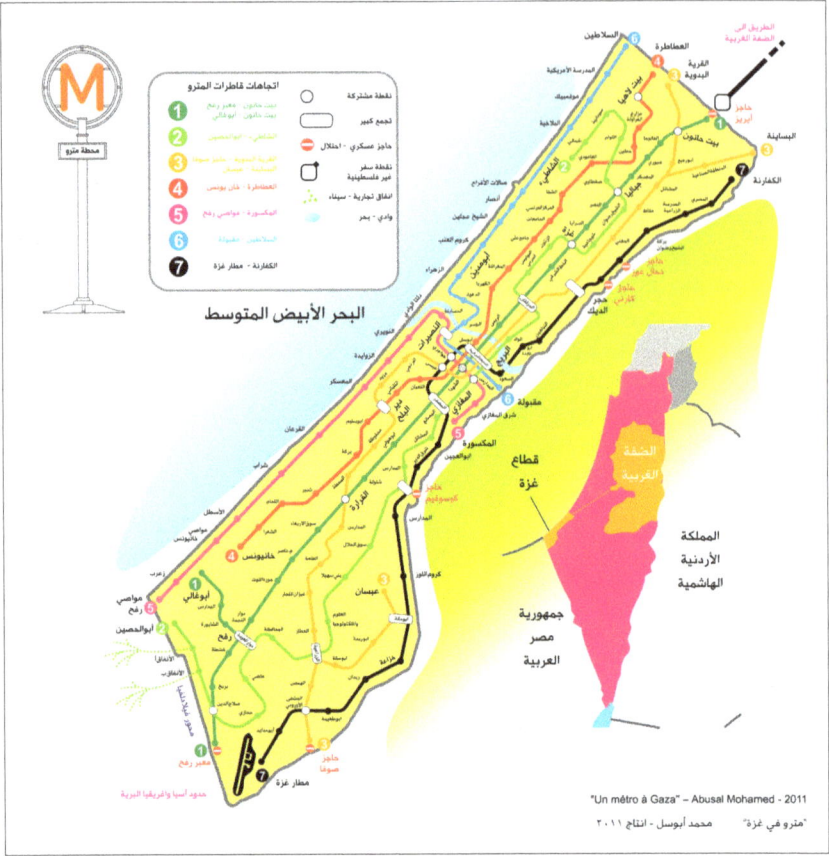

Figure 5.3 Gaza Metro map (Arabic). *(Source:* A Metro in Gaza *[Abusal, 2011].)*

graphed the reactions of locals as they came to inspect the signs. These photographs were exhibited at the French Cultural Center in Gaza City in 2011. Subsequently, he took his installation beyond Gaza to Jerusalem and Ramallah in 2012 and photographed reactions to his work in these sites. By making his installation mobile, Abusal immediately brought the imaginary of the Gaza Metro to life.

A Metro in Gaza harnesses the specter of a Palestinian subway system—a sleek, modern means of collective Palestinian mobility—to make a bold intervention into the Palestinian present. This intervention draws from the regional connectivity of the past mentioned earlier, which has since been foreclosed by the Israeli border-enclosures, and the present futurity of imagining the decolonized conditions required for such a project. Abusal recruits the past and the future to "haunt" (Gordon, 2008, 2018; Morrill et al., 2016; Tuck & Ree, 2013) the present with big red metro signs (Figure 5.5) and the rapid and collective mobility they represent. In the description on his website of a second, related project, *Reveal/A Metro in Gaza* (2014), he

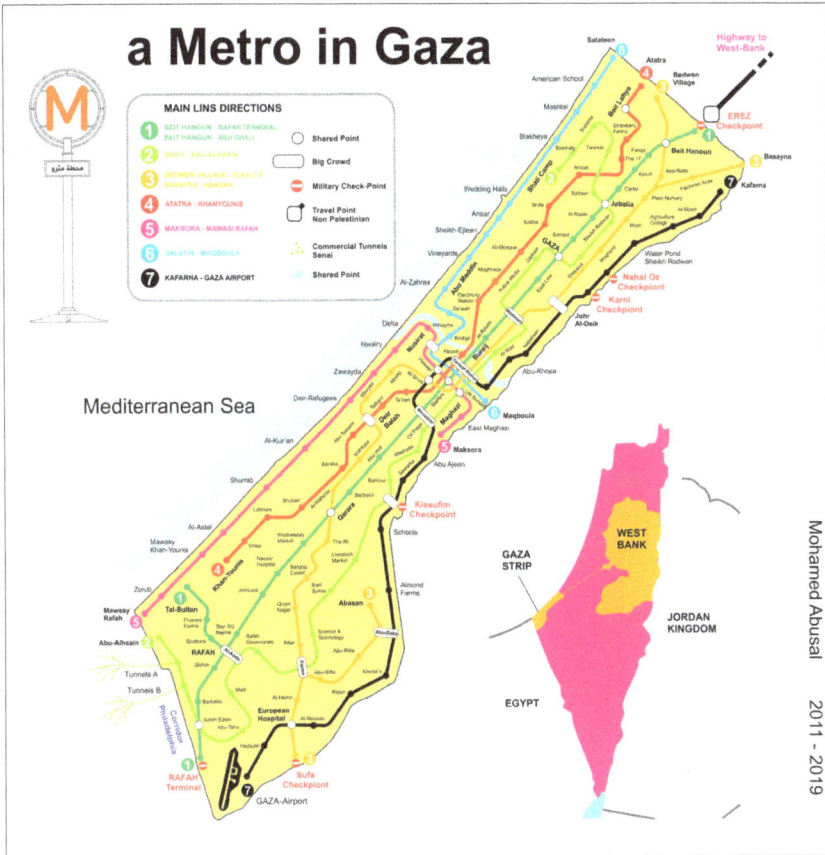

Figure 5.4 Gaza Metro map (English). *(Source:* A Metro in Gaza *[Abusal, 2011].)*

writes: "It is time to recount the past to understand the present and change our future, to get out of the limbo of being driven by processes, serving the optimization of occupation structure." Abusal asserts that moving beyond the conditions of the Israeli siege requires a Palestinian renarrativization of the relationships among the past, present, and future.

Abusal's vision of a Palestinian subway system is at once mundanely pragmatic and fantastical. In striking that chord, Abusal haunts his land-scapes, staging "singular yet repetitive instances when home becomes un-familiar, when your bearings on the world lose direction, when the over-and-done-with comes alive, when what's been in your blind spot comes into view" (Gordon, 2008, p. xvi). The idea of the Gaza metro materializes mul-tiple ghosts of settler colonialism—both the ongoing violence with which it conditions Palestinian life and the quotidian and fantastic ways that life persists anyway.

For example, in a review of the installation in the French newspaper *Le Monde*, Laurent Zaccheni (2012) commented that, for the project's central

Figure 5.5 Metro sign illuminated at night in front of "Welcome to Gaza" sign, Gaza. *(Source:* A Metro in Gaza *[Abusal, 2011].)*

provocation to materialize, it would require a guarantee from the Israelis to refrain from bombing the subway lines and to suspend their program of electricity cuts to which they subject the Gaza Strip regularly. In light of recent history, that requirement constitutes the most fantastical dimension of Abusal's metro proposal (Figure 5.6). The pragmatism of creating an art project out of a transit plan induces a pragmatic response in the audience (*It's impossible!*), which in turn immediately provokes a clear vision of what makes it impossible: the colonial confiscations of temporal and territorial self-determination that stand in the way of the proposal's practicality. Abusal's mobile installation, then, demands a full accounting of the effects of quotidian colonial violence, including im/mobilization strategies, that foreclose the possibility of a Palestinian metro.

In addition to provoking audiences with this generative question about pragmatism, the Gaza metro plan directly and indirectly presents elements of Israeli control and the dispossessions they continue to inflict. According to Abusal's metro map, the subway lines connect the existing landmarks of the Gaza Strip, including Israeli checkpoints and the refugee camps that house generations of families displaced by the establishment of Israel and its reverberations. The "Green Line," or Line 1, stretches the length of the Strip,

Figure 5.6 Metro sign in front of building façade riddled with bullet holes and damage, Gaza. *(Source:* A Metro in Gaza *[Abusal, 2011].)*

connecting the Rafah Checkpoint at the southwestern border with Egypt to the Eretz Checkpoint along the northeastern border imposed by Israel. In other words, Abusal is not waiting to open his metro in a future Palestine in which the right of return has already been fully realized; rather, he installs his system in the here and now (Figure 5.7). In the press release for the Gaza exhibit of *A Metro in Gaza*, the curator, Ala Younis (2012), notes, "A line of this sort would need to be direct, central, and fast in order to enable the inhabitants of the Gaza Strip to arrive at the main crossings as early as possible." Several of the proposed stations on Lines 2 and 3 would be placed at the various refugee camps in the Strip, "including Jabalia, Al-Shate', Al-Breij, Al-Maghazi, Al-Nseirat, Deir Al Balah, Khan Younis and Rafah" (Younis, 2012). Abusal also conjures memories of forms of Palestinian mobility that have been undermined by Israel. Another of his metro lines would provide service to the "Gaza International Airport"—which, in fact, existed from 1998 until the Israeli military destroyed it just two years after it was built, in 2000—at once reminding his audiences of Israel's denial of a crucial means for modern global connection to Gazan Palestinians and suddenly reasserting it as a present possibility (Abusal, 2011; Younis, 2012). Blending elements of infrastructures past, present, and future, Abusal establishes a rapid system

Figure 5.7 Men laughing in front of the metro sign with the seashore in the background, Gaza. (*Source:* A Metro in Gaza [*Abusal, 2011*].)

of collective transit for cross-country and international connection in the midst of, and in spite of, the effects of settler colonialism.

The pragmatism of *A Metro in Gaza* extends beyond critique to emphasize the presence and attainability of organized collective Palestinian movement and its significance against a colonial backdrop. In the description in Arabic of the project on his website, Abusal explains that the metro is an extension of the dreamlike situations in which Gaza Palestinians already live, but it is an alternative dream based on artistic suggestion. In other words, where the conditions of Palestinian life under Israeli siege are so unbelievable, nothing can be dismissed out of hand, including something as quotidian as rapid public transit. Moreover, he notes that the actual construction of the metro would present no problem, given that Gazan Palestinians have extensive experience in tunnel digging. In fact, Abusal's metro offers a clever response to public interest in (and media hysteria about) the vast network of tunnels built underground in Gaza to smuggle goods and people around Israel's land, air, and sea blockade of the Strip. The revolutionary potential of these tunnels, this "insurgent infrastructure" (Haddad, 2018), confronts the particular features of the Israeli settler colonial project that target the Gaza Strip. Indeed, the tunnels have been integral in both helping Palestinians of Gaza survive Israel's choking siege since 2006 by

Figure 5.8 Children playing around the metro sign, Gaza.
(*Source:* A Metro in Gaza *[Abusal, 2011].*)

carving out a way to move people and goods and in enabling, in key moments, the smuggling of weapons into Gaza to be used against Israeli targets (Haddad, 2018; Pelham, 2014). In this way, Abusal's Gaza metro recalls one aspect of the routine functioning of Palestinian public transit in the West Bank. As discussed in Chapter 3, practices of communality flourish in the service gaps caused by the interruptions of settler colonialism. Similarly, Abusal reveals a vision of Palestinian self-determined mobility flourishing in the tunnels necessitated by the Israeli blockade.

Abusal's metro builds on this revolutionary power. He still imagines that the tunnels will be used for smuggling goods and people—now in a faster, more streamlined way (Younis, 2012). But in imagining the metro as a way to deal with the congestion of Gaza traffic, Abusal presents another opposition front against settler colonialism: the reclamation of self-determined experiences of time and movement (Figure 5.8). The subway disrupts settler colonial confiscations of time in the quotidian sense, allowing Gaza Palestinians to stop losing time to blockade-related traffic and detours. According to Younis (2012), the envisioned metro was meant to be a regulated and reliable constant that would continue to run, and run on time, "despite the raids, people's poverty, and the intensification of the blockade." The project showcases a vision of predictable, even punctual, mobility in an otherwise chaotic situation, and that longing congeals in visions of a modern mode of public transportation.

Even in the way the project has been executed, the metro addresses a desire to break the extreme spatial fragmentation inside of Gaza and its separation from other Palestinian communities by proposing a vehicle for connection. The mobility of Abusal's spatial interventions was integral to his accomplishment of the project, and in that way, it is an example of site-oriented art (Kwon, 1997). Drawing from James Meyer's definition of the "functional site" in site-oriented art, Miwon Kwon (1997) notes that the "model [of the artwork's site] is not a map but an itinerary, a fragmentary sequence of events and actions *through* spaces, that is, a nomadic narrative whose path is articulated through the artist" (p. 95). The actual moving and positioning of the lighted sign brought Abusal's proposal to different in situ audiences, then his photographs of those encounters with the sign extended the mobility of the metro to gallery audiences. As Abusal moved with his sign from place to place around the Gaza Strip—and later in Jerusalem and Ramallah—he mapped the real route of the metro, even while that route differed from the one represented on his official system map.

This dimension of Abusal's metro came into view particularly sharply when, in 2012, the big red M, along with the subway map, went to Jerusalem and Ramallah, suggesting that the Gaza metro would become a system with service across historical Palestine. Abusal set up a metro stop at a lookout point on the Mount of Olives in Jerusalem, urging spectators to imagine a transit system that could swiftly carry Palestinians from the Gaza seashore to the spectacular view of Al-Aqsa Mosque's glinting gold dome, which, due to Israel's diffused bordering processes discussed in Chapters 1 and 2, today remains inaccessible to many Palestinians living in Gaza and the West Bank (Figure 5.9).

In another image from the Ramallah photo shoot, the metro stop sign seems to peer over a temporary sculpture in support of Palestine's bid to gain recognition as a member state in the United Nations (Figure 5.10). The sculpture, a gigantic blue chair representing a seat at the United Nations, features the demand, "Palestine's Right: Full Membership in the United Nations." Yet, as DAAR's *Right to Mobility* poignantly underscored, one might argue that Palestine's fundamental right is the internationally guaranteed right of return held by all Palestinians displaced by the establishment of Israel and their descendants. Capturing this meaningful juxtaposition, Abusal places his public transit sign, a symbol of collective movement, ahead of the stationary symbol of United Nations membership. The metro stop in Ramallah, then, suggests that meaningfully addressing the right to return with public transit might be a more urgent priority than, and perhaps even a prerequisite to, UN representation.

Figure 5.9 Metro sign behind what appear to be tourist children riding a camel, with Al-Aqsa Mosque visible in the distance, Jerusalem. *(Source: A Metro in Gaza [Abusal, 2012].)*

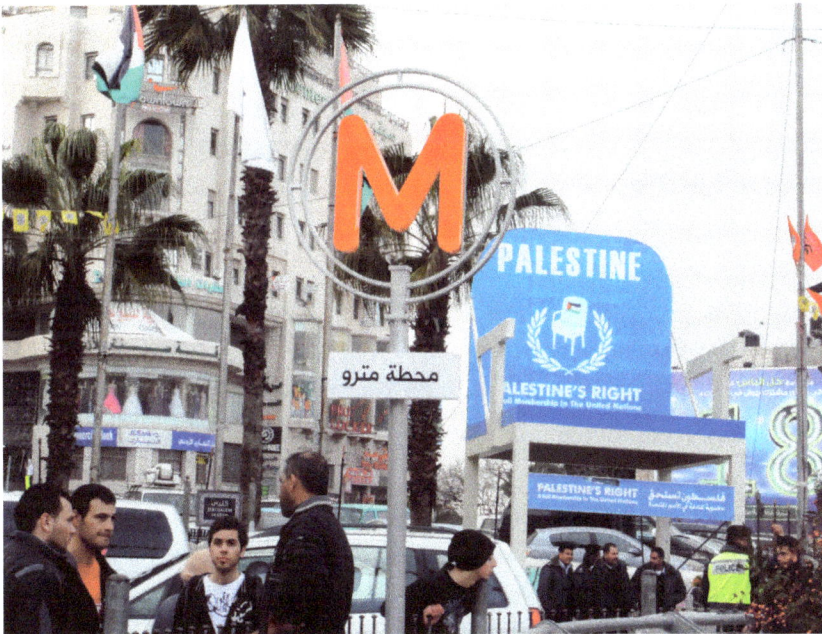

Figure 5.10 Metro sign in front of a temporary monument to the Palestine statehood bid, Ramallah. *(Source: A Metro in Gaza [Abusal, 2012].)*

While the idea of the Gaza metro would enable Palestinians to reclaim time, an object of routine colonial confiscation, as they travel by rapid transit around historical Palestine, it would be a mistake to imagine that Abusal is simply trying to propose technological advances to make life more livable in the shadow of the Israeli siege. Abusal's metro is meant to confront and exceed settler colonialism. In a subsequent, related project, *Reveal/A Metro in Gaza*, Abusal (2014) expanded his metro intervention by repurposing journalistic images of some of Gaza's tunnels and overlaying onto them graphics of familiar and mundane features of any modern subway system, such as turnstiles, line directories, illuminated signs, and even a pair of international travelers rolling their luggage. In the Arabic-language description of the project on his website, Abusal notes that, for *Reveal*, he selected images of the tunnels created and used by freedom fighters rather than those created for trade and the moving of goods. His selection underscores his message, delivered via metro, that the self-determined travel of Palestinians is a form of decolonization.

Moreover, we see in *A Metro in Gaza* Abusal using the method of haunting to invite his interlocutors to talk to ghosts (Gordon, 2008, 2018). Gordon (2008) explains that this invitation requires "the willingness to follow ghosts . . . where they lead, in the present, head turned backwards and forwards at the same time. To be haunted in the name of a will to heal is to allow the ghost to help you imagine what was lost that never even existed, really" (p. 57). Abusal's prominently placed metro signs haunt the spaces in which they are erected but do so in a way that resists total possession, that connects what was lost—the past and the future—with the immediacy and tangibility of "a something that must be done" in the present (Gordon, 2008, p. 174). There was never a subway system in Gaza, yet Abusal's project marks the loss of self-determined Palestinian mobility with the arresting presence of its immediate anticipation.

Abusal's metro as "ghostly matter" (Gordon, 2008) highlights the tension between a siege that seeks to seal off Palestinian territory and im/mobilize its residents and a metro system that enables mobility, and thus connection, far beyond colonial boundaries. He channels this tension in the erecting of his metro sign to haunt the Palestinian landscape with both loss and possibility. By starting on the ground (or, in the case of Abusal's Gaza metro, *under*ground) and centering seemingly mundane dreams of seamless transit, a suppressed truth emerges: Palestinian self-determined movement, quite fundamentally, asserts a radical refusal of Israeli colonial power and then exceeds it. The Gaza metro suggests that subway cars might become a vehicle for underground resistance that reclaims Palestinian control over Palestinian movement, across both space and time. *A Metro in*

Gaza, then, gestures to the radical potential and futures that emerge when we scrap the failed and failing "roadmap to peace" and replace it with a subway map.[9]

Movement in the Palestinian "Nation Estate"

Larissa Sansour, a Palestinian mixed-media artist born in Jerusalem and educated in Europe and the United States, has consistently engaged questions of displacement and diaspora, the persistent deformations of settler colonialism, and the active struggle over Palestinian futures. Sansour's *Nation Estate* project (2012), consisting of an eponymous short film and series of companion images (that look like film stills except they have different details), comments on the Palestinian statehood bid that was once again making headlines that year. Sansour's installation presents a droll science fiction rendering of one imaginative manifestation of Palestinian statehood: a "vertical" state in which the "entire Palestinian population" is contained in a single skyscraper. Sansour describes the project as a "clinically dystopian, yet humorous approach to deadlock in the Middle East" (larissasansour.com/Nation-Estate-2012). As a response to this deadlock—a state of immobility—*Nation Estate* advances a decolonial critique of the statehood project, with vehicles of collective movement playing a central role in delivering that critique.

This critique has two primary aspects, which I engage in this section. One aspect identifies im/mobilization as an enduring weapon of Israeli settler colonialism—so fundamental that Palestinian self-determination cannot be meaningfully realized without reclaiming autonomous control over movement. Another aspect presents a radical reimagining, and thus a reclamation, of Palestinian movement across space and time. *Nation Estate* and the series of four films of which it is part feature exercises of temporal self-determination, refusing to adhere to the limitations—in other words, the borders—of colonial arrangements of time and space (see Hochberg, 2018).[10] Even in the highly constrained dystopian landscape of *Nation Estate*, Palestinian life persists.

Sansour's *Nation Estate* has managed to cram all of Palestine into a single building, so the internal public transit system consists of not buses or taxis but, rather, a set of elevators (Figure 5.11). The elevator is the vantage point through which the protagonist (and the viewer riding alongside her) sees the many floors of the building and begins to understand its spatial and temporal logics. Much like a city bus line, the elevator makes its requested stops, and its opening doors reveal that each floor offers a facsimile of a different Palestinian city or landmark, to which I return in a moment. The elevator's

Figure 5.11 Elevators and directory in the lobby. Main Lobby, C-print, 75 × 150 cm. *(Source:* Nation Estate *[Sansour, 2012].)*

directory, located in the building's lobby, indicates that Gaza is located just one floor above Nablus, reducing some 130 kilometers to a few layers of steel and concrete. In that way, the elevator might appear to make the many cities of Palestine, now neatly layered on top of one another, more easily accessible to the residents of the state, many of whom would find it hard to obtain the permits necessary even to make such journeys in the real world of Israel's im/mobilization regime. There are no more checkpoints and segregated roads; no more buses and shared taxis. Jerusalem and Ramallah are no longer separated by the impossible traffic buildup at the infamous Qalandiya Checkpoint. Travelers need only take the elevator from the fourth floor to the fifth (or from the thirteenth floor to the fourteenth in the film short). The elevator is now the sole mechanism that connects the once and still fragmented cantons of Palestinian life.

Yet what appears to be impossibly easy geographical movement is far from unfettered. As Sansour (starring as the film's protagonist) rides up in the elevator, a screen embedded in the wall displays commercial advertisements and official announcements, including a video message that entreats passengers to "remember to have your documents validated for travel" while displaying an image of an "approved" Nation Estate passport above the fine print: "Restrictions may apply." The short film does not depict all of the bureaucratic processes of the Nation Estate, but I imagine that those validations might be obtained (along with the other ubiquitous hallmarks of bureaucratic state control over the means of movement) on the fifth floor, where the directory lists "permits and passports."[11] In a design reminiscent of the popular layout of major international airports around the world, the demands of state bureaucracy are reached only after travelers enjoy the shopping opportunities of the *souq* on the floor just below the lobby.[12] The film depicts passengers arriving on the Amman Express train moving from the train platform up the escalators to the lobby so they will pass the shopping on the way up.

Furthermore, the ease of elevator travel contrasts with the fact that the Nation Estate's cities are still separated from one another and contained on *all* sides. In fact, the windows at the edges of each city-floor appear with bars on them, which at first might seem to fit seamlessly into the sleek and sterile architectural style of the (e)state but also evoke the enclosing nature of the bars of a prison cell or cage. Sansour's visual representations of enclosure pointedly warn of the dangers of proceeding with declarations of Palestinian statehood without resolving the conditions of Israeli settler colonialism. When Sansour arrives at the Palestinian skyscraper, her entry is conditioned on the successful registration of both fingerprint and ocular iris scans linked to her identification number. These familiar features of modern border technologies might appear mundane, but they signal to the audience that, at best, the Palestine (e)state has succeeded only in reproducing these technologies of enclosure that have resulted, and continue to result, in Palestinian deterritorialization. Furthermore, while the very *Nation Estate* concept seems to suggest a negotiated settlement that results in the condensing of all of Palestine into a single building, it is still not free of the circling presence of the Israeli military, whose various mechanisms of control appear just outside the barred windows. A military helicopter casts its shadow in the Mediterranean Sea's water as it laps onto the beach on what could be the Gaza floor, and a panoptic guard tower peers into Sansour's apartment, while the ominous concrete slabs of the Apartheid Wall seem to surround the building.

At the end of the film, the view from the protagonist's apartment reveals what was traded for the streamlined mobility of the Nation Estate: while the golden dome of the real Aqsa Mosque, situated in its rightful place, can be seen glinting in the distance beyond the militarized Wall, Sansour encounters the same mosaicked façade, a convincing replica of Al-Aqsa, when the elevator door opens on the Jerusalem floor. Juxtaposing the smooth movement of the building's internal elevator with the harsh immobilization that still surrounds Palestinian life, Sansour underscores the dangers of formalizing Palestinian statehood in the shadow of unfettered Israeli settler colonialism.

The primary danger is the continued depopulation of Palestine, palpable in the relative emptiness of the building. The premise of *Nation Estate*—that this high-rise building is now the national home of all Palestinians—might elicit an expectation of busy, congested spaces, but there are only a few people visible in its public areas, such as the lobby and the elevator. At the tourist sites of Bethlehem's Nativity Church and Jerusalem's Aqsa Mosque (Figures 5.12–5.13), Sansour encounters people, some of whom may be foreign visitors, given that all of the signs are written in English. But she is the only person in the small room with barred windows that contains an otherwise deserted Mediterranean seashore (Figure 5.14). Where are all of the people in this single-building home for the entire Palestinian nation? Sansour reminds the audience that the compound enclosure of Palestinian life—first within single city floors, and then within a single state building—has been a critical technology of Palestinian deterritorialization and, if left unopposed in an official Palestinian estate, will surely result in the continued depopulation of Palestine.

In *Nation Estate*, a "two-state solution" that at first appears to have created a home for all Palestinians in a contiguous "state" is soon revealed to be premised on the evacuation of Palestinian self-determination, if not also of Palestine itself. In issuing this reminder that the repression of the past and present will disfigure the future if it is not actively dismantled, Sansour's intervention recalls Edward Said's critiques of earlier bids for Palestinian statehood that traded away territorial integrity for formal declarations (e.g., 1993, 1998, 1999). Said's (1998) critique of the planned declaration of a Palestinian state by Yasser Arafat, then the leader of the Palestine Liberation Organization, underscored the dangers of declaring a state even though both sovereignty and territorial contiguity had been denied to the Palestinians through the Oslo Accords, whose failures had begun to reveal themselves. By legitimizing the geographic fragmentations of the Oslo Accords, Arafat's statehood declaration "would definitively divide the Palestinian population and its cause more or less forever" (Said, 1998). Moreover, the repeated denial of Palestinian sovereignty would make Arafat's statehood declaration a formal betrayal of Palestinian self-determination, which Said (1999) emphatically noted was "unworkable . . . in a separate state." The Nation Estate building represents a shortcut around the question of territorial contiguity by putting everyone in a single high-rise building while avoiding the urgent

Facing page:

top: Figure 5.12 The Church of the Nativity on the Bethlehem floor. Manger Square, C-print, 75 × 150 cm. *(Source:* Nation Estate *[Sansour, 2012].)*

middle: Figure 5.13 View of Al-Aqsa Mosque on the Jerusalem floor. Jerusalem Floor, C-print, 75 × 150 cm. *(Source:* Nation Estate *[Sansour, 2012].)*

bottom: Figure 5.14 The contained Mediterranean seashore. Mediterranean Floor, C-print, 75 × 150 cm. *(Source:* Nation Estate *[Sansour, 2012].)*

issue of land repatriation that is key to a decolonial project. While this itinerary might be pleasing to the proponents of colonialism in Palestine, Sansour "haunts" (Gordon, 2008, 2018; Morrill et al., 2016; Tuck & Ree, 2013) this route with ghosts of Indigenous survivance (Vizenor, 1999), and one of the vehicles to accomplish this haunting is a train.

The *Nation Estate* film begins with the camera adopting the perspective of the front of a subway train speeding through a modern, well-lit tunnel. The subway, we learn, is the Amman Express, a mode of public transit that enables the collective return to Palestine, the building. Sansour's selection of a train to accomplish this feat of return underscores the importance of collectivity for such a return to be meaningful. Inside the train we encounter the protagonist, Sansour herself, who sits listening to announcements in Arabic and English. In preparation for arrival, she effortlessly slides up the retractable handle of her suitcase before exiting the train onto the arrivals platform. This opening scene subtly provokes a contrast between the mundane ease of traveling from Amman to the Palestinian Nation Estate on the subway and the intensely burdensome current-day conditions of crossing from Jordan through Israeli military installations into the West Bank. The latter experience, which has changed over the years since the Oslo Accords to incorporate increased Israeli security technology, typically involves taking multiple buses; lengthy waits and stops where vehicles are repeatedly searched; porters helping passengers lug around their belongings for inspection; and travelers being subjected, body and mind, to the invasive scrutiny of border control. The mundane simplicity of a trip on the Amman Express is a clear improvement, and Sansour's itinerary starting with the train subtly indicts the unnecessarily troublesome current route from Amman to Bethlehem.

Easing the experience of travel into Palestine is one important part of the Nation Estate's subway, but the vehicle also evokes an imperiled past and present of interregional dis/connection. The opening footage's object perspective of the Amman Express moving through its subway shaft brings to mind one means of guerrilla mobility in the present: the underground tunnels of the Gaza Strip that enable the movement of people and goods beyond the strangling confines of Israel's siege, which otherwise forcibly separates the territory from the rest of the world (Haddad, 2018; Pelham, 2014). The concept of the Amman Express also conjures the historical train system in Palestine, first built under the Ottomans and then developed under the British, which previously connected Palestinian cities to one another and to Egypt, Syria, Saudi Arabia, and beyond (Mansour, 2006). This train system enabled the transportation of people and goods before the train was annexed, and the international routes were severed through the establishment of the Israeli state.

In the vehicle that represents a return to Palestine (the Nation Estate), the resonance among past, present, and future means of collective Palestinian movement, transit that sustains and reproduces social life, congeals. This temporal self-determination, which resists and overwrites settler colonial ruptures, erasures, and foreclosures, infuses Sansour's *Nation Estate*. In fact, more than half of the film follows Sansour moving by various means on her journey home. Excluding the closing credits, the film itself is seven-and-a-half minutes long. Starting with the first moments of the film in the Amman Express tunnels, Sansour reaches the door of her apartment only at the five-minute mark. As she physically moves through the spaces of the Nation Estate, she moves among the past, present, and future, here interwoven together. The building's aesthetic is thoroughly futuristic, yet its features are historical. The stony façade of the Church of the Nativity, recreated on the Bethlehem floor, now sits bathing in fluorescent lights, surrounded by steel tunnel walkways.

Moreover, hallmarks of Palestinian culture appear throughout the project (both the film and companion images), enduring despite renewed containment. In both the film and one of the images, the black-and-white *keffiyeh* pattern adorns the plates in which Sansour sets out prepared tabbouleh, kibbeh, and *marmaoun* (a couscous dish). A pinwheel pattern (which symbolizes the moon) common to Palestinian embroidery is emblazoned on the sleeve of Sansour's futuristic thatched uniform, the cover of the Nation Estate passport that appears in the elevator announcement, and the tote bags carried by other people in the elevator. And a brief glimpse of Sansour's wide jacket pocket reveals another reference to embroidery—this time a floral pattern made with the couching technique for which the traditional Bethlehem style is famous (and distinct from the typical Palestinian cross stitch). These allusions to two methods of embroidery not only represent enduring Palestinian cultural practices; they also reference the immense cultural circulation—of artistic styles and textiles among different villages and from other countries—that shaped the embroidery tradition in Palestine and has been threatened by the Israeli enclosures (see Kawar, 2011; Weir, 2008).

What appears to be a mature olive tree, judging by its thick, knotted trunk, sprouts from the ground of Sansour's apartment as she waters it (Figure 5.15), nurturing its persistence, however dislocated. The olive tree recalls a history of struggle over both the existence and the meaning of such trees in Palestine. It evokes a history of using the tree as a symbol of Palestinian rootedness in the land of Palestine as it became subject to settler colonialism (Abufarha, 2008), as well as Israeli practices of uprooting and otherwise restricting Palestinian interactions with olive trees (Braverman, 2009). The tree and the rootedness it represents are breaking through the confines of

Figure 5.15 The protagonist watering an olive tree sprouting from the ground of her apartment. Olive Tree, C-print, 75 × 150 cm. *(Source:* Nation Estate *[Sansour, 2012].)*

the Nation Estate, literally sending cracks up the walls. Despite the context of enclosure and its expulsive logic, the tree and its nurturing signal a permanence, a refusal to move that is itself an important component of truly self-determined mobility—in other words, the power to stay.[13] Here, too, Sansour deploys the method of haunting by practicing self-determined movement, even while directly in the shadow of its denial. The fecundity of the olive tree is then paralleled in the next image, where we see the protagonist suddenly growing to be pregnant. It is from this view that the camera zooms out, ultimately escaping from the confines of the skyscraper. Mixing symbols of rootedness in the past with planting seeds for the future, these final images of self-determined (im)mobility and temporal reconnection across past, present, and future represent a decolonized mode of living that seems sure to outlast each new colonial configuration on Palestinian land.

In its movement among past, present, and future, the journey of return to Palestine at the center of *Nation Estate* asserts Indigenous survivance, an active, moving presence that belies "victimry" (Vizenor, 1999, 2000), even under conditions of extreme and renewed enclosure. Sansour deploys haunting as a method to disrupt the spatial and temporal monopoly claimed by colonial power. Her films enact temporal self-determination, refusing to adhere to the limitations—in other words, the borders—of colonial arrangements of time and space. This self-determination is portrayed in *Nation Estate* through an emphasis on movement, including two vehicles of collective movement (the train and the elevator). Sansour's assertion of Palestinian temporal self-determination delivers a searing indictment of settler colonialism while simultaneously insisting on the continuation of Indigenous life.

This book has examined vehicles of collective Palestinian movement as sites of social struggle against and beyond settler colonialism. In that vein, this chapter has analyzed artistic representations of Palestinian transit. In response to the impasse over "solutions" often associated with the Palestinian struggle, I round out this book with a chapter on the speculative power of art that can transcend the limitations of other political activities. At the beginning of the chapter, I noted an often expressed frustration with repeated international political denials of Palestinian self-determination, reflected in Abourahme's (2011) discussion of the phrase "Shou nisawee? . . . Ma fee hal" (What can we do? . . . There is no solution). The artists whose work I have analyzed here play with the problem of searching for solutions on a terrain that has already defined them as impossible. Rather than capitulate to the predeterminations of this miserly political calculus, the artists exercise haunting, a method by which the repressed violence of colonialism, as well as the lives and communities that it has attempted to obliterate, is brought (back) into view. Each of these projects is animated by a practical impulse of thinking through the accomplishment and representation of collective Indigenous movement across space and time, in contravention of the settler colonial consumption of both. The pragmatic nature of public transit anchors their speculative visions in present-day practices, as well as once possible but foreclosed histories of collective Palestinian mobility. By doing so in ways that rewrite given relationships among past, present, and future, the artists use their conceptualizations of public transit to expose the effects of colonial im/mobilizations and demonstrate Indigenous self-determination that will outlast them.

Conclusion

In examining collective Palestinian mobility in the West Bank via public transit, this book asserts that mobility is a highly contested arena of social struggle in the context of settler colonialism. Israeli colonization of the West Bank has come to revolve around an enclosures strategy toward West Bank Palestinians that undermines Palestinian economic independence, political stability, and social cohesion to accomplish the maximum annexation of territory for Jewish Israelis while attempting to frustrate, destroy, and "vanish" (Sharif, 2016) Palestinian life on Palestinian land. The Israeli enclosures are animated by the logics of im/mobilization, a programmatic denial of Palestinian self-determined mobility that manifests by forcing, forbidding, and otherwise burdening movement. Im/mobilization is imposed as a collective condition through a network of diffused borders, a linked web of potential encounter points with the Israeli military, that makes Palestinian movement dangerous, tedious, and unpredictable.

In this context, even mundane forms of mobility such as public transit take on political significance. As a literal vehicle for collective movement, Palestinian public transportation hosts alternatives to the settler colonial logics of im/mobilization. Through the normal course of its operations, Palestinian transit in the West Bank fosters communality among its participants that enables travel for a variety of socially reproductive purposes and bolsters Indigenous claims to spatial knowledge, each of which are threatened by Israeli settler colonialism. Through its spectacular deployment by activists as both vehicle and symbol of collective movement, Palestinian public transit carries accounts of experiences of Israeli settler colonialism beyond the jagged edges of the Israeli border-enclosures to promote solidarity among separated Palestinian communities and with international civil society audiences. And as a symbol representing collective mobility across space and time, Palestinian public transit is a site where artists work through and propose decolonial interventions based on Palestinian movement. In all cases, Palestinian public transportation hosts radical exercises of self-determined movement that defy the constrictions of settler colonialism while cultivating lasting alternatives to conquest and confiscation. I have highlighted collective Palestinian mobility via public transportation in this book precisely because it represents the power of the Palestinian mobile commons, a space where Palestinian autonomy and self-determination have been, and continue to be, practiced in opposition to, but also in excess of, settler colonial logics of im/mobilization.

When I began researching the public transportation system in the West Bank, the routine riders with whom I spoke would listen to my explanation of the project with puzzlement. *What transit system?* they'd say, or *Bus 11, that's the most important mode of transit.* The number 11, the joke went, represented one's own two legs. Bus 11—or, in other words, walking— is often the fallback form of "transportation" in a system plagued by unpredictable delays, unreliable service, and colonial intervention. However, I also heard that the current condition of transit was a marked improvement from the days of the second Intifada, which were defined by curfew and closure. Before an early interview at the Ministry of Transportation (Wizarat an-Naql w al-Muwasalat), Issa, an administrative assistant, told me that during the second Intifada and due to Israeli closures, his workday commute was broken into nine segments each way, including transfers among taxis, mules, and horse carts. He explained that the transit system as it functions now is a marked improvement. These initial reactions to the provocation of my research topic indicated the urgency of attending to the conditions and logics of the Israeli im/mobilization regime that have frustrated, and continue to frustrate, Palestinian movement. They also indicated that despite the burdens of im/mobilization, West Bank Palestinians have continued to collectively develop ways of moving.

One of my interlocutors, Zahi, once asked me how I came up with the idea to study public transportation, commenting that he had never thought of it as a site of research. His question alongside the Bus 11–type jokes caused me to consider whether my interlocutors viewed public transit as an insignificant topic for consideration. But when I asked directly about this, their answers indicated that public transportation plays a central role in their lives. Zahi at the time of my research was a resident of Beit Sahour in his early twenties and relied on public transit vehicles to get to his job in food service at a hotel and to visit his sister who lived in Ad-Doha, on the far side of Bethlehem, among other activities. He responded that his question was motivated not by the *insignificance* of transit but, rather, by the fact that he was surprised because he had not before considered just how significant it was. In his words, "Transportation is the most important thing for life in the West Bank. It is how everyone gets around."[1] In a similar conversation, Zeina, then a student who was living with her parents in Beit Sahour and studying primary education at Al-Quds Open University in Bethlehem, remarked, "Public transit connects us. We all use it to get anywhere in the West Bank." This recognition of widespread reliance on and the critical function of Palestinian transit does not negate the accompanying complaints about its unreliability, unpredictability, costliness, and danger. Rather, it underscores the social stakes of preserving collective mobility in the face of these challenges.

The answer to Zahi's question about the origins of my research topic, emerging from a confluence of events and observations, not only responds to his inquiry but also illuminates the "So what?" of this book's assertions. In what follows, I outline the significance of conceptualizing public transit engagements as vehicles of decolonization in a continuously changing landscape.

My idea to research the significance of public transportation in the West Bank originally emerged from the interplay between my first impressions in 2012 of a well-organized and user-friendly Palestinian transit system and the context of the 2011 bid by the Palestinian Authority (PA) for Palestine to be recognized as a full member of the United Nations. After the bid was blocked by the United Nations Security Council, the UN General Assembly passed Resolution 67/19 to upgrade Palestine to the position of "non-member observer state" (an elevation from "observer entity") on November 29, 2012.[2] This diplomatic campaign, like earlier statehood bids by Palestinian leadership, met with criticism from Palestinians living in the West Bank, Gaza Strip, and elsewhere. Some of the diverse concerns focused on the meaninglessness of declaring Palestinian statehood on the land of the West Bank and Gaza Strip (WBGS) without the means to address Israel's fragmentation of these territories or its denial of Palestinian sovereignty at every register.

With these concerns in mind, I first visited Palestine in 2012 and encountered there an organized public transit system, what I had initially taken to be a marker of a functioning state. Vehicles are painted in recognizable colors (the shades of yellow, orange, and white depicted in the figures in Chapter 2); for many (but not all) routes, drivers wait for passengers in

stations or lots designated by their destination; and the routes (if not schedules) are somewhat set (except for the disruptions and improvisations I discussed in Chapter 3). I became interested in investigating the significance
of such an organized system that enables collective movement within a context shaped by the im/mobilizations of settler colonialism. Once I learned
the relationship between the PA and the transit operators in a public-private
partnership, public transportation as a site of social struggle came into view.
I observed that the routine functioning of the public transit system in the
West Bank appeared to reject the attempted containment of Palestinian life
into the shards of fragmented Palestinian territory, working instead to connect them and assert regular access to the routes among them.

In a 2007 report on the humanitarian impacts of expanding Israeli settlements in the West Bank, the UN Office for the Coordination of Humanitarian Affairs, Occupied Palestinian Territory highlighted the contrast between
the robust connectedness of the various settlements and the separation of
Palestinian areas. The report's concluding remarks note:

> Palestinians now mostly move from one enclave to another via a net-
> work of checkpoints, alternative roads or through tunnels or bridges
> under roads primarily reserved for settlers. This provides a measure
> of transport contiguity—in the sense that enclaves are linked—but
> not territorial contiguity because West Bank land is divided by Is-
> raeli roads and other infrastructure. Transport contiguity may sat-
> isfy short-term humanitarian needs but cannot ultimately lead to a
> sustainable economy. It also does not provide the basis for a two state
> solution. (p. 8)

Certainly, the report captured the fragmenting effects of Israel's bordering
processes and identified their deleterious effects on Palestinian economic
independence and political and territorial cohesion. But to reduce this transport contiguity to the "satisf[action of] short-term humanitarian needs"
overlooks or underestimates the lasting significance of practiced, collective
reassertions of self-determination through the medium of mobility in the
context of intensifying settler colonialism.

This significance appears more clearly when one considers Israel's attempts to delegitimize and frustrate any and all forms of Palestinian resistance to settler colonialism, which, in turn, have severely restricted the
spaces and idioms of struggle. The political landscape in the WBGS is constrained by Israeli efforts to imprison Palestinian activists; delegitimize
grassroots campaigns, such as the Boycott, Divestment, and Sanctions
(BDS) movement; and brand any remaining Palestinian activity that is

not under direct or indirect Israeli control as "violent," "terrorist," or "anti-Semitic." Furthermore, the im/mobilization regime, which was developed as an anti-Indigenous counterinsurgent response to the successes of the first Intifada (as I explained in Chapter 1), has further conditioned the terrain on which the Palestinian struggle operates. The shattering effects of the Oslo Accords and the bordering practices that have been imposed in their shadow have hindered the ability for Palestinian communities particularly in the WBGS to connect with one another; with other Palestinian communities inside Jerusalem and 1948 Palestine; and with international communities, including the Palestinian diaspora and other allies (see, e.g., Dana & Jarbawi, 2017). It has also decreased the possibility for direct Palestinian contact with the Israeli population, restricting the elements of Israeli society with which Palestinians interact to military personnel and infrastructure. The multiple effects of this spatial fragmentation have frustrated collective political organizing (Baylouny, 2009). Of course, the Palestinian struggle continues to dynamically respond and transform. Here I mean simply to identify Israeli colonial pressures, diffused through the PA, that have necessitated a proliferation in forms and registers of Palestinian people power.

A multidisciplinary set of scholarship attempts to reach beyond the boundaries of traditional social movements literature to engage multiple notions of people power: what to call them, how to recognize them, how they are related, and why and to what extent they matter (see, e.g., Abu-Lughod, 1990; Bayat, 2010; Jeffress, 2008; Jones, 2012; Scott, 1985, 1990, 2009, 2012; Y. Sharif, 2017; Sharp et al., 2000). Different scholars pursue this project for a variety of purposes—many rooted in solidarity with the oppressed—whether to better understand the logics or tactics of domination, to identify overlooked sources of consequential power that materially alter the dynamics of domination, or to demonstrate the limits of supposedly totalizing forms of domination. One particular strand of the "resistance" scholarship, a term I use for convenience but whose insufficiency is a central debate in that very literature, examines the political import of small-scale everyday acts. This strand has extended to the study of mundane activities in Palestine. On the importance of recognizing such activity as "resistance," Timothy Seidel (2019) argues that such a conceptual move illuminates the everyday nature of Israeli rule in the West Bank, as well as anticipating and rejecting efforts to invalidate Palestinian resistance as decontextualized violence (pp. 731–732). An examination of the political dimensions of everyday resistance also avoids frameworks that dismiss it as mere passivity, a label that can also be dehumanizing. I suggest that, in addition to defending Palestinian political life against continued efforts to invalidate it in all its forms, a consideration of the decolonial nature of everyday engagements with transit illuminates the ways that the politics of mundane activity intertwine with more explicitly political actions and, together, cultivate alternative patterns of Indigenous life that exceed the limits of settler colonialism.

In his study of "street politics" in multiple urban centers in the Middle East, Asef Bayat (2010) notes the "epidemic potential" of street politics evident in numerous moments when "a small demonstration . . . grow[s] into a massive exhibition of solidarity" (p. 12). He explains that the *circulation* of people in the public spaces of the city establish "latent communication with one another by recognizing their mutual interests and shared sentiments" (p. 12). I contend that the operation of West Bank transit and the *recognition of mutual interests and shared sentiments* that it fosters—about the power of exercising self-determined mobility across colonized space—can and do feed into the direct political expressions of activists and artists.

By examining these distinct and interrelated forms of people power at one site of their expression, public transportation, I mean to suggest that they are related components in an overall process of decolonization. In particular, I argue that the mundane, political, and artistic engagements with public transit I have discussed in this book make up a constellation of decolonizing activity, a repertoire of self-determination practices. Considering these practices together illuminates the ebb-and-flow dynamics of decolonization that actively respond to political opportunities as they open and close. When the Israeli military intensifies its closure to lock down Palestinian life, as it did during the second Intifada, public transit vehicles and routes united Palestinians in fugitive defiance and resilience, even though it also created opportunities for internal price gouging. These exercises of collective mobility across the terrain subject to border-enclosures continue to influence the operation of a more regulated and regularized transit system after the loosening of lockdown. Collective self-determined mobility via transit generates friction with settler colonial im/mobilization, and Palestinian activists then identify moments when they can use this friction to create sparks or spectacles for multiple audiences. Although their physical movement may be constrained, these sparks call for nuanced solidarity with Palestinian decolonization across divided Palestinian communities and beyond to global comrades. Palestinian artists, in turn, recognize collective Palestinian movement via public transportation as a site to further crystallize the drive to decolonize in their creative representations of Palestinian self-determined mobility through time and space.

Furthermore, one might consider the links between Palestinian public transit engagement as vehicles of decolonization and other exercises of self-determined movement in contravention of Israeli settler colonialism that extend beyond the boundaries of the West Bank. I discussed in Chapter 5 some connections to the system of mobility enabled by the underground tunnels in and out of Gaza. Another set of resilient engagements with collective mobility can be seen in the networks that move West Bank Palestinians across the Apartheid Wall, in contravention of the border-enclosures strategy to which it contributes. Yara Sharif (2017) has generatively conceived of this system that responds to the "blurry boundaries" of the occupation as "community patterns of capturing spaces" that become the basis for an "architecture of resistance" (pp. 59–62, 69). The stealth nature of such crossings echoes the routes of the second Intifada's off-road taxis discussed in Chapter 3. I propose that we consider all of these vehicles of collective movement in contravention of the settler colonial enclosures together to reveal a moving map of active decolonization as Palestinians continue to harness the means of mobility to exercise self-determined relationships with and on their land across the entire territory of Palestine.

Examinations of mundane sites of resistant or resilient activities might appear "romanticizing." Indeed, Lila Abu-Lughod (1990) diagnosed and responded to this concern, suggesting that studies of resistance are more productively deployed as "diagnostics of power" (i.e., domination) and its contextualized particularities. Yet in the case of Indigenous modes of living, a singular focus on the instrumental value of people's everyday activities as a lens for understanding domination can have the adverse effect of reinforcing the self-declared supremacy of settler colonialism. Recognizing instead how these activities both instantiate and anticipate alternative modes of life, beyond dispossession and displacement, challenges the settler colonial myth of its own completeness and permanence. By avoiding the "grave error" of "mistak[ing] the conceits of authority and the ambitions of the powerful for the realities of people's worldly existence" (A. Gordon, 2004, p. 210), this approach highlights the incompleteness of settler colonialism and the fact that it is the reactive (or *resistant*) force against the resilient indigeneity it is constantly attempting to uproot and eliminate (see, e.g., Barakat, 2018; Goeman, 2014; Kauanui, 2016; Wolfe, 2006).

In an early conversation about this book, an editor suggested the title "Vehicles of Resistance," a phrase that is clever, evocative, and lyrical. It is for these reasons that I regret I could not use it, but as I reflected on my fieldwork, I realized that "resistance" was an insufficient word for what I have sought to highlight. In terms of mundane transit operation, this resilient mode of inter- and intracity travel did not take the form of traditional resistance. Instead, it comprised a set of activities whose intention was primarily practical, but whose significance in and for a politically overdetermined landscape was palpable. Then, while considering other forms of engagement with public transit that were more intentionally political but invested in something beyond opposition, I came to recognize a repertoire of decolonization. Taken together, these engagements advance a collective (re)assertion of self-determination through resilient relations of mobility that link people, life, and land.

This is different from a demand for self-determined movement. A demand is addressed to an audience from which action is expected. Instead, these repertoires of self-determined mobility are an exercise without waiting for a demand to be recognized or fulfilled. This is reminiscent of the exercised self-determination of the Zapatistas (Speed & Reyes, 2005; Subcomandante Insurgente Marcos, 1996) or the activities in/of the utopian margins curated by the keeper of *The Hawthorn Archive* (2018), Avery Gordon (particularly in the files "the scandal of the qualitative difference" and "a means of preparation"). Locating the current study in relation to these literatures suggests that exercises of self-determination can take place alongside active struggles, e.g., resistance, against limitations on that self-determination. In other words, the systematic denial of self-determination does not negate the fact of its practice. But where self-determination is exercised in spite of its denial, that practice is more than, or even different from, opposition. Here, the goal is to "audaciously assert" an unauthorized autonomy (Gordon, 2018, p. viii).

We might consider what is being practiced, created, preserved, prefigured, and claimed (or reclaimed) not only in opposition to domination but also beyond it. For example, Gerald Vizenor (1999, 2000) links Native "transmotion," "survivance," and sovereignty into an aesthetic theory to address how movement animates and is animated by the exercise of a "*sui generis* sovereignty" (1999, p. 15). This "sovereignty" is not nationalistic but rather an assemblage of collective narratives that "[renounce] . . . dominance, tragedy, and victimry" (p. vii). For Vizenor, at the core of *survivance*, which includes transmotion as one of its forms, is an "active sense of presence" (p. vii). Vizenor's *survivance* resonates with Bayat's (2010) "art of presence," which connotes "the courage and creativity to assert collective will in spite of all odds, to circumvent constraints, utilizing what is available and discovering new spaces within which to make oneself heard, seen, felt, and realized" (p. 26). These repertoires of self-determined presence are bound up in the collective movement of people according to their own motivations, which navigates but is not wholly constrained by the forces of im/mobilization, whether colonial or national (or both). And, reading Vizenor and Bayat together, the significance of this "active presence" in motion emits from the fact that it materializes robust if fugitive social relations that endure dominant efforts to impose separation, alienation, and victimization.

Returning to the concept of transformative *sumud* that I addressed in the Introduction, we can see a connection between Palestinian survivance and active presence. Although it has reflected many different definitions, the core of *sumud* is the steadfastness that enables Palestinians to stay and live in Palestine. My proposal to consider engagements with public transit as expressions of transformative *sumud* underscores how self-determined collective movement contributes to this project of staying, of practicing the art of active presence, of survivance in motion.

Given the significance of the vehicles of decolonization at the center of this book, how might we understand this significance in a changing landscape? The active processes of domination and decolonization in the Palestinian West Bank continue to transform, even at the time of final editing of this book. There are two developments in particular that I address here to signal some of the ways I hope the insights of this book will extend beyond the necessarily limited period of my fieldwork. The first is an increase in individual Palestinian debt that has enabled a rise in personal car ownership, and the second is Israel's aggressive pursuit of further territorial annexation in the West Bank. In both of these arenas, the decolonizing energy exercised through engagements with public transit are imperiled, and they both underscore the urgency of recentering the necessary imbrication of decolonization and self-determination.

In the Introduction, I noted that in recent years the number of private cars registered in the West Bank is increasing at a higher rate than public transportation. Automobile purchase is quite expensive in the West Bank due to double taxation by both the Palestinian Authority and Israel, and I suggested that, in the apparent absence of proportional improvements in income or wealth, an increase in private car ownership is likely the result of the increased availability of personal loans. The proliferation of banks, the relaxation of lending requirements, and advertising have all led to a rise in individual bank loan taking in the Palestinian West Bank (Harker, 2017; Hatuqa, 2013). Christopher Harker (2017) identifies a popular sense among West Bank Palestinians that almost everyone now carries some debt. Harker notes that this at first blush seems to contradict the Palestinian Monetary Authority's (PMA) figures, which indicate that only 9 percent of the working population has taken loans from banks or microcredit institutions (p. 603). But he argues that the public perception of wide-scale indebtedness is accounting for a kind of debt that the PMA's calculations do not—namely, loans taken directly from nonbank entities, such as people within the borrower's social network, employers, and property owners (p. 603). Taken together, these developments have resulted in an intensified condition of individual indebtedness in the West Bank (Bahour, 2012; Harker, 2017; Hatuqa, 2013). This growing personal debt is largely linked to "consumption spending" on housing, car purchases, and other personal loans (Harker, 2017, p. 603; Hatuqa, 2013).

In the years since I began traveling to the West Bank in 2012, six of the interlocutors with whom I have stayed in touch have obtained loans to purchase cars. Because the purchased vehicles are shared among family members, my interlocutors have reduced, but not entirely eliminated, their reliance on public transit; they still use shared vans, shared taxis, and buses to accomplish some of their inter- and intracity movement when the car is in use by someone else. The motivation for these acquisitions is expressly linked to the increased convenience of private car use compared with public transportation—particularly the convenience of controlling one's schedule that derives from having a conveyance ready to go at one's door rather than having to find a way to a transit route and wait for the vehicle to fill. In exchange for this increased individual autonomy, car buyers across the West Bank are accepting the curtailment of autonomy that comes with debt, and while these loan decisions are made individually, they amount to an increasingly collective condition of indebtedness.

As this expanding debt regime decreases reliance on public transportation, we might consider what is lost. The loss of collective autonomy through indebtedness can be considered a recent consequence of what Seidel (2019) calls the "invisible occupation," or a program of domination that masquerades as development and improvement, especially as Israel creates the restricted conditions in which the PA then maneuvers.[3] As indebtedness is linked to the individuation of mobility through private car ownership, public transportation as the primary means of collective mobility may lose its salience. Research on the condition and effects of individual loans on West Bank Palestinians is emerging alongside this growing trend. I suggest that, as this research deepens, it is worth considering the effects of collective indebtedness on collective mobility and the collective expressions of self-determination that public transit has heretofore fostered.

Alongside the expansion of debt, Palestinian self-determination is facing intensified siege as Israel's colonial annexation of West Bank territory enjoys renewed vigor. On January 28, 2020, the United States' Trump administration unveiled the official version of its plan to advance Israeli settler colonialism in Palestine. This "Deal of the Century" involved a coerced transaction in which Palestinians would sacrifice, among other things, their internationally guaranteed Right of Return in exchange for the imposition of an expanded neoliberal economic program facilitated by international investments. The Trump administration's plan then encouraged Israeli Prime Minister Benjamin Netanyahu to pursue formal annexation of 30 percent of West Bank territory, formally and permanently confiscating the land as part of Israel. Netanyahu's desperate plan to impose annexation despite the crisis of his own leadership was then walked back in the late summer as part of a normalization agreement between Israel and the United Arab Emirates. Still, Netanyahu has referred to this decision as merely placing annexation plans on hold.

This aggressive campaign of planned dispossession continues a convention of pursuing settler colonialism through the denial of Palestinian self-determination and the spatial and social relations that constitute the indigeneity on which such self-determination is based. It is my hope that a look at Palestinian public transportation, a means of enabling collective Palestinian mobility across Palestinian territory, will reinvigorate a focus on Palestinian self-determination and territoriality that underscores the inseparability of the two. In other words, the exercise of and demand for self-determined mobility that is evident across multiple engagements with Palestinian public transportation in the West Bank exceeds its denial, forging the connections among people and land that advance Indigenous decolonization. As Israel continues to pursue its settler colonial agenda, the endurance, feasibility, and urgency of alternatives—beyond state-based solutions—must be rooted in moving practices of Palestinian decolonization.

.

Appendix on Methodology

As stated in the Introduction, to collect the data on which this book is based I used a variety of methods over the course of six trips to Palestine in 2012–2014, 2016, and 2018. I accomplished the bulk of the data collection over two-and-a-half months in the summer of 2013 and seven-and-a-half months in 2014. During those extended stays, I rented apartments in Beit Sahour, a suburb of Greater Bethlehem, and made day or overnight trips to other locations as needed. From 2012 to 2014, I visited Ramallah and Akka, Al-Bireh, Battir, Haifa, Hebron, Jaffa, Jericho, Jerusalem, Nablus, and Tel Aviv, all via public transportation that originated in Bethlehem. Nonetheless, I anchored my research efforts in Bethlehem because operating out of one city allowed me to make more sustained social connections.

My research does not cover Gaza, Jerusalem, or the rest of 1948 Palestine, even though Palestinians use public transportation in all of those places. In the Introduction I discussed how my focus on the West Bank reflects the particularities and distinctions among experiences of collective mobility in different areas where Palestinians live as the result of settler colonial fragmentation. This focus was also influenced by logistical considerations. I could not travel to the Gaza Strip, which required extremely rare Israeli permission. In addition, in March 2014, as part of my visa renewal, Israel restricted my presence to the Palestinian Authority (PA) territories—that is, only parts of the West Bank—and thereby prohibited me from entering Jerusalem and 1948 Palestine. Moreover, the transportation system in 1948

Palestine and Jerusalem is controlled by Israeli law and primarily owned by Israelis (with some exceptions), although there are many Palestinian operators. For this research, I focused on Palestinian-owned, -organized, and -operated public transportation because it is a means of facilitating collective Palestinian movement; this does not rank among the main purposes of Israeli transportation. However, in Chapter 4 I address Israeli transportation that operates inside the West Bank to the extent that it has been engaged by Palestinian passengers, including workers who hold Israeli permits to enter 1948 Palestine and political activists who organize bus-related protests. And in Chapter 5 I discuss artistic representations of public transit that traverse the whole of historical Palestinian territory.

Throughout the time of my research, I used mixed methods to learn about Palestinian public transportation. I interviewed some sixty West Bank residents, the vast majority of whom lived in Bethlehem. Most of those with whom I spoke belonged to the working and middle classes and relied heavily on transit to get around. Their occupations included shop owners and employees, restaurant staff, retail workers, construction workers, students, and office staff mostly employed by nongovernmental organizations. The majority of my interlocutors, approximately 60 percent, were men. Due to the cost of private car ownership, affluent families are more likely to own cars, but I did speak with some wealthy people who also rely on public transportation. The slight majority of my respondents hailed from 1948 refugee families—that is, they were descendants of refugees who fled their hometowns located in 1948 Palestine, the lands that Israel considers its uncontested territory. This corresponds to the socioeconomic makeup of my sample because, in Bethlehem, "refugees" (a term applied to even those who have been living in Bethlehem for three generations) tend to, but do not always, occupy a slightly lower socioeconomic stratum due to discriminatory employment and consumer practices.

I also interviewed approximately twenty Palestinian public transportation drivers (mostly of taxis and shared vans) and six officials from the PA Ministry of Transportation (Wizarat an-Naql w al-Muwasalat) and from the Bethlehem Traffic Department (Da'irat as-Seir). Conversations with transit drivers usually occurred while they were waiting to fill their vehicles at a station or while on the road somewhere. Meetings with Ministry of Transportation and Traffic Department officials were arranged in advance. At one point, as part of an ongoing research collaboration with the Applied Research Institute–Jerusalem (ARIJ), I accompanied officials from the Ministry of Transportation and Traffic Department and ARIJ researchers to visit each of the stations of the shared *Ford* vans in the Bethlehem area. These visits were organized as part of an ARIJ effort to map the transit system in Bethlehem, beginning with the van routes. During these site visits I spoke with many drivers of different intercity routes and continued informal conversations with Ministry of Transportation and Traffic Department officials.

One significant force that shaped my methods of researching Palestinian public transportation is related to the very characteristics that make it resilient. Public transit is coordinated by the PA, but it is operated by hundreds of private owners, companies, and drivers. Furthermore, the Israeli occupation of the West Bank fragments Palestinian communities through a system of physical and bureaucratic restrictions on movement, which function erratically. To operate in this environment, Palestinian transit maintains a flexibility and decentralization to improvise solutions to the unpredictable disruptions of the occupation. One of the results of this organization is that the availability of official system data is limited and diffuse. Sometimes, speaking with transit drivers yielded more accurate data or detailed information than conversations with the government officials. For example, toward the end of my last stay in 2014, one of the Ministry of Transportation officials told me that private taxis are supposed to turn on their meters and charge accordingly. However, in twelve months and, easily, one hundred taxi rides, I never once saw a driver use his meter. When I asked about this, a private taxi driver I knew well explained that the Ministry of Transportation sets the meter rates too low, and most locals already know the standard fares anyway, give or take the typical bargaining window of five shekels. Thus, to understand how West Bank transit functions, I had to consult government officials, transit drivers, and frequent and casual riders, but I also had to ride and observe public transportation myself. The reader may notice missing information about the transit system, especially with reference to cities in which I did not frequently ride public transportation, precisely because in a flexible system, some details can only be ascertained through practice. In her ethnographic study of Palestinian driving on many different routes across historical Palestine, Amahl Bishara (2015) argues that the mobility conditions Palestinians encounter mean that knowledge about movement and space takes many forms, including "gestures . . . , jokes, silences, or embodied skills and maneuvers" (p. 37). While she was describing privately organized trips, the same can be said about the knowledge generated, circulated, and deployed in the context of Palestinian public transportation. For these reasons, it was necessary to combine sensitive observation with direct interlocution. In addition, because the conditions of Israeli im/mobilization and Palestinian movement have always been uneven and continue to change, this book may contain details that are not applicable to some parts of the West Bank or have since become outdated.

The restrictive conditions of the Israeli military occupation also posed a challenge for my research. It is not easy to access any part of the lands that once constituted historical Palestine unless you are Israeli. I never flew into

Ben Gurion Airport in Tel Aviv, because I was typically traveling from Lebanon (which does not have diplomatic relations with Israel, so direct travel is not possible) or Jordan, making the King Hussein/Allenby Bridge at the Jordanian border crossing the most convenient choice. It is routine for Palestinians as well as foreign travelers to be interrogated at any of the Israeli border crossings, and my experiences were no exception. The subjectively determined intensity and duration of the interrogation depends on a number of factors, including religion, ethnicity, nationality, age, dress, appearance, purpose of visit, and intended duration of visit. Of course, the inconvenience, delays, and searches are the worst and most severe and humiliating for Palestinians, the people whom these tactics are meant to dispossess. Ultimately, border crossings are permitted at the (often arbitrary) discretion of the Israeli border agents, so it is hard to determine the exact criteria used in any given case. This creates a climate of anxiety and insecurity for Palestinians, who must build time for delays into their travel plans, anticipating harassment and interrogation, denial of entry, or a permanent ban.

Another set of methodological issues that shaped my research emerged from my status as a foreigner and, specifically, a holder of a U.S. passport. As a non–Palestinian Arab American (half-Lebanese, half-white American), my experience of public transportation, and mobility more generally, in the field was very different from that of a Palestinian West Bank resident. Certainly, there were some commonalities: I rode the same vehicles on the same routes and according to the same timetable (or lack thereof). Where there were checkpoints, I had to submit to inspection and produce my identity documents. But there were stark and important differences, beginning with how those identity documents were received. For example, as a holder of a U.S. passport (and of no other country's passport or identity papers),[1] I was not required to obtain an Israeli permit to cross into Jerusalem or 1948 Palestine during the time I held a visa that was not geographically limited. As mentioned earlier, after some months of fieldwork, my passport was marked with a stamp that prohibited me from entering Jerusalem and 1948 Palestine. I was once able to cross Checkpoint 300, going from Bethlehem to Jerusalem, by flashing the cover of my U.S. passport and was not asked by Israeli border agents to show the visa. This was a gamble because here, too, crossing is at the discretion of the checkpoint soldiers, but clearly the consequences for me as a U.S. citizen and visitor would have been vastly different from those for a Palestinian without a permit. Similarly, when soldiers would board a transit vehicle inside the West Bank, either at a flying or activated checkpoint, they would sometimes pass over me when they saw the cover of my U.S. passport. These represent some of the ways that foreigners enjoy much easier movement than do Palestinians on Palestinian land.

My methodology was also influenced by the sociopolitical context of the research. Palestinian society is highly politicized and very familiar with international researchers coming to study all facets of Palestinian life. "Research fatigue" is common. I interviewed almost exclusively in Arabic, and the people with whom I spoke were all thoroughly prepared to articulate the various ways that the Israeli occupation affects their lives. Their testimonies guided my research in productive ways, leading me to consider the effects of settler colonialism on Palestinian spatial, social, political, and economic life through the modality of mobility control. At the same time, I sought to present an accurate picture of Palestinian mobility via transportation in the West Bank that would include a full accounting of the myriad forms of Israeli domination, while also recognizing the significance of a variety of engagements with collective mobility in spite of the restricted circumstances. In general, my interlocutors confirmed my observations of Palestinian mobility, but they were often more interested in describing other dimensions of the occupation and more invested in my ability to communicate its oppressive nature to audiences beyond the boundaries of the West Bank. This shaped how I constructed the book, as I was careful to convey the conditions on which Palestinian collective movement occurs, as well as the deep significance of that movement.

Notes

INTRODUCTION

1. Following common practice, I use the terms "public transportation" and "public transit" interchangeably throughout the book.

2. The Union Internationale des Transports Publics (International Association of Public Transportation) provides a broad definition:

> Public transport, public transportation, public transit or mass transit comprises all transport systems in which the passengers do not travel in their own vehicles. While it is generally taken to include rail and bus services, wider definitions include scheduled ferries, taxicab services etc [*sic*]—in other words, any system that transports members of the general public. Public transport is usually regulated as a common carrier and is usually configured to provide scheduled service on fixed routes on a non-reservation basis. The majority of transit passengers are traveling within a local area or region between their homes and places of employment, shopping, or schools. (Union Internationale des Transports Publics, n.d.).

I discuss the complex nature of coordinating service schedules and fixed routes in the context of a settler colonial occupation in Chapter 3.

3. I note that these are statistics for the Palestinian population in the West Bank because the figures for car ownership and population do not include Israeli settlers, although these settlers are present in West Bank territory.

4. Here I also note the important scholarship that has exposed uses of "the commons" and commoning as justifications or excuses for colonial dispossession (see, e.g., Fortier, 2017; Greer, 2012; Tuck & Yang, 2012). Petti, Hilal, and Weizman note that this was

precisely the case for Israeli settler colonialism, which expropriated Palestinian land as Israeli "state land . . . in the name of 'the public'" (pp. 179–181).

5. In Chapter 3 I discuss how the mobile commoning involved in mundane Palestinian transit use resembles the concept as defined by Papadopoulos and Tsianos (2013) but differs from Sheller's more expansive definition.

6. Reading the essay "Reflections on Trump" (Butler, 2017), Sheller (2018) elaborates on the polysemy of the commons as both shared space (and/as the variety of economic, political, and social relationships that that space entails) and a collective that articulates political power (p. 31).

7. See also Sheller (2016) for a more generalized discussion of "unsustainable mobility" to describe colonial mobility logics that produce movement as a zero-sum affair, conditioning the mobility of settlers on the control of the movement of native populations (pp. 20–22) and "uneven mobility" to depict the phenomenon of differential access to and experiences of mobility attached to different subjectivities (p. 16). Tawil-Souri further analyzes the interdependence of Israeli mobility on Palestinian im/mobilization through a focus on the system of Israeli-issued travel permits (2011a, 2011b, 2012) and the effects of Israeli checkpoints on time (2017).

8. Leila Farsakh (2005a), among other scholars, has written about the shattering of West Bank territory into semi-separate bantustans, analogizing the economic, political, and geographic functioning of these shards to their South African counterparts.

9. For an elaboration of the difference between exercising the principle of nondomination versus only removing direct foreign rule, see Adom Getachew's (2019) theorization of self-determination based on the decolonial projects of Black Anglophone intellectuals and leaders in the 1950s–1970s.

10. Tuck and Yang (2012) also warn against collapsing as identical the necessarily different decolonizing projects that emerge in distinct but connected settler colonial contexts. In particular, they argue that "*decolonization 'here' is intimately connected to anti-imperialism elsewhere. However, decolonial struggles here/there are not parallel, not shared equally, nor do they bring neat closure to the concerns of all involved—particularly not for settlers. Decolonization is not equivocal to other anti-colonial struggles. It is incommensurable*" (p. 31, italics in the original). In drawing from Tuck and Yang's (2012) reassertion of the concrete meaning of decolonization in opposition to its widespread metaphorical deployments, I do not mean to suggest that all decolonization projects are the same. Still, I also do not read decolonization in Palestine as being one among "other anti-colonial struggles" or "anti-imperialism elsewhere" (ibid.). Instead, I see Palestinians' decolonization against active settler colonialism on their lands as linked to the decolonization Tuck and Yang describe precisely in its centering of the repatriation of land and Indigenous relationships to and on it.

11. *Sumud* as a concept has been mobilized to reflect different meanings by social actors from various social positions advancing distinct or overlapping interests (Ali, 2018; Meari, 2014; Rijke & van Teeffelen, 2014; Tamari, 1991). Tamari (1991) traces the emergence of the ideology of steadfastness in the 1970s and early 1980s and its use by multiple actors for multiple reasons. He notes that Arab states anchored their decision to donate "guilt money" (which was only ever partially delivered) after "abandoning the confrontation with Israel" in their purported support of Palestinian *sumud*; he also describes the use of *sumud* by some local leaders who called for adherence to conservative family models as a way to preserve Palestinian communities in the face of colonial attempts at erasure (pp. 61–62). He continues, "The net effect of this conception of steadfastness was an assertion of traditionalism, both in the cultural domain and in the reinforcement of

political hierarchies that had been hegemonic prior to Israeli rule (notable urban families and rural potentates)" (p. 62). Against this "regressive" definition of *sumud*, Tamari identifies a populist reclamation of the term that represented a more active form of community organizing and that laid the foundation for the first Intifada (pp. 66–68).

12. Where applicable, I use the formulation "1948 Palestine" to refer to the territory confiscated through the establishment of the Israeli state in 1948. This follows common linguistic practice among Palestinians to use the Arabic phrase *tamaniya w arba'een* (forty-eight) in reference to that territory. Following public exhortations of Steven Salaita, I do so to draw attention to the contested nature of all of the Indigenous lands on which Israel claims authority. Doing so is especially important for this book, as I focus mainly on the West Bank frontier of Israeli settler colonialism; thus, I must take care to signal the connections between that frontier and the earlier annexation of land that Israel now considers uncontested. Still, I acknowledge that "1948 Palestine," like any term (including "Israel" itself) that refers to particular swaths of the territories, is not geographically precise or consistent but is a function of the very geographic manipulations that Israel has imposed as part of its settler colonial project.

13. Ali's (2019) argument addresses the particular circumstances of life for Palestinians living inside 1948 Palestine, typically with Israeli citizenship. Although *sumud* is a term layered with significance for Palestinians across all contexts, it may not be appropriate to apply her concept of "active *sumud*" to the situation of West Bank Palestinians because of the fragmenting consequences of the enclosures discussed earlier in the Introduction. Still, Ali's work opens up the idea of *sumud* to consider the ways that steadfastness can be embodied and practiced in multiple ways.

14. I return in the Conclusion to a discussion of "resistance" in relation to the core arguments of this book.

15. As I explain in the Appendix, I was barred from entering 1948 Palestine in March 2014.

CHAPTER 1

1. In agreement with my interlocutors, I have used pseudonyms and created amalgams out of personal details to protect anonymity. This is especially important due to the sensitive nature of the movement I discuss here.

2. For a helpful diagram of the checkpoint's spatiality, see Rijke and Minca (2018, p. 39). They also confirm my observation that the humanitarian lane has since been deactivated.

3. Between 2013 and 2014, Israel remodeled the entrance to the terminal, closing the roof of the lanes. This reduced opportunities to cut in line, although the practice still occurred through the vertical bars separating the humanitarian and regular lanes. My last trip to the West Bank was in 2018, but more recently, in 2020, friends reported that the military had increased the number of processing windows to check permits and fingerprints in the main building of Checkpoint 300, dramatically reducing waiting times for morning commuters. This is heralded as an improvement but not as a marker of any relinquishing of control.

4. See also Y. Sharif (2017), whose account of such "invisible" journeys across the Wall illuminates the coordination, improvisation, and intimate (though also unstable) spatial knowledge that make this movement possible.

5. According to Federici (2004), peasant self-sufficiency was one factor that emboldened them to revolt against the lords, drove up wages, drove down rent, and resulted

in the ultimate demise of feudalism. In response to this crisis, through the passage of laws, the erection of physical barriers, and the circulation of discursive mechanisms, the enclosures were imposed to annex commonly held land for private use and profit. Marx originally explained that the enclosures also had the effect of alienating peasants from their land and labor and subsequently created a new population that had to find wage-based work to sustain itself. This, in turn, enabled the primitive accumulation on which the burgeoning capitalist system relied. But, Federici explains, there were other important purposes of the enclosures. Among them, attacking the commons was an effective repression campaign against rebellious peasants. By undermining the communal self-sustenance of the peasants, the enclosures, in turn, undermined their social relationships and the communal basis of their political power.

6. As Seikaly (2015) demonstrates, the history of the ascension of capitalism as the dominant economic system in Palestine was not entirely determined by settler colonial agents and logics. It was also shaped by the ideas and practices of bourgeois Palestinian nationalists.

7. Tuck and Yang (2012) cite Grande (2004) to note that, while capital accumulation and settler colonialism can take, and have taken, intertwined forms, they are not necessarily or always coexistent (fn2).

8. Here I include only specific citations for concepts that were primarily defined and used by a particular thinker. The others are used widely. In addition to the use of particular terms, there are others who propose hybrid perspectives. See, e.g., Ghanim's (2018) analysis of Israel's ruling regime as a hybrid strategy straddling the conceptual categories of colonialism, apartheid, and occupation.

9. As noted in the Introduction, the trajectory of Israel's approach to the Gaza Strip has diverged, particularly since the dismantling of Israeli settlements in 2005 and their replacement with a comprehensive blockade by land, air, and sea, punctuated by repeated bouts of intensified military siege. This has resulted in differences between how Israel has shaped the space of Gazan life and that of the West Bank, although they remain interrelated as parts of the broader settler colonial project in historical Palestine. In this book, I focus on the particularities of collective mobility and im/mobilization in the West Bank, but an exploration of how these modes of decolonization and dispossession relate to the Gaza Strip and other parts of historical Palestine is also needed.

10. During this period, the famed Palestinian writer Ghassan Kanafani was assassinated by the Mossad, Israel's national intelligence agency, in Beirut, where he had been active in writing against the Zionist project (Qumsiyeh, 2011, p. 120). Also, in his book dedicated to the subject of Palestinian resistance, Qumsiyeh (2011) recounts protests, demonstrations, and strikes that occurred nearly every year throughout the history of the Israel-Palestine conflict. I mention the 1967–1973 period to note how tensions rose after the invasion, but he says there also were small-scale protests in 1974–1976 (p. 123).

11. Using newspaper sources, Qumsiyeh (2011) methodically describes these incidents in October and November 1987 as alternatives to the more typical narrative that the uprising began in December, after an Israeli truck driver killed four Palestinian workers in a car accident in Gaza. Qumsiyeh (2011) muses that the truck driver incident may frequently be cited as the origin of the Intifada because "the Israeli-influenced media could score a PR point by stating that Palestinians overreacted to a 'traffic accident'" (p. 135). In any case, his account of the rapid succession of civilian killings and subsequent protests in October and November 1987 as the beginning of the first Intifada is compelling.

The first Intifada is often referred to simply as "the Intifada" because it was the only one that had occurred at the time. The second Intifada is sometimes distinguished from the first as "Al-Aqsa Intifada."

12. Notwithstanding its original grassroots character, the first Intifada had changed course by late 1989, when the PLO leadership attempted to centralize the uprising under its direction, sidelining and sometimes undermining the local leaders who had been instrumental in launching the Intifada in the first place. While the PLO's ambitions began to influence the rebellion's course, Israeli military violence worsened, subjecting Palestinians of all ages and genders to indefinite detentions, torture, and assassinations. This second half of the Intifada witnessed the increased involvement of armed para-military groups, whose use of violence necessarily displaced many of the Palestinian civilians involved in the uprising (Andoni, 2001, p. 212).

13. After surveying much of the literature, I did not find many accounts of rebellious forms of public transportation during the first Intifada, likely for multiple reasons. The first is that transportation is such a mundane part of life that it is less likely to feature in memories from this tumultuous period of frequent and visible protests. The second is that the elaborate regime of im/mobilization of the Palestinian West Bank had not yet been thoroughly established, so overcoming mobility restrictions had not yet become primary. This presents a contrast to the circumstances of the second Intifada, as I elabo-rate later.

14. Naomi Klein (2008) notes that the Soviet emigrants selected Israel as their desti-nation not out of an ideological commitment to Zionism but, rather, because it was the only country that would accept them without delay (p. 545).

15. Some scholars argue that the closure policy was inaugurated in earnest in April 1993, when the Israeli military responded to the killing of Israeli settlers and soldiers with a blanket closure of the WBGS (Nakhal, 1996). However, the revocation of the general exit orders and the rollout of travel permits suggest that closure was already well underway by 1993.

16. In Chapter 2, I address the multiple names used to reference this Wall. Here, I use "Apartheid Wall" to signal the connection between Israel's policy of racial spatial segregation and settler colonialism.

17. This characterization resembles Patrick Hayden's (2008) conception of "inclusive exclusion" as the relationship that sovereign states have applied to a growing number of stateless people in the world. He explains that this approach exposes stateless people to the violence of state power without affording them any rights as lawful subjects of the state (p. 262). Hayden notes that, across a variety of contexts, inclusive exclusion is accomplished through a strategy of physical "containment" that applies state power to the contained population while holding it outside the geographical space that might otherwise trigger certain rights (p. 258). Relatedly, scholars have argued that "abandon-ment" has become a strategy favored by the racial state in many contexts to contain and demobilize aggrieved populations who have been made redundant by global racial capi-talism without providing for their welfare (see, e.g., Gilmore, 2008; A. Gordon, 2006). Considering all of these analyses, it is clear that settler colonialism is one among many exploitative programs that benefit from deploying only their repressive apparatuses while shirking all other responsibilities to the targeted population.

18. Parsons and Salter (2008) refer to "external closure" and "internal closure," the former denoting the separation of Palestinians from 1948 Palestine and the latter denot-ing the separation of Palestinian enclaves inside the West Bank (p. 705). Here, I use

the terms "separation" and "fragmentation" to correspond, roughly, to "external" and "internal" closure, respectively. What is internal and external to the West Bank is itself a highly contested product of Israeli settler colonialism. In addition, I shy away from the term "closure," which carries the connotation of containment. While containment is, of course, a pronounced element of Israeli im/mobilization of West Bank Palestinians, it is also intertwined with efforts to compel movement and to otherwise affect the experience of movement, as I argue in the Introduction.

19. Importantly, this was not the case with Palestinian workers from Gaza. By the start of the first Intifada, Israel had already begun decreasing its reliance on Gazan labor, and this trend continued during the Oslo period (Farsakh, 2002, pp. 16–18). I do not analyze this split in depth because the chapter's ultimate focus is the emergence of the im/mobilization regime that imposed settler colonial enclosures in the West Bank.

20. In *Jil Oslo,* her ethnographic study of Palestinian hip hop, street art, and youth culture as media for expressing alternative political visions, Maira (2013) depicts the depth of frustration among Palestinian youth with the Oslo Accords, in particular, the PA's reluctance to combat Israeli aggression while simultaneously exercising political repression against Palestinian youth (pp. 120, 122, 132–138).

21. Calculated based on figures obtained from Adam (2020) and the tables in B'Tselem (n.d.). From 1987 to September 13, 1993, the date on which the Oslo process began with the signing of the Declaration of Principles, approximately 1,087 Palestinians were killed (B'Tselem, n.d.). According to Adam (2020), during the Al-Aqsa Intifada, at least 4,973 Palestinians were killed.

22. The other major catalyst was a collapse in the value of Internet stocks around the world (Graham, 2011, p. 143).

CHAPTER 2

1. Of course, some passengers and drivers wear seatbelts throughout the journey. Nevertheless, the sounds I speak of here are sufficiently common to indicate that wearing seatbelts is not a majoritarian practice. Yazan Al-Khalili (2011) has suggested that "it is a very small minority who would actually put [the seatbelt] on and these will always be the rich, upper class who are imitating the West in their life-style" (p. 45). Al-Khalili's analysis indicates that the wearing of seatbelts is also embedded in a broader international politics of colonialism and contestation.

2. Tawil-Souri (2012) uses the term "im/mobility" to describe how Israel combines elements of forcing and forbidding Palestinian mobility in a zero-sum calculus that favors Israeli settler mobility in the West Bank (p. 11). I invoke the same term, building on Tawil-Souri's generative formulation, to emphasize the colonial effects of this regime on Palestinian self-determination.

3. Dana (2017) also notes that alongside fragmentation, the Wall, along with the interlocking systems of checkpoints and travel permits to which I turn shortly, has the effect of "potentially strengthening a sense of community and national identity through the shared experience of oppression" (p. 905). While this is an important insight, I focus my analysis here on the consequences of the Wall that advance settler colonialism.

4. In June 2012, just before I began my fieldwork in the West Bank, OCHA OPT (2012) had reported 542 physical obstacles, 15 percent of which were characterized as "passable" (p. 4). The office notes that its 2020 figure excludes "passable" impediments. In addition, according to the Applied Research Institute–Jerusalem (ARIJ) (2012), OCHA OPT's 2012 figure does not include an additional 112 obstructions installed in

the section of Hebron City under direct Israeli control, seventy-three agricultural gates along Israel's Apartheid Wall that lead to private Palestinian land on the western side of the Wall, and as many as 410 flying checkpoints, which move around and activate without warning. In OCHA OPT's 2020 report, the organization notes that its updated figure still does not include these other obstructions (identified by ARIJ).

5. OCHA OPT (2013) has noted that, while most of the checkpoints along the Apartheid Wall are run by the Israeli army, some are administered by an entity of the Israeli Ministry of Defense called the Crossing Point Administration, and "the latter implements stricter and more invasive inspections of Palestinians crossing the checkpoints" (p. 39).

The year 2017 is the latest for which a figure representing the total number of checkpoints was available. For comparison, as of February 2014, during one of my extended research stays in the West Bank, B'Tselem reported that there were ninety-nine fixed checkpoints, forty of which were "points of entry to Israel."

6. I place "and back" in parentheses because the movement of Palestinians from 1948 Palestine back into the West Bank is somewhat less strictly monitored. Israel's main focus is targeting Palestinians' movement in the other direction.

7. Here I note that the permits affect "WBGS Palestinian" movement because the system is applied only to Palestinians in the West Bank and Gaza Strip. The movement of Palestinian residents of Jerusalem and Palestinian citizens of Israel is not subject to the permit regime (Al-Qadi, 2018, pp. 1–2).

8. This is based on my observations during 2012 and 2013. In 2014, my visa was restricted so I could no longer travel into Jerusalem or 1948 Palestine (including through the Qalandiya Checkpoint).

9. Shortly after the shooting, an Israeli police commander led Anas's brother Ismail a few meters away from where Anas had been shot to show him a knife. The police commander claimed that Anas was armed, which Ismail vehemently denies. Nonetheless, the official story, echoed by Israeli newspapers, became that Anas had rushed the soldiers while holding a knife, and they shot to disarm him. The checkpoint thus has become the scene not only of summary execution but of manufacturing its justification.

10. In this context, the term "refugee" (*laji'* in Arabic) refers to people and families who were forced to flee their ancestral land. Many of these refugees fled after the 1948 war, which resulted in the creation of the State of Israel, while others left for different (though typically derivative) reasons and at different times. Many live in refugee camps across the West Bank, but some live outside of the camps in cities or villages. Karim is a third-generation refugee, meaning that his grandparents were the last generation to live in their ancestral hometown in an area northeast of the Gaza Strip.

11. According to 2019 figures, the proportion of registered private cars was approximately 0.075 per capita in the Palestinian West Bank, calculated based on data from the Palestinian Central Bureau of Statistics (2019, 2020).

12. In terms of Palestinian air travel, there are three relevant sites in historical Palestine: the airports in Tel Aviv, Gaza, and Jerusalem. The Israeli airport in Tel Aviv is not accessible to Palestinians from Gaza or the West Bank, except in rare cases of travelers with special permits. The airport in Gaza, known as the Yasser Arafat International Airport, opened during the Oslo period in 1998 but was destroyed by Israel in 2001 during the second Intifada (Norris, 2017, p. 281). According to Nahed Awwad (2008), who has written and made a film about the topic, the airport in Jerusalem, located in Qalandiya, opened in the 1920s as a military landing strip for the British Mandate forces and was subsequently converted into a civilian airport under the Jordanian Authority

in the 1950s (p. 55). Jacob Norris (2017) adds that Jerusalem Airport "was viewed as a triumph of Arab postcolonial modernity" until it was confiscated and closed down by the Israelis during the 1967 invasion (p. 281).

13. It is possible that there are some exceptions to this statement, as I did not interact with every bus company that operates inside the West Bank.

14. I do not have an updated figure for the number of taxi companies today. In addition, the Palestinian Central Bureau of Statistics, on which I have relied for figures on registered transit vehicles, does not distinguish among for-hire taxis, shared taxis, and shared transit van taxis. The bureau reports that in 2014, there were 9,285 taxi vehicles (including all three of those types), and by 2019 that number had increased only slightly, to 9,655.

15. *Service* is the common name for shared, non-bus vehicles throughout the Levant, including in Lebanon and Jordan, although the *service* is not operated in the same way across local contexts. In this chapter, I also use the plural *services* to denote when I mean multiple *service* vehicles, but the final *s* is not pronounced.

16. "Im" and "Abu" mean "mother" and "father," respectively, and are widely used before the name of a person's first-born son (or other salient referent) to address her or him with respect.

CHAPTER 3

1. Ariel Handel (2009) describes the expression of resistance through quotidian Palestinian mobility as "*sumud* and smuggling," in which physical and communicative practices enable Palestinians to remain on their land and smuggle themselves (along with necessary goods) through restricted space (pp. 215–216). The concept of mobile commoning adds to this generative formulation by emphasizing the collective nature of these practices and their tendency to create lasting alternatives to settler colonialism.

2. Placing these geographically distinct practices in relation to one another illuminates repertoires of mobile commoning that Sheller (2018) identifies as the basis for a global movement for mobility justice (p. 167).

3. Even during the years of my field research, one might have observed permanent bus stops in the greater Ramallah metropolitan area—for example, between Ramallah's downtown and the university town of Birzeit. Certainly, there were informal stops, such as the corner in front of Beit Sahour's famous Souq ash-Sha'ab supermarket, that were generally unmarked but nonetheless were, and continue to be, commonly used and recognized by passengers and drivers as a pick-up and drop-off site. Again, while the installation of more bus stop shelters is an advantage for passengers waiting in the sun, the shelters do not currently constrain the social negotiation that occurs among passengers and drivers about where to get on or off a bus or van.

4. Spatial and territorial knowledge have a long history as a terrain of struggle shaped by different colonial enterprises. The British Mandate's imposition of its Torrens title system in Palestine is one powerful example (see, e.g., Bhandar, 2018; Bunton, 2007; Quiquivix, 2013). This system was an essential tool in enabling the enclosure and privatization of land in several invaded territories. Originally developed in Australia and then practiced throughout territories subjected to British control, including Egypt, the registration of land to particular owners was premised on the extensive surveying and mapping of the territory (Bhandar, 2018, pp. 84–96; Quiquivix, 2013, p. 11). These official fabrications had the effect of abstracting and extracting the land from the socio-spatial

relations in which it is always embedded (Pottage, 1994, p. 383, cited in Bhandar, 2018, p. 93; see also Quiquivix, 2013).

5. Foucault (1977) advances the concept of knowledge-power to describe the productive relationship through which the field of the knowable is defined. Foucault does not collapse the ideas of knowledge and power as if they were one in the same; rather, he argues "that power and knowledge directly imply one another; that there is no power relation without the correlative constitution of a field of knowledge, nor any knowledge that does not presuppose and constitute at the same time power relations" (p. 27).

6. I focus here on *Fordaat* drivers because they were the group I approached for this small part of my research, but I could have asked drivers of any of the transit system's vehicles—bus or sedan taxis on inter- or intracity routes—to draw maps. I chose to approach them because, of all the stations in Bethlehem at the time, the *Fordaat* level of the Mujama' was the most populated with vehicles and drivers of multiple routes.

7. As noted in Chapter 2, there are also taxis available for individual parties, but I did not inquire about them in this questionnaire because the private nature of their service makes their prices incomparable with the other forms of public transportation about which I was asking.

8. For a variety of reasons, the results of the pilot questionnaire are not included in this volume. I mention the exercise because it figured as a provocation in my conversation with the drivers.

9. As noted in Chapter 2, I have used pseudonyms and created amalgams out of personal details to protect the identities of those with whom I spoke. Drivers are not identifiable by their routes because dozens of them work the same route. Furthermore, most of the drivers who spoke with me had several years of experience, which included working a variety of intercity routes in the area. Thus, the information provided here does not risk identifying them in any way.

10. Ahmad, a private taxi driver, and Abu Khalil, one of my interlocutors who had used the Intifada-era taxis, each separately noted that the off-road taxis were not always driven by public transit drivers. Some people who were not employed in the transit sector took their own cars on illicit trips to make extra cash.

11. Both Rolston (2014) and a report conducted twenty years earlier by the Palestinian Academic Society for the Study of International Affairs (Steinberg & Oliver, 1994) note that the use of graffiti as a communication tool during an uprising actually began with the first Intifada. In Chapter 1, I also discussed the collective activities at the heart of the first Intifada. This fact, along with my argument connecting mobile commoning to *sumud*, situates these everyday activities within a longer tradition of decolonial politics practiced at mundane registers. Here I mean only to emphasize the elements of rebellious mobility of the second Intifada that the current system has inherited.

12. For a description of the system of traversing another, similar second Intifada-era roadblock, the Hawara Checkpoint at the eastern edge of Nablus, see Doumani (2004).

13. Hammami (2005) richly describes two alternative versions of how the porters came to work the Surda Checkpoint. One version credits the governor of Ramallah for contacting the market porters to seek their services at the checkpoint. The other version originates with a young boy who was selling bananas from a cart at the al-Jawwal Checkpoint (one of the Surda road's two alternative routes, which were also blocked at the time) when he was run off by Israeli soldiers. In his escape down a hillside, he lost his inventory and found himself at the Surda Checkpoint with nothing but an empty cart. An elderly traveler enlisted his help to transport luggage, and porter services at Surda were born (Hammami, 2005).

14. Doumani (2004) notes that some of the drivers of these expensive mid-Intifada taxis were Samaritans, members of an ancient Nabulsi community whose living conditions markedly improved while the rest of Nablus suffered under the conditions of Israeli military siege (p. 41). Even here, while the Samaritans used their relatively privileged ability to move around the West Bank to make money from their neighbors who could pay for their taxi services, it can be argued that this movement itself proceeded against the designs of Israeli colonial control. In fact, this is why the high prices could be demanded in the first place.

CHAPTER 4

1. For a discussion of how, despite Israel's facility in the use of walls and borders to enclose Palestinian life, the Israeli military has also perfected the craft of "moving through walls," or laying siege to Palestinian homes by breaking through house walls, see Weizman (2007, p. 194 and the surrounding chapter).

2. In this chapter, I focus on mobility-themed Palestinian activism in historical Palestine, but in light of the weaponization of borders across the world, Palestinian activists outside Palestine also organize political actions that contest imperial mobility regimes. In fact, Quintanilla and Mogannam (2015) demonstrate that collective movement (in the form of a 5K run), along with activists' movements across the U.S.-Mexico border in San Ysidro, California, presented opportunities for a diverse coalition of organizers to generate and exchange support, analysis, and resources.

3. Veolia used to operate some of the bus lines that serviced the settlements, but in 2013 it sold its remaining routes to Afikim (Nieuwhof, 2013).

4. As noted in Chapter 2, as of January 2017 Israel operated ninety-eight checkpoints in the West Bank. B'Tselem reported that in March 2014, the total number was ninety-nine, and in March 2013, it was ninety-eight. In 2017, fifty-nine of these checkpoints were positioned in the interior of the West Bank, and in 2014, the number was the same.

5. This is true even if they find themselves driving a car with yellow Israeli license plates. However, Palestinians with Israeli citizenship are permitted to drive through checkpoints.

6. I derived these numbers from B'Tselem's list of checkpoints (2019). While B'Tselem's total checkpoint count was last updated in 2017, its list of individual checkpoints of different types was updated in 2019. According to those figures, the number of border checkpoints rose to forty-three, and I identified thirteen of them that could be crossed by Palestinian holders of non-residence-related permits. Thirteen was a generous estimate; I am unsure about the crossing rules for the "a-Za'ayem–West Bank" Checkpoint, and while I suspect it is not in fact open to Palestinian permit holders, I decided to include it here to present the best-case scenario. Also, one of the thirteen checkpoints accessible to all permit holders, Jalameh, in the northern district of Jenin, allows "entry into Israel" only from 5 A.M. to 12 P.M.

By "residence-related permits," I mean those issued to a small number of Palestinians who require entry across the checkpoint to access their land just on the other side or residents of the "Seam Zones," those pockets of land created where the Apartheid Wall hews east of the Green Line. There are roughly twelve additional checkpoints open to holders of residence-related permits, but the permit holder is allowed to cross through only the particular checkpoint assigned to her.

7. I am unclear as to whether there are any lines that connect multiple settlements, and if so, what would happen if a Palestinian passenger wanted to continue on the route

past the first settlement. Given settlement entry rules, it is highly likely that this is not an option for the Palestinian passenger.

8. Ghanim (2018) argues that this "hybridity" is a product of Israel's transformative invasion and occupation of the West Bank and Gaza Strip. Historical evidence suggests that Israel deployed apartheid practices against Palestinians even before the 1967 invasion of the WBGS. But Ghanim's point about the hybrid integration of settler colonialism, military occupation, and apartheid is particularly resonant with the development of Israeli rule in the Palestinian West Bank after 1967.

9. See, e.g., Benvenisti (2008), who summarizes the original two responsibilities imposed by occupation law on the occupiers as "the obligation to protect the life and property of the inhabitants and the obligation to respect the sovereign rights of the ousted government" (p. 622).

10. An investigation by *Ha'aretz* noted that in 2014, only one complaint was filed alleging sexual harassment on the bus, and the complainant was a Palestinian with Israeli citizenship (Levinson, 2014a).

11. For a study of racialized sexual tropes about Palestinians crystalized in the Israeli antimiscegenation movement, see Ihmoud (2018).

12. In the question portion of Abdel Jawad's testimony, Cynthia McKinney comments that, similar to his concept of "sociocide," the system of slavery systematically obliterated cultural and social ties of enslaved Africans. Her comment suggests that racial segregation may also be insufficient to describe the condition of African Americans as their descendants.

13. For additional discussion of the limits of cross-movement, cross-historical, and cross-issue analogy, see Chandan Reddy's (2008) critique of the analogy between anti-gay marriage laws and antimiscegenation laws.

14. Maha Nassar (2019) demonstrates that this transnational organizing was itself part of an earlier legacy, beginning in the 1930s, of Palestinian intellectuals drawing parallels between their anticolonial struggles and the antiracist organizing of Black Americans.

CHAPTER 5

1. See also Lori Allen (2008), who references the rhetorical refrain, "Shu bidna nsawy?" (another formulation of 'What can we do?') during the second Palestinian Intifada (p. 459). Allen notes that this question represented an assertion that the Palestinians who uttered it would indeed continue to go about their lives, despite the arresting conditions of colonial occupation. She connects this rhetorical question to the declaration "Ta'wwudna" (We've gotten used to it) and argues that this adaptation constitutes a resistant agency that literally "gets by" and "goes around" the occupation's restrictions. The resilient valence of this *ta'weed* (*ta'wwudna*'s infinitive) is illuminated by John Berger's (2006) observation of "undefeated despair" in Palestine, practices of continuing life with a precise diagnosis of the oppressive present and a stalwart refusal of its attempt to foreclose the future.

2. See also Derek Gregory (2004), whose book of the same name examines the enduring British and American colonial legacies that have shaped the Middle East, including Palestine. Gregory argues that the "colonial present" combines traditional approaches of colonial rule, technological advances in biopolitics, and the declarations of states of emergency. These structures create material conditions that threaten the imagination of alternative models for living.

3. In fact, several Palestinian artists have engaged with the problem of im/mobilization, and while I cannot mention all of them, I would like to note a few others. Hany Abu-Assad's 2002 film *Ford Transit* showcases the shared van as both a vehicle for making life work (as a source of income and travel) under repressive colonial conditions and a venue for practices of Palestinian sociality, particularly in the form of political debates and social commentary. In her 2006 photo essay "Retracing Bus No. 23 on the Historic Jerusalem-Hebron Road," Emily Jacir attempted to reconstruct her father's 1960s-era commute between Bethlehem and Hebron, but her inability exposes the colonial confiscations effected by Israel's diffused bordering processes. In "The Slaughterhouse" (2011), Yazan Al-Khalili sets out from Ramallah at night to reach the sea, but Israel's borders block his way, and he instead lands in a dump for dismantled car parts, which eerily conjure the current fragments of a once contiguous Palestine. Khaled Jarrar (2011) imagined, created, and indeed issued "State of Palestine" postage stamps and passport stamps, reclaiming from Israel's purported monopoly the authority to legitimize movement (of both people and post). And Iyad Issa and Sahar Qawasmi (2011) invited guests of the Cities Exhibition at the Birzeit University Museum to reinhabit, through travel, a connected Palestine by "boarding" the projected image of a train arriving at the long-defunct Nablus station as part of their *Palestine Connected* installation.

4. For a similar consideration of spatial and temporal movement in the work of the artist Hulleah Tsinhnahjinnie (Dine, Seminole, Muscogee), see Goeman (2014).

5. I refer here to scholarly and artistic interventions that include Morrill et al., 2016; Tuck & Recollet, 2017; Tuck & Ree, 2013; and Tuck & Yang, 2012, as well as the work of Super Futures Haunt Qollective (SFHQ), featured in the "After Life (What Remains)" exhibit curated by Thea Quiray Tagle at the Alice Gallery in Seattle, Washington, which the SFHQ visited—or, in other words, performed a visitation—during the show's opening. Quiray Tagle (2018) described the SFHQ's work as manifesting "random appearances in sites of fast fashion, luxury accommodation, and coastal isolation [that] insist on revealing to us the simultaneous presence of indigeneity and militarism everywhere; their persistence is a call for decolonization that needs to be practiced by all non-Indigenous people, even those who experience racism themselves as people of color."

6. See also Lila Sharif's (2016) analysis of Raja Shehadeh's award-winning *Palestinian Walks: Forays into a Vanishing Landscape* (2007), in which she argues that Shehadeh uses haunting to challenge settler colonialism by making visible the hidden bureaucratic policies, legal contrivances, and eco-logics that accomplish the "vanishment" of Palestine.

7. The quotation was pulled from the site when I accessed it in July 2019. As of July 2020, the "About" section of the site had been updated and no longer contained this passage.

8. "Peace Park" is the site's official name, which I learned from some of its former employees, but I only ever heard residents refer to it as *oush ghrab*.

9. This phrase refers to the failed plan, designed by the George W. Bush administration in the United States, to broker a two-state solution between Israelis and Palestinians.

10. Gil Hochberg (2018) refers to Sansour's "trilogy" of films, which includes *A Space Exodus* (2008), *Nation Estate* (2012), and *In the Future, They Ate from the Finest Porcelain* (2015). I use the term "series" because Sansour has since released a fourth film, *In Vitro* (2019), which could be considered part of the collection in that it explores similar themes of exile, decolonization, and temporal self-determination.

11. In the film, "permits and passports" are on the fifth floor, but in the image that I use in Figure 5.11, the directory indicates that they are located on the second floor.

12. Here, too, the floors in the image stills are slightly different. The image in Figure 5.11 indicates that the souq is on the first floor.

13. For an exploration of the "politics of staying in place" through a study of the Palestinian feminist collective *murabitat al-Haram*, see Ihmoud (2019).

CONCLUSION

1. The quotations in this section are my translations into English of remarks made in Arabic.

2. Susan Rice, then the U.S. ambassador to the United Nations, disagreed, declaring to the General Assembly that "this resolution does not establish that Palestine is a state." Despite the U.S. denial, the United Nations' resolution to include the State of Palestine led to the later acceptance of Palestine to join the International Criminal Court in early 2015.

3. Indeed, the programmatic laundering of the colonial character of Israeli rule in the West Bank echoes the plan formulated late in 1967 by then Defense Minister Moshe Dayan that he termed the "invisible administration" (Berda, 2018, p. 17; Shehadeh, 2012).

APPENDIX ON METHODOLOGY

1. It must be noted that even among U.S. citizens, Palestinian Americans with West Bank or Gaza Strip identity papers are not allowed to cross into Jerusalem or 1948 Palestine without an Israeli permit.

References

Abdel Jawad, S. (2013). Testimony at the Russell Tribunal on Palestine. New York.

Abourahme, N. (2011). Spatial collisions and discordant temporalities: Everyday life between camp and checkpoint. *International Journal of Urban and Regional Research, 35*(2), 453–461.

Abu-Assad, H., dir. (2002). *Ford Transit*. Augustus Films, Amsterdam.

Abufarha, N. (2008). Land of symbols: Cactus, poppies, orange and olive trees in Palestine. *Identities, 15*(3), 343–368.

Abu-Lughod, L. (1990). The romance of resistance: Tracing transformations of power through Bedouin women. *American Ethnologist, 17*(1), 41–55.

Abusal, M. (2011). *A Metro in Gaza*. Retrieved August 29, 2020. https://abusalmohamed .com/project/a-metro-in-gaza.

———. (2014). *Reveal/A metro in Gaza*. Retrieved August 29, 2020. https://abusalmo hamed.com/project/reveal-a-metro-in-gaza.

Abu-Zahra, N. & Kay, A. (2013). *Unfree in Palestine: Registration, documentation and movement restrictions*. London: Pluto.

Adam, A. (2020, September 28). Palestinian Intifada: How Israel orchestrated a bloody takeover. *Al Jazeera*. Retrieved February 23, 2021. https://www.aljazeera.com/news/2020 /9/28/palestinian-intifada-20-years-later-israeli-occupation-continues.

Addameer. (2018). Statistics: December. Retrieved April 13, 2020. http://www.addameer .org/statistics.

Agence France-Presse. (2013, March 5). Arson attempt on second day of Israel's segregated bus programme. *The National*. Retrieved February 23, 2021. http://www.the national.ae/news/world/middle-east/arson-attempt-on-second-day-of-israels-segre gated-bus-programme.

Alayan, S. (2017). White pages: Israeli censorship of Palestinian textbooks in East Jerusalem. *Social Semiotics, 28*(4), 512–532.

Ali, N. (2018). Lifestyle of resistance: Palestinian *sumud* in Israel as a form of transformative resistance. *Journal of Conflict Transformation & Security, 6*(2), 143–162.

———. (2019). Active transformative *sumud* among Palestinian activists in Israel. In Tartir, A. & Seidel, T. (Eds.), *Palestine and rule of power: Local dissent versus international governance* (pp. 71–103). London: Palgrave Macmillan.

Al Jazeera. (2013, March 5). Israel's Palestinian-only buses "torched." Retrieved April 13, 2020. http://www.aljazeera.com/news/middleeast/2013/03/20133514230798542.html.

———. (2019, September 25). Football final canceled as Israel denies Gaza team travel permit. Retrieved April 13, 2020. http://www.aljazeera.com/news/2019/09/football-final-cancelled-israel-denies-gaza-team-travel-permit-190925133252447.html.

Al-Khalili, Y. (2011). (R&B) rhythm and blues: Post-traffic lights in Ramallah and Al-Bireh city. *Race and Class, 52*(3), 43–49.

Allam, H. (2019, April 11). U.S. denies entry to leader of movement to boycott Israel. National Public Radio. Retrieved April 13, 2020. http://www.npr.org/2019/04/11/712189791/u-s-denies-entry-to-leader-of-movement-to-boycott-israel.

Allen, L. (2008). Getting by the occupation: How violence became normal during the second Palestinian intifada. *Cultural Anthropology, 23*(3), 453–487.

Al-Qadi, N. (2018). The Israeli permit regime: Realities and challenges. Applied Research Institute–Jerusalem. Bethlehem, Palestine.

Alqasis, A. & Al-Azza, N. (2015, December). Forced population transfer: The case of Palestine. Installment of a permit regime. Working paper no. 18, BADIL Resource Center for Palestinian Residency and Refugee Rights. Bethlehem, Palestine.

Alsaafin, L. (2011a, November 9). Freedom rides in the 21st century. Retrieved February 19, 2021. https://electronicintifada.net/blogs/linah-alsaafin/freedom-rides-21st-century.

———. (2011b, November 14). Palestinians clarify goal of "Freedom Rides" challenge to segregated Israeli buses. Retrieved February 19, 2021. http://electronicintifada.net/blogs/linah-alsaafin/palestinians-clarify-goal-freedom-rides-challenge-segregated-israeli-buses.

Anderson, B., Sharma, N. & Wright, C. (2009). Editorial: Why no borders? *Refuge, 26*(2), 5–18.

Andoni, G. (2001). A comparative study of intifada 1987 and intifada 2000. In Carey, R. (Ed.), *The new intifada: Resisting Israel's apartheid* (pp. 209–220). New York: Verso.

Applied Research Institute–Jerusalem. (2012). Internal closure and the West Bank labor market. Retrieved February 23, 2021. http://arij.org/files/admin/latestnews/Internal%20ClosureNovember20_2012.pdf.

Ashcroft, B. (2016). *Utopianism in postcolonial literature.* London: Routledge.

Awwad, N. (2008, Summer). In search of Jerusalem airport. *Jerusalem Quarterly, 35,* 51–63.

Azeb, S. (2014). Palestine made flesh. *Funambulist Papers,* (59), 31–35

BADIL Resource Center for Palestinian Residency and Refugee Rights. (2003, November). The permit maze: Palestinians need permits to move, to live, for everything. *BADIL Occasional Bulletin,* no. 12. Retrieved August 19, 2020. https://www.badil.org/phoca download/Badil_docs/Working_Papers/Bulletin-12.htm.

Bahour, S. (2012, January). Palestine's economic hallucinations. *This Week in Palestine* (165). Retrieved August 5, 2020. https://epalestine.blogspot.com/2011/12/epalestine twip-palestines-economic.html.

Bakhtin, M. (1968). *Rabelais and his world* (H. Isowolsky, Trans.). Cambridge, MA: MIT Press.

Barakat, R. (2018). Writing/righting Palestine studies: Settler colonialism, indigenous sovereignty, and resisting the ghost(s) of history. *Settler Colonialism Studies, 8*(3), 349–363.

Barghouti, O. (2009). Derailing injustice: Palestinian civil resistance to the "Jerusalem Light Rail." *Jerusalem Quarterly, 38,* 46–58.

———. (2011). *Boycott, divestment, sanctions: The global struggle for Palestinian rights.* Chicago: Haymarket.

———. (2019, April 16). I co-founded the BDS movement. Why was I denied entry to the U.S.? *The Guardian.* Retrieved April 13, 2020. http://www.theguardian.com/comment isfree/2019/apr/16/bds-movement-omar-barghouti-denied-entry.

Batarseh, A. (2019). *An unsettling state: Thinking through Palestine as a critical reading practice* [Conference presentation]. Critiques of Violence/Languages of Critique Conference, University of California, Riverside.

Bayat, A. (2010). *Life as politics: How ordinary people change the Middle East.* Palo Alto, CA: Stanford University Press.

———. (2017). *Revolution without revolutionaries: Making sense of the Arab spring.* Palo Alto, CA: Stanford University Press.

Baylouny, A. M. (2009). Fragmented space and violence in Palestine. *International Journal on World Peace, 26*(3), 39–68.

BBC News. (2011, November 15). Palestinian "freedom riders" board settlers' bus. Retrieved April 8, 2020. http://www.bbc.co.uk/news/world-middle-east-15744576.

BDS Movement. (2005, July 9). Palestinian civil society calls for boycott, divestment and sanctions against Israel until it complies with international Law and Universal Principles of Human Rights. Retrieved March 6, 2021. http://www.bdsmovement.net/call#sthash .AXaNZfQc.dpuf.

Bennett, A., Nashashibi, K., Beidas, S., Reichold, S. & Toujas-Bernaté, J. (2003, September 15). Economic performance and reform under conflict conditions. Retrieved February 23, 2021. https://www.imf.org/external/pubs/ft/med/2003/eng/wbg/wbg.pdf.

Benvenisti, E. (2008). The origins of the concept of belligerent occupation. *Law and History Review, 26*(3), 621–648.

———. (2013). *The International Law of Occupation.* Oxford: Oxford University Press.

Berda, Y. 2018. *Living emergency: Israel's permit regime in the occupied West Bank.* Palo Alto, CA: Stanford University Press.

Berger, J. (2006, January 13). Undefeated despair. Retrieved February 23, 2021. https://www .opendemocracy.net/en/palestine_3176jsp.

Bhandar, B. 2018. *Colonial lives of property: Law, land, and racial regimes of ownership.* Durham, NC: Duke University Press.

Bhandar, B. & Ziadah, R. (2016, January 14). Acts and omissions: Framing settler colonialism in Palestine studies. Retrieved February 23, 2021. https://www.jadaliyya.com /Details/32857.

Bishara, A. (2015). Driving while Palestinian in Israel and the West Bank: The politics of disorientation and the routes of a subaltern knowledge. *American Ethnologist, 42*(1), 33–54.

Black, F. (2013, March 9.) Israel moves to segregate buses. *Palestine Monitor.* Retrieved February 23, 2021. http://palestinemonitor.org/details.php?id=emf3uza3049ye191xklnv.

Brambilla, C. (2015). Exploring the critical potential of the borderscapes concept. *Geopolitics, 20*(1), 14–34.

Branton, W. E. (1983). Little Rock revisited: Desegregation to resegregation. *Journal of Negro Education, 52*(3), 250–269.

Braverman, I. (2009). Uprooting identities: The regulation of olive trees in the occupied West Bank. *PoLAR, 32*(2), 237–264.

———. (2010). Civilized borders: A study of Israel's new crossing administration. *Antipode, 43*(2), 264–295.

B'Tselem. (N.d.). Fatalities in the first intifada. Retrieved March 6, 2021. http://www.b tselem.org/statistics/first_intifada_tables.

———. (2004, August). Forbidden roads: Israel's discriminatory road regime in the West Bank. Retrieved February 23, 2021. https://www.btselem.org/download/200408_for bidden_roads_eng.pdf

———. (2007). Ground to a halt: Denial of Palestinians' freedom of movement in the West Bank. Retrieved February 23, 2021. http://www.btselem.org/publications/summaries /200708_ground_to_a_halt.

———. (2014, October 26). Minister of Defense not content with moving Palestinians to the back of the bus, means to keep them off entirely. Press release. Retrieved February 23, 2021. http://www.btselem.org/press_releases/20141026_separation_in_buses.

———. (2017a, January 1). Closure. Retrieved February 23, 2021. https://www.btselem .org/freedom_of_movement/copy%20of%20closure.

———. (2017b, November 11). Restrictions on movement. Retrieved August 18, 2020. https://www.btselem.org/freedom_of_movement.

———. (2017c, November 11). The separation barrier. Retrieved February 23, 2021. http:// www.btselem.org/separation_barrier.

———. (2019, September 25). List of military checkpoints in the West Bank and Gaza Strip. Retrieved February 18, 2021. http://www.btselem.org/freedom_of_movement /checkpoints_and_forbidden_roads.

Bunton, M. P. (2007). *Colonial land policies in Palestine, 1917–1936.* Oxford: Oxford University Press.

Burris, G. (2019). *The Palestinian idea: Film, media, and the radical imagination.* Philadelphia: Temple University Press.

Butler, J. (2017). Reflections on Trump. In *The rise of Trumpism*, series, Society for Cultural Anthropology. Retrieved August 19, 2020. https://culanth.org/fieldsights/reflec tions-on-trump.

Byrd, J. A. (2011). *The transit of empire.* Minneapolis: University of Minnesota Press.

Byrd, J. A., Goldstein, A., Melamed, J. & Reddy, C. (2018). Predatory value: Economies of dispossession and disturbed relationalities. *Social Text, 36*(2), 1–18.

Camp, S. (2002, August). The pleasures of resistance: Enslaved women and body politics in the plantation South, 1830–1861. *Journal of Southern History, 68*(3), 533–572.

Chamberlin, P. T. (2012). *The global offensive: The United States, the Palestine Liberation Organization, and the making of the post–Cold War order.* Oxford: Oxford University Press.

Chemerensky, E. (2002–2003). The segregation and resegregation of American public education: The court's role. *North Carolina Law Review, 81,* 1597–1622.

Clarno, A. (2017). *Neoliberal apartheid: Palestine/Israel and South Africa after 1994.* Chicago: University of Chicago Press.

Collins, J. (2011). *Global Palestine.* New York: Columbia University Press.

Corntassel, J. (2008). Toward sustainable self-determination: Rethinking the contemporary Indigenous-rights discourse. *Alternatives, 33,* 105–132.

Coulthard, G. S. (2014). *Red skin, white masks: Rejecting the colonial politics of recognition.* Minneapolis: University of Minnesota Press.

Crenshaw, K. W. (1988). Race, reform and retrenchment: Transformation and legitimation in antidiscrimination law. *Harvard Law Review, 101*(7), 1331–1387.

Cresswell, T. (2010). Towards a politics of mobility. *Environment and Planning D: Society and Space, 28,* 17–31.

Dana, K. (2017). The West Bank apartheid/separation wall: Space, punishment and the disruption of social continuity. *Geopolitics, 22*(4), 887–910.

Dana, T. & Jarbawi, A. (2017). A century of settler colonialism in Palestine: Zionism's entangled project. *Brown Journal of World Affairs, 24*(1), 197–219.

De Angelis, M. (2019). Migrants' inhabiting through commoning and state enclosures. A postface. *Citizenship Studies, 23*(6), 627–636.

Decolonizing Architecture Art Residency. (2011). *Right to mobility*. Retrieved February 23, 2021. http://www.decolonizing.ps.

Doha Institute, Policy Analysis Unit—ACRPS. (2012). The Palestinian protests of September 2012: The birth of a social protest movement. Retrieved February 23, 2021. https://www.dohainstitute.org/en/PoliticalStudies/Pages/The_Palestinian_Protests_of_September_2012_The_Birth_of_a_Social_Protest_Movement.aspx.

Dorr, L. L. (2004). *White women, rape, and the power of race in Virginia, 1900–1960*. Chapel Hill: University of North Carolina Press.

Doumani, B. (1995). *Rediscovering Palestine: Merchants and peasants in Jabal Nablus, 1700–1900*. Berkeley: University of California Press.

———. (2004, Autumn). Scenes from daily life: The view from Nablus. *Journal of Palestine Studies, 34*(1), 37–50.

———. (2009). Archiving Palestine and the Palestinians: The patrimony of Ihsan Nimr. *Jerusalem Quarterly, 36*, 4–12.

Duschinski, H. & Bhan, M. (2017). Introduction: Law containing violence: critical ethnographies of occupation and resistance. *Journal of Legal Pluralism and Unofficial Law, 49*(3), 253–267.

Ehrenreich, B. (2013, December 1). The death of Anas Al-Atrash. *Los Angeles Review of Books*. Retrieved August 19, 2020. https://lareviewofbooks.org/article/the-death-of-anas-al-atrash.

Erakat, N. (2019). *Justice for some: Law and the question of Palestine*. Stanford, CA: Stanford University Press.

Erakat, N. & Hill, M. L. (2019). Black-Palestinian transnational solidarity: Renewals, returns, and practice. *Journal of Palestine Studies, 48*(4), 7–16.

Fadda, R. (2009). Not-yet-ness. In Danon, E. & Eilat, G. (Eds.), *Liminal spaces 2006–2009* (pp. 223–231). Retrieved August 19, 2020. https://galiteilat.files.wordpress.com/2018/11/liminal-spaces-reader.pdf.

Falk, R. (2008). *Achieving human rights*. New York: Routledge.

———. (2010, December 24). The Palestinian "legitimacy war." Retrieved February 23, 2021. https://www.aljazeera.com/opinions/2010/12/24/the-palestinian-legitimacy-war.

———. (2014). *Palestine: The legitimacy of hope*. Washington, DC: Just World Books.

———. (2017). *Palestine's horizon: Toward a just peace*. London: Pluto.

Farsakh, L. (2002). Palestinian labor flows to the Israeli economy: A finished story? *Journal of Palestine Studies, 32*(1), 13–27.

———. (2005a). Independence, cantons, or bantustans: Whither the Palestinian state? *Middle East Journal, 59*(2), 230–245.

———. (2005b). *Palestinian labour migration to Israel: Labour, land and occupation*. New York: Routledge.

———. (2010). The Palestinian economy and the Oslo "Peace Process" (Arab Research Institute, Trans.). Retrieved February 23, 2021. http://www.tari.org/index.php?option=com_content&view=article&id=9:the-palestinian-economy.

Federici, S. (2004). *Caliban and the witch: Women, the body and primitive accumulation*. Brooklyn, NY: Autonomedia.

Feldman, K. (2009). Representing permanent war: Black power's Palestine and the end(s) of civil rights. In Aidi, H. D. & Marable, M. (Eds.), *Black routes to Islam* (pp. 79–98). London: Palgrave Macmillan.

Fields, G. (2010). Landscaping Palestine: Reflections of enclosure in a historical mirror. *International Journal of Middle East Studies, 42*(1), 63–82.

———. (2017). *Enclosure: Palestinian landscapes in a historical mirror.* Oakland: University of California Press.

Fortier, C. (2017). *Unsettling the commons: Social movements within, against, and beyond settler colonialism.* Winnipeg, MB: ARP Books.

Foucault, M. (1977, February). Governmentality [Lecture]. Collège de France, Paris.

Freeman, V. (2010). "Toronto has no history!" Indigeneity, settler colonialism, and historical memory in Canada's largest city. *Urban History Review, 38*(2), 21–35.

Friedberg, R. M. (2001). The impact of mass migration on the Israeli labor market. *Quarterly Journal of Economics, 116*(4), 1373–1408.

Getachew, A. (2019). *Worldmaking after empire: The rise and fall of self-determination.* Princeton, NJ: Princeton University Press.

Ghanim, H. (2018). The composite framing of a hybrid regime: The controversy of settler colonialism, occupation, and apartheid in Palestine. In *Israel and the apartheid: Comparative studies* (pp. 15–53). Ramallah: Palestinian Forum for Israeli Studies (MADAR).

Gilmore, R. W. (2008). Forgotten places and the seeds of grassroots planning. In Hale, C. (Ed.), *Engaging contradictions: Theory, politics, and methods of activist scholarship* (pp. 31–61). Berkeley: University of California Press.

Goeman, M. R. (2014). Disrupting a settler colonial grammar of place: The visual memoir of Hulleah Tsinhnahjinnie. In Simpson, A. & Smith, A. (Eds.), *Theorizing Native Studies* (pp. 235–265). Durham, NC: Duke University Press.

Gordon, A. (2004). *Keeping good time: Reflections on knowledge, power, and people.* Boulder, CO: Paradigm.

———. (2006). Abu Ghraib: Imprisonment and the war on terror. *Race and Class, 48*(1), 42–59.

———. (2008). *Ghostly matters: Haunting and the sociological imagination* (2d ed). Minneapolis: University of Minnesota Press.

———. (2018). *The Hawthorn archive: Letters from the utopian margins.* New York: Fordham University Press.

Gordon, N. (2008a). From colonization to separation: Exploring the structure of Israel's occupation. *Third World Quarterly, 29*(1), 25–44.

———. (2008b). *Israel's occupation.* Berkeley: University of California Press.

Graham, S. (2011). Laboratories of war: Surveillance and U.S.-Israeli collaboration in war and security. In Zureik, E. (Ed.), *Surveillance and control in Israel/Palestine: Population, territory, power* (pp. 133–152). New York: Routledge.

Grande, S. (2004). *Red pedagogy: Native American social and political thought.* Lanham, MD: Rowman and Littlefield.

Greenwald, C. S. (1973). *Recession as a policy instrument: Israel 1965–1969.* Madison, NJ: Fairleigh Dickinson University Press.

Greer, A. (2012). Commons and enclosure in the colonization of North America. *American Historical Review, 117*(2), 365–386.

Gregory, D. (2004). *The colonial present: Afghanistan, Palestine, Iraq.* Malden, MA: Blackwell.

Ha'aretz. (2014, October 31). Livni: Settlers want "apartheid" buses. Retrieved August 18, 2020. https://www.haaretz.com/livni-settlers-want-apartheid-buses-1.5322583.

Haddad, T. (2018). Insurgent infrastructure: Tunnels of the Gaza Strip. *Middle East—Topics and Arguments, 10*, 71–85.

Hajjar, L. (2005). *Courting conflict: The Israeli military court system in the West and Gaza.* Berkeley: University of California Press.

Halper, J. (2000, Fall). The 94 percent solution: A matrix of control. *Middle East Report, 216*. Retrieved February 23, 2021. https://merip.org/2000/09/the-94-percent-solution.

Hammami, R. (2005). On the importance of thugs: The moral economy of a checkpoint. *Jerusalem Quarterly, 22–23*, 16–28.

Hammami, R. & Tamari, S. (2000). Anatomy of another rebellion. *Middle East Report, 217*, 2–15.

Hanafi, S. (2009, January–March). Spacio-cide: Colonial politics, invisibility, and rezoning in Palestinian territory. *Contemporary Arab Affairs, 2*(1), 106–121.

Handel, A. (2009). Where, where to and when in the occupied Palestinian territories: An introduction to geography of disaster. In Ophir, A., Givoni, M. & Hanafi, S. (Eds.), *The power of inclusive exclusion: Anatomy of Israeli rule in the occupied Palestinian territories* (pp. 179–222). New York: Zone.

———. (2013). Gated/gating community: The settlement complex in the West Bank. *Transactions of the Institute of British Geographers, 39*(4), 504–517.

———. (2015). What are we talking about when we talk about "geographies of occupation"? In Abdallah, S. L. & Parizot, C. (Eds.), *Israelis and Palestinians in the shadow of the wall: Spaces of separation and occupation* (pp. 71–86). Farnham, UK: Ashgate.

Hanieh, A. (2003, May 15). A roadmap to the Oslo cul-de-sac. *Middle East Report* (online). Retrieved February 23, 2021. https://merip.org/2003/05/a-road-map-to-the-oslo-cul-de-sac.

Hansen, T. B. & Stepputat, F. (Eds.). (2005). *Sovereign bodies: Citizens, migrants, and states in the postcolonial world*. Princeton, NJ: Princeton University Press.

Harker, C. (2017). Debt space: Topologies, ecologies and Ramallah, Palestine. *Environment and Planning D: Society and Space, 35*(4), 600–619.

Hass, A. (2002). Israel's closure policy: An ineffective strategy of containment and repression. *Journal of Palestine Studies, 31*(3), 5–20.

———. (2005, February 23). The natives' time is cheap. *Ha'aretz*. Retrieved February 23, 2021. https://www.haaretz.com/1.4753348

Hatuqa, D. (2013, September 12). Banking on West Bank property. Retrieved August 5, 2020. https://www.aljazeera.com/indepth/features/2013/09/201391275625391674.html.

Hayden, P. (2008). From exclusion to containment: Arendt, sovereign power, and statelessness. *Societies without Borders, 3*(2), 248–269.

Hochberg, G. (2018). "Jerusalem, We Have a Problem": Larissa Sansour's sci fi trilogy and the impetus of dystopic imagination. *Arab Studies Journal, 26*(1), 34–57.

Hodkinson, S. (2012). The new *urban* enclosures. *City, 16*(5), 500–518.

Horowitz, A. (2011, November 15). Six Palestinian freedom riders arrested traveling on Israeli-only bus. Retrieved February 23, 2021. http://mondoweiss.net/2011/11/follow-the-freedom-rides.

Hudson, J., Eglash, R., Dawsey, J. & Bade, R. (2019, August 15). Israel denies entry to Reps. Omar and Tlaib hours after Trump's push for a ban. Retrieved August 18, 2020. http://www.washingtonpost.com/world/national-security/netanyahu-considers-blocking-omar-tlaib-from-entering-israel-ahead-of-a-planned-weekend-visit/2019/08/15/d69983ce-d15b-4074-8590-c6f69bd4a084_story.html.

Human Rights Council. (2019, February 25). *Report of the Independent International Commission of Inquiry on the protests in the occupied Palestinian Territory*. Retrieved April 13, 2020. https://www.ohchr.org/Documents/HRBodies/HRCouncil/CoIOPT/A_HRC_40_74.pdf.

Ihmoud, S. (2018). Policing the intimate: Israel's anti-miscegenation movement. *Jerusalem Quarterly, 75*, 91–103.

———. (2019). *Murabata: The politics of staying in place. Feminist Studies, 45*(2–3), 512–540.

International Court of Justice. (2004, July 9). Advisory Opinion. Legal consequences of the construction of a wall in the occupied Palestinian territories. Retrieved February 18, 2021. https://www.icj-cij.org/public/files/case-related/131/131-20040709-ADV-01-00-EN.pdf

Issa, I. & Qawasmi, S. (2011). *Palestine Connected.* Part of "Between Ebal and Gerzim," Cities Exhibition, 3rd Edition. Birzeit, Palestine: Birzeit University. Retrieved February 23, 2021. https://universes.art/en/nafas/articles/2011/nablus/img/iyad-issa-sahar-qawasmi.

Jabary Salamanca, O., Qato, M., Rabie, K. & Samour, S. (2012). Past is present: Settler colonialism in Palestine. *Settler Colonial Studies, 2*(1), 1–8.

Jarrar, K. (2011). *State of Palestine.* Retrieved February 23, 2021. https://artmuseum.pl/en/archiwum/archiwum-7-berlin-biennale/1891?read=all.

Jeffress, D. (2008). *Postcolonial resistance: Culture, liberation, and transformation.* Toronto: University of Toronto Press.

Jeffrey, A., McFarlane, C. & Vasudevan, A. (2012). Rethinking enclosure: Space, subjectivity and the commons. *Antipode, 44*(4), 1247–1267.

Johnson, P., O'Brien, L. & Hiltermann, J. (1989). The West Bank rises up. In Lockman, Z. & Beinin, J. (Eds.), *Intifada: The Palestinian uprising against Israeli occupation* (pp. 29–41). Cambridge, MA: South End Press.

Jones, R. (2012). Spaces of refusal: Rethinking sovereign power and resistance at the border. *Annals of the Association of American Geographers, 102*(3), 685–699.

Kauanui, J. K. (2016, Spring). "A structure not an event": Settler colonialism and enduring indigeneity. Forum: Emergent critical analytics for alternative humanities. *Lateral: Journal of the Cultural Studies Association, 5*(1). Retrieved February 23, 2021. http://csalateral.org/issue/5-1/forum-alt-humanities-settler-colonialism-enduring-indigeneity-kauanui.

Kawar, W. K. (2011). *Threads of identity: Preserving Palestinian costume and heritage.* Limassol, Cyprus: Rimal.

Kay, A. & Abu-Zahra, N. (2012). *Unfree in Palestine: Registration, documentation and movement restriction.* London: Pluto.

Kelley, R. D. G. (2002). *Freedom dreams: The black radical imagination.* Boston: Beacon.

———. (2019). From the river to the sea to every mountain top: Solidarity as worldmaking. *Journal of Palestine Studies, 48*(4), 69–91.

Kelly, J. L. (2016). Asymmetrical itineraries: Militarism, tourism, and solidarity in occupied Palestine. *American Quarterly, 68*(3), 723–745.

Khalidi, R. (1997). *Palestinian identity: The construction of modern national consciousness.* New York: Columbia University Press.

———. (2005, February 3). After Arafat. *London Review of Books, 27*(3). Retrieved February 23, 2021. https://www.lrb.co.uk/the-paper/v27/n03/rashid-khalidi/after-arafat.

———. (2007). *The iron cage: The story of the Palestinian struggle for statehood.* Boston: Beacon.

———. (2010, April 15). Bad faith in the holy city: How Israel's Jerusalem policy imperils the peace process. *Foreign Affairs.* Retrieved February 23, 2021. https://www.foreignaffairs.com/articles/middle-east/2010-04-15/bad-faith-holy-city.

Khalili, L. (2012). *Time in the shadows: Confinements in counterinsurgencies.* Palo Alto, CA: Stanford University Press.

Khan, M. (2014, October 26). Palestinians banned from Israeli public transport system in the West Bank. *International Business Times.* Retrieved April 13, 2020. https://www.ibtimes.co.uk/palestinians-banned-israeli-public-transport-system-west-bank-1471842.

Kimmerling, B. (2006). *Politicide: The real legacy of Ariel Sharon.* London: Verso.

Kipnis, B. A. (1987). Geopolitical ideologies and regional strategies in Israel. *Tijdschrift voor Economische en Sociale Geografie [Journal of Economic and Social Geography],* 78(2), 125–138.

Klein, N. (2008). *The shock doctrine: The rise of disaster capitalism.* New York: Picador.

Kotef, H. (2015). *Movement and the ordering of freedom: On liberal governances of mobility.* Durham, NC: Duke University Press.

Kuntsman, A. & Stein, R. (2015). *Digital militarism: Israel's occupation in the social media age.* Stanford, CA: Stanford University Press.

Kwon, M. (1997, Spring). One place after another: Notes on site specificity. *October, 80,* 85–110.

Landau, I. (2013, October 7). A journey into the dark heart of Israel's permit regime (J. Michaeli, Trans.). *+972 Magazine.* Retrieved February 23, 2021. http://972mag.com /a-journey-into-the-dark-heart-of-israels-permit-regime/80096.

Levinson, C. (2011, December 22). Israel has 101 different types of permits governing Palestinian movement. *Ha'aretz.* Retrieved August 18, 2020. https://www.haaretz.com/1 .5222134.

———. (2014a, October 26). Ya'alon bans Palestinians from Israeli-run bus lines in West Bank, following settler pressure. *Ha'aretz.* Retrieved August 18, 2020. http://www .haaretz.com/news/israel/.premium-1.622414.

———. (2014b, October 28). Bus rides with Jews "a victory" for Palestinians, say settlers. *Ha'aretz.* Retrieved August 18, 2020. https://www.haaretz.com/.premium-idf-split -with-settlers-on-bus-issue-1.5321149.

Lien, S. (2013, November 2013). Villages east of Ramallah plea to reopen road to the city. *Palestine Monitor.* Retrieved August 18, 2020. http://palestinemonitor.org/details.php? id=3fnlmla5662y6mffh40xq.

Linebaugh, P. (2010, Fall). Enclosures from the bottom up. *Radical History Review,* (108), 11–27.

Lockman, Z. (1996). *Comrades and enemies: Arab and Jewish workers in Palestine, 1906–1948.* Berkeley: University of California Press.

Lubin, A. (2014). *Geographies of liberation: The making of an Afro-Arab political imaginary.* Chapel Hill: University of North Carolina Press.

Ma'an News Agency. (2012, September). P[alestinian] A[uthority] threatens to sue union over transport strikes. Retrieved April 29, 2013. http://www.maannews.com/Content .aspx?id=522855.

Maira, S. (2013). *Jil Oslo: Palestinian hip hop, youth culture, and the youth movement.* Washington, DC: Tadween.

Makdisi, S. (2008). *Palestine inside/out: An everyday occupation.* New York: W. W. Norton.

Mansbach, D. (2009). Normalizing violence: From military checkpoints to "terminals" in the occupied territories. *Journal of Power, 2*(2), 255–273.

Mansour, J. (2006). The Hijaz-Palestine Railway and the development of Haifa. *Jerusalem Quarterly, 28,* 5–21.

Marcuse, H. (1964). *One-dimensional man.* Boston: Beacon.

Masalha, N. (2012). *The Palestine Nakba: Decolonizing history, narrating the subaltern, reclaiming memory.* London: Zed.

Matar, H. (2012, August 25). Bus company backs driver who refused Palestinian passengers on board. *+972 Magazine.* Retrieved August 18, 2020. http://972mag.com/bus -company-backs-driver-who-refused-palestinian-passengers-on-board/54461.

———. (2019, March 15). A spike in censorship: Israel censored on average one news piece a day in 2018. *+972 Magazine.* Retrieved April 13, 2020. https://972mag.com/idf-censor-press-freedom-israel-2018/140594.

Mbembe, A. (2003). Necropolitics. *Public Culture, 15*(1), 11–40.

McGahern, U. (2019). Making space on the run: Exercising the right to move in Jerusalem. *Mobilities, 14*(6), 890–905.

Meari, L. (2014). *Sumud:* A Palestinian philosophy of confrontation in colonial prisons. *South Atlantic Quarterly, 113*(3), 547–578.

Meneley, A. (2019). Walk this way: Fitbit and other kinds of walking in Palestine. *Cultural Anthropology, 31*(1), 130–154.

Mezzadra, S. & Neilson, B. (2013). *Border as method, or, The multiplication of labor.* Durham, NC: Duke University Press.

Middle East Monitor. (2017, November 27). Israel arrests 280 Palestinians for Facebook posts. Retrieved February 23, 2021. https://www.middleeastmonitor.com/20171127-israel-arrests-280-palestinians-for-facebook-posts.

Midnight Notes Collective. (1990). The new enclosures. *Midnight Notes, 10.* Retrieved February 23, 2021. http://www.midnightnotes.org/newenclos.html.

Miller, E. (2015, May 20). Netanyahu puts the brakes on "segregated" West Bank buses. *Times of Israel.* Retrieved April 13, 2020. http://www.timesofisrael.com/netanyahu-puts-the-breaks-on-segregated-west-bank-buses.

Mills, C. W. ([1959] 2000). *The sociological imagination* (40th anniversary ed.). Oxford: Oxford University Press.

Morrill, A., Tuck, E., and Super Futures Haunt Qollective. (2016). Before dispossession, or surviving it. *Liminalities, 12*(1), 1–20.

Nader, L. (1994). Comparative consciousness. In Borofsky, R. (Ed.), *Assessing cultural anthropology* (pp. 84–96). New York: McGraw-Hill.

Nakhal, M. (1996). Closure and borders: An examination of Israeli closure policies as unique in the world, their implementation and consequences. *The Road Ahead [Palestine-Israel Journal of Politics, Economics and Culture], 3*(3–4). Retrieved February 23, 2021. https://pij.org/articles/529.

Nassar, M. (2019). Palestinian engagement with the black freedom movement prior to 1967. *Journal of Palestine Studies, 48*(4), 17–32.

Nieuwhof, A. (2013, September 29). Veolia, feeling pressure, launches attack on Israel boycott movement. *Electronic Intifada.* Retrieved February 23, 2021. https://eletronicintifada.net/blogs/adri-nieuwhof/veolia-feeling-pressure-launches-attack-israel-boycott-movement.

Nitzan, J. & Bichler, S. (2002). *The global political economy of Israel: From war profits to peace dividends.* London: Pluto.

Norris, J. (2017). Transforming the Holy Land: The ideology of development and the British Mandate in Palestine. *Humanity, 8*(2), 269–286.

Nusseibeh, S. (2011). *What is a Palestinian state worth?* Cambridge, MA: Harvard University Press.

Oliver, P. E. & Johnston, H. (2000). What a good idea! Ideologies and frames in social movement research. *Mobilization, 4*(1), 37–54.

Pacheco, A. (2001). Flouting convention: The Oslo Agreements. In Carey, R. (Ed.), *The new intifada: Resisting Israel's apartheid.* New York: Verso.

Palestinian Central Bureau of Statistics. (2013). Statistics of transport and communications in Palestine: Annual report, 2020 (in Arabic, with English-language data). Retrieved August 29, 2020. http://www.pcbs.gov.ps/Downloads/book2065.pdf.

———. (2019). Statistics of transport and communications in Palestine: Annual report, 2019 (in Arabic, with English-language data). Retrieved August 29, 2020. http://www.pcbs.gov.ps/Downloads/book2530.pdf.

———. (2020). Estimated population in the Palestinian territory mid-year by governorate, 1997–2021. http://www.pcbs.gov.ps/site/803/default.aspx.

Papadopoulos, D. & Tsianos, V. S. (2013). After citizenship: Autonomy of migration, organisational ontology and mobile commons. *Citizenship Studies, 17*(2), 178–196.

paperson, l. (2010). The postcolonial ghetto: Seeing her shape and his hand. *Berkeley Review of Education, 1*(1), 5–34.

Pappé, I. (2008, March 4). The mega prison of Palestine. *Electronic Intifada*. Retrieved February 23, 2021. https://electronicintifada.net/content/mega-prison-palestine/7399.

Paq, A. (2018). Palestine marathon puts spotlight on right of movement. *Al Jazeera*. Retrieved April 13, 2020. https://www.aljazeera.com/indepth/inpictures/palestine-marathon-puts-spotlight-movement-180323183108289.html.

Parizot, C. (2012). An undocumented economy of control: Workers, smugglers and state authorities in Israel/Palestine. In Anteby-Yemini, L., Baby-Collin, V., Mazzella, S., Mourlane, S., Parizot, C., Regnard, C. & Sintès, P. (Eds.), *Borders, mobilities and migrations: Perspectives from the Mediterranean, 19th–21st century*. Brussels: Peter Lang.

———. (2018). Viscous spatialities: The spaces of the Israeli permit regime of access and movement. *South Atlantic Quarterly, 118*(1), 21–42.

Parsons, N. & Salter, M. B. (2008). Israeli biopolitics: Closure, territorialisation, and governmentality in the occupied territories. *Geopolitics, 13*(4), 701–723.

Pelham, N. (2014). The role of the tunnel economy in redeveloping Gaza. In Turner, M. & Shweiki, O. (Eds.), *Decolonizing Palestinian political economy* (pp. 200–219). London: Palgrave Macmillan.

Peteet, J. (2005). *Landscape of hope and despair: Palestinian refugee camps*. Philadelphia: University of Pennsylvania Press.

———. (2017). *Space and mobility in Palestine*. Bloomington: Indiana University Press.

———. (2018). Closure's temporality: The cultural politics of time and waiting. *South Atlantic Quarterly, 117*(1), 43–64.

Petti, A., Hilal, S. & Weizman, E. (2013). *Architecture after revolution*. Berlin: Sternberg.

Pottage, A. (1994). The measure of land. *Modern Law Review, 57*(3), 361–384.

Qato, D. (2004). The politics of deteriorating health: The case of Palestine. *International Journal of Health Services, 34*(2), 341–364.

Quintanilla, L. & Mogannam, J. (2015). Borders are obsolete: Relations beyond the "borderlands" of Palestine and U.S.-Mexico. *American Quarterly, 67*(4), 1039–1046.

Quiquivix, L. (2013). When the carob tree was the border: On autonomy and Palestinian practices of figuring it out. *Capitalism Nature Socialism, 24*(3), 1–20.

Quiray Tagle, T. (2018). After life (what remains) (Curatorial essay). Alice Gallery, Seattle. Retrieved February 23, 2021. https://www.thealicegallery.com/after-life-what-remains.html.

Qumsiyeh, M. B. (2011). *Popular resistance in Palestine: A history of hope and empowerment*. New York: Pluto.

Qutami, L. (2014). Rethinking the single story: BDS, transnational cross-movement building and the Palestine analytic. *Social Text* (online). Retrieved February 23, 2021. https://socialtextjournal.org/periscope_article/rethinking-the-single-story-bds-transnational-cross-movement-building-and-the-palestine-analytic.

Qutami, L. & Zahzah, O. (2020, Winter–Spring). The war of words: Language as an instrument of Palestinian national struggle. *Arab Studies Quarterly, 42*(1–2), 66–90.

Rainey, V. (2010, April 29). Separate roads increasingly part of West Bank map. *Jerusalem Media and Communication Centre.* Retrieved February 23, 2021. http://www.jmcc.org /news.aspx?id=816.

Reardon, S. F., Grewal, E. T., Kalogrides, D. & Greenberg, E. (2012). Brown fades: The end of court-ordered desegregation and the resegregation of American public schools. *Journal of Policy Analysis and Management, 31*(4), 876–904.

Reddy, C. (2008). Time for rights? Loving, gay marriage, and the limits of legal justice. *Fordham Law Review, 76*(6), 2849–2872.

Reinhart, T. (2006). *The road map to nowhere: Israel/Palestine since 2003.* New York: Verso.

Reuters (2013, 4 March). Israel opens Palestinians-only bus lines in W[est] Bank. Retrieved April 13, 2020. http://www.reuters.com/article/2013/03/04/palestinians-israel -buses-idUSL6N0BW1RN20130304.

Reynolds, J. (2017). Repressive inclusion. *Journal of Legal Pluralism and Unofficial Law, 49*(3), 268–293.

Rifkin, M. (2017). *Beyond settler time: Temporal sovereignty and indigenous self-determination.* Durham, NC: Duke University Press.

Rijke, A. & Minca, C. (2018). Checkpoint 300: Precarious checkpoint geographies and rights/rites of passage in the occupied Palestinian territories. *Political Geography, 65,* 35–45.

Rijke, A. & van Teeffelen, T. (2014). To exist is to resist: Sumud, heroism, and the everyday. *Jerusalem Quarterly, 59,* 86–99.

Robinson, C. (2007). *Forgeries of memory and meaning: Blacks and the regimes of race in American theater and film before World War II.* Chapel Hill: University of North Carolina Press.

Rolston, B. (2014). Messages of allegiance and defiance: The murals of Gaza. *Race and Class, 55*(4), 40–64.

Roy, S. (1995). *The Gaza Strip: The political economy of de-development* (1st ed.). Washington, DC: Institute for Palestine Studies.

Sabella, B. (1993, May/June). Russian Jewish immigration and the future of the Israeli-Palestinian conflict. *Middle East Report, 182.* Retrieved February 23, 2021. https://merip .org/1993/05/russian-jewish-immigration-and-the-future-of-the-israeli-palestinian-con flict.

Sa'di, A. H. (2002). Catastrophe, memory and identity: Al-Nakbah as a component of Palestinian identity. *Israel Studies, 7*(2), 175–198.

Said, E. (1993, October 21). The morning after. *London Review of Books, 15*(20). Retrieved February 23, 2021. https://www.lrb.co.uk/the-paper/v15/n20/edward-said/the-morn ing-after.

———. (1994). *Culture and imperialism.* New York: Vintage.

———. (1995). *The politics of dispossession: The struggle for Palestinian self-determination, 1969–1994.* New York: Vintage.

———. (1998, October 1–7). A real state needs real work. *Al-Ahram Weekly* (online), reprinted in *Palestine Chronicle* (online). Retrieved February 23, 2021. http://www.pal estinechronicle.com/a-real-state-means-real-work/#.UzAelK2Sy50.

———. (1999, January 10). The one-state solution. *New York Times Magazine.* Retrieved February 22, 2021. https://www.nytimes.com/1999/01/10/magazine/the-one-state-solu tion.html.

———. (2001a). *The end of the peace process: Oslo and after.* New York: Vintage.

———. (2001b). Palestinians under siege. In Carey, R. (Ed.), *The new intifada: Resisting Israel's apartheid* (pp. 27–44). New York: Verso.

Salaita, S. (2006). *Holy Land in transit: Colonialism and the quest for Canaan*. Syracuse, NY: Syracuse University Press.

———. (2016). *Inter/nationalism: Decolonizing Native America and Palestine*. Minneapolis: University of Minnesota Press.

Sansour, L. (2012). *Nation estate* (Film). Accessed June 20–21, 2020. http://www.larissasansour.com/nation_estate.html.

Sayegh, F. A. (1965). *Zionist colonialism in Palestine*. Beirut: Palestinian Liberation Organization Research Center.

Sayigh, Y. (1986, Summer). The Palestinian economy under occupation: Dependency and pauperization. *Journal of Palestine Studies, 15*(4), 46–67.

Scott, J. C. (1985). *Weapons of the weak: Everyday forms of peasant resistance*. New Haven, CT: Yale University Press.

———. (1990). *Domination and the arts of resistance: Hidden transcripts*. New Haven, CT: Yale University Press.

———. (2009). *The art of not being governed: An anarchist history of upland Southeast Asia*. New Haven, CT: Yale University Press.

———. (2012). Infrapolitics and mobilizations: A response by James C. Scott. *Revue Française d'Études Américaines*, (131), 112–117.

Segal, R. & Weizman, E. (Eds.) (2003). *A civilian occupation: The politics of Israeli architecture*. London: Verso.

Seidel, T. (2019). Neoliberal developments, national consciousness, and political economies of resistance in Palestine. *Interventions, 21*(5), 727–746.

Seidel, T. & Tartir, A. (2019). The rule of power in Palestine: Settler colonialism, neoliberal governance, and resistance. In Tartir, A. & Seidel, T. (Eds.), *Palestine and rule of power: Local dissent versus international governance* (pp. 1–19). London: Palgrave Macmillan.

Seikaly, S. (2015). *Men of capital: Scarcity and economy in Mandate Palestine*. Palo Alto, CA: Stanford University Press.

Sela, R. (2017). The genealogy of colonial plunder and erasure—Israel's control over Palestinian archives. *Social Semiotics, 28*(2), 201–229.

Sharif, L. (2016). Vanishing Palestine. *Critical Ethnic Studies, 2*(1), 17–39.

Sharif, R. (2014). Bodies, buses, and permits: Palestinians navigating care. *Feminists@law, 4*(1), 1–15.

Sharif, Y. (2017). *Architecture of resistance: Cultivating moments of possibility within the Palestinian/Israeli conflict*. London: Routledge.

Sharp, J., Routledge, P., Philo, C. & Paddison, R. (2000). *Entanglements of power: Geographies of domination/resistance*. London: Routledge.

Shehadeh, R. (2007). *Palestinian walks: Forays into a vanishing landscape*. New York: Scribner.

———. (2012, November 9). My father's peace proposal. Updated July 14, 2017. *The Daily Beast*. Retrieved September 15, 2020. https://www.thedailybeast.com/my-fathers-peace-proposal.

Sheller, M. (2016). Uneven mobility futures: A Foucauldian approach. *Mobilities, 11*(1), 15–31.

———. (2018). *Mobility justice: The politics of movement in an age of extremes*. Brooklyn, NY: Verso.

Shihade, M. (2014). Not just a picnic: Settler colonialism, mobility, and identity among Palestinians in Israel. *Biography, 37*(2), 451–473.

Simpson, A. (2014). *Mohawk interruptus: Political life across the borders of settler states*. Durham, NC: Duke University Press.

Snow, D. A. & Benford, R. D. (2000). Framing processes and social movements: An overview and assessment. *Annual Review of Sociology, 26*, 611–639.

Snow, D. A., Rochford, Jr., E. B., Worden, S. K. & Benford, R. D. (1986). Frame alignment processes, micromobilization and movement participation. *American Sociological Review, 51*(4), 464–481.

Speed, S. & Reyes, A. (2005). Rights, resistance, and radical alternatives: The Red de Defensores Comunitarios and Zapatismo in Chiapas. *Humboldt Journal of Social Relations, 29*(1), 47–82.

Stacher, J. (2018, May 3). Running as resistance in occupied Palestine. *Middle East Report* (online). Retrieved April 13, 2020. https://merip.org/2018/05/running-as-resistance -in-occupied-palestine.

Steinberg, P. & Oliver, A. M. (1994, May). *The graffiti of the Intifada: A brief survey* (2d ed). Jerusalem: Palestinian Academic Society for the Study of International Affairs.

Stoler, A. (2016). *Duress: Imperial durabilities in our times*. Durham, NC: Duke University Press.

Subcomandante Insurgente Marcos. (1996, August 29). To the soldiers and commanders of the Popular Revolutionary Army. Retrieved August 9, 2020. http://www.struggle.ws /mexico/ezln/ezln_epr_se96.html.

Tabar, L. & Desai, C. (2017). Decolonization is a global project: From Palestine to the Americas. *Decolonization: Indigeneity, Education and Society, 6*(1), i–xix.

Tamari, S. (1991). The Palestinian Movement in transition: Historical reversals and the uprising. *Journal of Palestine Studies, 20*(2), 57–70.

Tartir, A. & Seidel, T. (Eds). (2019). *Palestine and rule of power: Local dissent versus international governance*. London: Palgrave Macmillan.

Tawil-Souri, H. (2011a). Colored identity: The politics and materiality of ID cards in Palestine/Israel. *Social Text, 29*(2), 67–97.

———. (2011b). Orange, green and blue: Color-coded paperwork for Palestinian population control. In Zureik, E. E. (Ed.), *Surveillance and control in Israel/Palestine: Population, territory and power* (pp. 219–238). London: Routledge.

———. (2012). Uneven borders, coloured (im)mobilities: ID cards in Palestine/Israel. *Geopolitics, 17*(1), 153–176.

———. (2017). Checkpoint time. *Qui Parle, 26*(2), 383–422.

Tawil-Souri, H. & Aouragh, M. (2014). Intifada 3.0? Cyber colonialism and Palestinian resistance. *Arab Studies Journal, 22*(1), 102–133.

Thomsen, C. (2015). The politics of narrative, narrative as politics: Rethinking reproductive justice frameworks through the South Dakota abortion story. *Feminist Formations, 21*(2), 1–26.

Torpey, J. (2000). *The invention of the passport: Surveillance, citizenship, and the state*. Cambridge: Cambridge University Press.

Tuck, E. & Recollet, K. (2017). Visitations (You are not alone). In *#Callresponse* (Exhibition catalogue). Retrieved August 20, 2020. https://static1.squarespace.com/static/557744ffe4 b013bae3b7af63/t/5b06f6d80e2e720b9835fe9e/1527183064966/Visitations+%28You+ are+not+alone%29+2017+Tuck+%26+Recollet.pdf.

Tuck, E. & Ree, C. (2013). A glossary of haunting. In Jones, S. H., Adams, T. E. & Ellis, C. (Eds.), *Handbook of autoethnography* (pp. 639–658). Walnut Creek, CA: Left Coast.

Tuck, E. & Yang, K. W. (2012). Decolonization is not a metaphor. *Decolonization: Indigeneity, Education & Society, 1*(1), 1–40.

Union Internationale des Transports Publics. (N.d.) Why public transit? Retrieved August 29, 2020. https://ceec.uitp.org/why-public-transport.

United Nations Office for the Coordination of Humanitarian Affairs (OCHA). (2006, May). Territorial fragmentation of the West Bank. Retrieved February 23, 2021. https://unispal.un.org/DPA/DPR/unispal.nsf/85255db800470aa485255d8b004e349a/bb027df1429e73c6852571720054c874?OpenDocument.

United Nations Office for the Coordination of Humanitarian Affairs, Occupied Palestinian Territory (OCHA OPT). (2007, July). The humanitarian impact on Palestinians of Israeli settlements and other infrastructure in the West Bank. Retrieved August 7, 2020. https://www.ochaopt.org/sites/default/files/ocharpt_update30july2007.pdf.

———. (2012, September). West Bank movement and access update. Retrieved August 18, 2020. https://www.ochaopt.org/sites/default/files/ocha_opt_movement_and_access_report_september_2012_english.pdf.

———. (2013). Fragmented lives: Humanitarian overview 2012. Retrieved August 18, 2020. https://www.ochaopt.org/content/fragmented-lives-humanitarian-overview-2012.

———. (2020, March–May). Longstanding access restrictions continue to undermine the living conditions of West Bank Palestinians. *Humanitarian Bulletin.* Retrieved August 18, 2020. https://www.ochaopt.org/content/longstanding-access-restrictions-continue-undermine-living-conditions-west-bank-palestinians.

United Nations Security Council. (1967). Resolution 242: The situation in the Middle East. Adopted November 22. Retrieved February 23, 2021. https://unispal.un.org/unispal.nsf/0/7D35E1F729DF491C85256EE700686136.

———. (1979). Resolution 446: Territories occupied by Israel. Adopted March 22. Retrieved February 23, 2021. https://unispal.un.org/UNISPAL.NSF/0/BA123CDED3EA84A5852560E50077C2DC.

———. (2016, December 23). Resolution 2334. Retrieved February 18, 2021. https://www.un.org/webcast/pdfs/SRES2334-2016.pdf.

Vanneschi, M. (2014, July 14). Israel denies exit for Palestinian artist in new museum show. *Hyperallergic.* Retrieved April 13, 2020. https://hyperallergic.com/137643/israel-denies-exit-for-palestinian-artist-in-new-museum-show.

Virilio, P. (2006). *Speed and politics* (M. Polizzatti, Trans.). Los Angeles: Semiotext(e).

Vizenor, G. (1999). *Manifest manners: Narratives on postindian survivance.* Lincoln: University of Nebraska Press.

———. (2000). *Fugitive poses: Native American Indian scenes of absence and presence.* Lincoln: University of Nebraska Press.

Walters, W. (2006). Border/control. *European Journal of Social Theory, 9*(2), 187–203.

———. (2015). Migration, vehicles, and politics: Three theses on viapolitics. *European Journal of Social Theory, 18*(4), 469–488.

Weir, S. (2008). *Palestinian costume.* Northampton, MA: Interlink.

Weizman, E. (2007). *Hollowland: Israel's architecture of occupation.* London: Verso.

Wolfe, P. (2006). Settler colonialism and the elimination of the native. *Journal of Genocide Research, 8*(4), 387–409.

———. (2013). Recuperating binarism: A heretical introduction. *Settler Colonial Studies, 3*(3–4), 257–279.

Woods, C. (2009). Les misérables of New Orleans: Trap economics and the asset stripping blues, part 1. *American Quarterly, 61*(3), 769–796.

World Bank. (1969, July 22). Current economic position and prospects for Israel. Report no. EMA-7b. Retrieved February 23, 2021. http://documents1.worldbank.org/curated/en/445481468038666133/pdf/multi0page.pdf.

———. (2003). Twenty-seven months—Intifada, closures and Palestinian economic crisis: An assessment. Retrieved February 23, 2021. https://openknowledge.worldbank.org /handle/10986/14614.

———. (2008, October). The economic effects of restricted access to land in the West Bank. Retrieved February 23, 2021. https://documents.worldbank.org/en/publication/docu ments-reports/documentdetail/654801468176641469/west-bank-and-gaza-the-eco nomic-effects-of-restricted-access-to-land-in-the-west-bank.

Younis, A. (2012). Exhibition of the month: *A metro in Gaza*. Press release. *This Week in Palestine,* (165). Retrieved February 23, 2020. https://www.artsy.net/show/eltiqa-a -metro-in-gaza/info.

Zaccheni, L. (2012, January 14). Un métro à Gaza (in French). Retrieved February 23, 2021. http://www.lemonde.fr/proche-orient/article/2012/01/14/lettre-du-proche-orient -un-metro-a-gaza_1629771_3218.html.

Index

Page numbers in italics refer to illustrations

Abdel Jawad, Saleh, 117–118, 181n12
'Abediyya, Al-, 65
Abourahme, Nasser, 123, 126, 151
Abu Dis, 58, 83
Abusal, Mohamed, 19, 123, 133–142
active presence, 97, 128, 160–161. *See also* art
   of presence; staying/remaining; survivance
Addameer Prisoner Support and Human
   Rights Association, 103
Afikim, 105, *107*–108, 180n3
Agence France-Presse, 114
air travel: air blockades, 138, 174n9; airports,
   47, 60, 137, 144, 168, 177n12; and deportations, 16
Ali, Nijmeh, 14
alienation, 2, 5, 10, 26, 50, 83–84, 160, 173n5
Al Jazeera, 114–115
Allon, Yigal, 28, 30
Allon Plan, 28–29
annexation, 14, 17, 19, 37, 84, 107, 111, 173n5;
   and Apartheid Wall, 42, 49–50; as Israeli
   settler colonial goal, 1, 4–7, 23–33, 153,
   161–163, 173n12; of time, 55–56
apartheid: Israeli, 18, 26, 104–105, 115–116,
   118–120, 174n8, 181n8; South African, 111,
   114, 117

Apartheid Wall, 9, 22, *63*, 145, 159, 180n6; and
   checkpoints, 17, 51, 101, 105, 108, 177nn4–
   5; construction of, 37, 42–43, 48–49; use of
   term, 49, 175n16
Applied Research Institute–Jerusalem (ARIJ),
   16, 176n4
Aqsa Intifada, Al-, 8, 175n11, 176n21. *See also*
   Palestinian Intifada, second
Aqsa Mosque, Al-, 41, 140–*141*, 145–146
Arab-Israeli War (1967), 5, 27. *See also* Naksa,
   an-; Six-Day War (1967)
Ariel settlement, *107*, 109, 114
art of presence, 96–97. *See also* active pres-
   ence; staying/remaining; survivance
Ashcroft, Bill, 126
Atrash, Anas, al-, 58
Azeb, Sophia, 124

bantustanization, 10
Barak, Ehud, 37, 41
Barakat, Rana, 4
Barghouti, Marwan, 93
Barghouti, Omar, 103
Barkan settlement, 108
Bayat, Asef, 96–97, 158, 160
Baylouny, Anne Marie, 41, 103

Beit Fajjar, 66–67, 67
Beit Jala, 50, 60–62, 65, 72, 107
Beit Sahour, 34, 60–62, 81, 129, 155, 165,
    178n3; and public transportation, 65–66,
    70, 72–74, 178n3
Beit Sahour Bus Company, 61–62, 74
Ben Gurion Airport, 168, 177n12
Benjamin, Walter, 126
Berda, Yael, 54
Bethlehem, 16, 21–22, 29, 58–74, 81, 94, 103,
    129, 148–149; and the Apartheid Wall, 50,
    107–108; and public transit, 155, 179n6;
    and van routes, 85–90, 182n3. See also
    Bethlehem–Al-Khalil/Hebron van route;
    Bethlehem–Ireeha/Jericho van route;
    Bethlehem–Ramallah van route
Bethlehem–Al-Khalil/Hebron van route,
    86–90, 182n3
Bethlehem–Ireeha/Jericho van route, 65,
    87–89
Bethlehem–Ramallah van route, 45, 53, 83
Bethlehem Traffic Department (Da'irat as-
    Seir), 16, 67, 166–167
Bhandar, Brenna, 9, 23
Birzeit, 92–93, 178n3
Bishara, Amahl, 82, 85
Black, Felix, 114–115
Black September War, 33
border-enclosures, 7, 9, 11, 18, 26, 75, 78, 80,
    96–97, 115, 124–125, 134, 154, 158–159,
    180n1
bordering, diffused, 3, 9–10, 16–17, 38, 51,
    140, 156–157, 182n3; and checkpoints/
    permits, 23, 55, 59, 74; definition, 7–8; and
    enclosures, 25–26; and im/mobilization, 44,
    46–48, 56, 59, 78, 91–92, 153; and mobile
    commoning, 98; and service gaps, 75; and
    temporality, 56, 125, 143, 150–151
borders, 83, 90, 107–108, 119, 137, 145, 156–
    157; and Allon Plan, 28; border economies,
    22; border police, 41, 110, 148, 168; and
    settlements, 42; weaponization of, 180n2.
    See also border-enclosures; bordering, dif-
    fused; borderscapes; checkpoints
borderscapes, 7, 17, 44–75, 98
Boycott, Divestment, and Sanctions
    Movement (BDS Movement), 78, 99, 103,
    156
British Mandate period, 7, 177n12, 178n4
B'Tselem, 51, 53, 114, 176n21, 177n5, 180n4,
    180n6
Burris, Greg, 126
Buttu, Diana, 41
Byrd, Jodi, 4

Canada, 6, 23, 106
capitalism, 6, 23–25, 94, 174nn5-7
Cauter, Lieven De, 130
Checkpoint 300, 21, 43, 61–63, 101, 173n3
checkpoints, 8, 10, 23, 39, 48, 51, 53–55,
    57–58, 156, 180nn4-6; and Apartheid Wall,
    176n3, 177n5; "border," 107–110; dangers
    of, 94, 103; "flying," 7, 9, 17, 42, 53, 81, 168,
    177n4; and Gaza metro plan, 136, 144; and
    im/mobilization, 36, 41–43, 172n7; mili-
    tary, 61, 89; rules of, 84, 119; and time, 127,
    172n7; and West Bank, 105–106. See also
    Checkpoint 300; Container Checkpoint;
    Eyal Checkpoint; Hizma Checkpoint;
    Nablus Checkpoint; Qalandiya Checkpoint;
    Rafah Checkpoint; Tunnel Checkpoint
civilian occupation, 29–31
Clarno, Andy, 117
Closure Policy, Israel's, 35–36, 175n15
collective mobility/movement, 98, 121, 131,
    134, 151, 156, 169; expectations of, 77; and
    im/mobilization, 11, 25; rebellious, 91–92,
    127–130, 133; self-determined, 95, 97;
    significance to project, 1–2, 11–12, 16–17,
    46–48, 162–163, 174n9; symbols of, 102,
    104, 140, 153–155; vehicles of, 3, 104, 123,
    143, 150, 153, 158–159
Collins, John, 125
commons, the, 6, 17, 23–24, 94, 171n4, 172n6,
    174n5. See also mobile commons
Container Checkpoint, 57–59, 66
Corntassel, Jeff, 12
Coulthard, Glenn Sean, 4, 6
counterinsurgency, 17, 25, 27, 33, 42, 157
Crenshaw, Kimberlé, 118
Cresswell, Tim, 13
critical border studies, 17, 47
curfews, 3, 34, 42–43, 91, 154

Damascus Gate, 61, 63
Dar Salah, 66, 81
Darwazah, Mais, 126
decolonization, 18–19, 25, 78, 84, 99, 123,
    150, 174n9; definition, 172n10; and haunt-
    ing, 128–130, 134; and rehabitation, 85,
    90; and resistance, 2, 120; and self-deter-
    mination, 11–13, 102, 142, 182n10; stakes
    of, 155, 158–163; and sumud, 14–15; and
    viapolitics, 1
Decolonizing Architecture Art Residency
    (DAAR), 19, 123, 129–131, 133, 140
denationalization, 4–5, 10, 31
deterritorialization, 4–5, 10, 31, 145–146
Dheisheh refugee camp, 61, 89

diffused bordering, 3, 9–10, 16–17, 38, 51, 140, 156–157, 182n3; and checkpoints/permits, 23, 55, 59, 74; definition, 7–8; and enclosures, 25–26; and im/mobilization, 44, 46–48, 56, 59, 78, 91–92, 153; and mobile commoning, 98; and service gaps, 75; and temporality, 56, 125, 143, 150–151

dispossession, 50, 75, 78, 90, 96, 120, 174n9; and checkpoints, 58–59, 94, 107, 127–128; and enclosures, 4–11, 23–26, 55, 98, 125; and Israeli settler colonialism, 15, 31, 131, 133, 136, 159, 163, 171n4; and Oslo Accords, 38, 41–42

Doumani, Beshara, 8, 93, 180n14

Durrah, Muhammad, 41

Egged, 105

Egypt, 47, 130, 137, 148, 178n4

Eizariya, Al-, 45

enclosures, 105, 117, 149–150, 173n5, 178n4; border-enclosures, 7, 11, 18, 96–97, 115, 125, 134; challenges to, 19, 36, 80, 92, 97–98, 158–159; and fragmentation, 11, 13, 124, 173n13; and im/mobilization, 11, 17, 21–44, 78, 176n19; as Israeli settler colonial method, 5–9, 23–27, 30, 36, 39, 75, 145–146, 153–154

England, 23, 26

Erakat, Noura, 12, 119–120

Erekat, Ahmed, 58

extraction, 5, 7, 17

Eyal Checkpoint, 119

Facebook, 114

Fadda, Reem, 56

Farsakh, Leila, 28, 35, 39, 172n8

Federici, Silvia, 23, 173n5

Feldman, Keith, 117

Fields, Gary, 23

First Nations people, 6, 23

Fordaat (shared vans), 2, 21, 58, 60, 162, 166, 179n6, 182n3; and methodology, 16; routes, 45–47, 65–74, 82–83, 85–95; stations, 79

fragmentation, 30, 36–44, 49–50, 89, 107, 112, 117, 121, 124; challenges to, 18, 91, 140; and Oslo Accords, 103, 146, 157; and sumud, 78, 95, 97, 173n13; use of term, 2, 10–11, 26–27, 176n18

freedom, 26, 103, 105, 120, 142; of expression, 102; instinct for, 97–98; many faces of, 112–113; of movement, 15, 93, 110, 112, 121, 133; and self-determination, 12, 121

Freedom Bus, 18, 102, 111–113, 115, 121

Freedom Rides (Palestinian), 18, 102, 109–111, 114–115, 119

Freedom Rides (U.S. Civil Rights Movement), 109–110

Freedom Theater (Jenin), 111

Gaza International Airport/Yasser Arafat International Airport, 137, 177n12

Ghanim, Honaida, 115, 174n8, 181n8

Gordon, Avery, 97, 127–130, 142, 160

Great Britain, 3, 7, 60, 130, 177n12, 178n4, 181n2. See also England

Green Line, 105, 113, 115, 136; and the Apartheid Wall, 42, 49–50, 107, 180n6; and Palestinian workers, 23, 39

Ha'aretz (newspaper), 54, 116, 181n10

Hammami, Rema, 14, 93–95, 179n13

Handel, Ariel, 43, 178n1

Har Homa settlement, 29

Harker, Christopher, 161

Hass, Amira, 55, 125

haunting, 123–124, 129–130; as method, 127–128, 131, 133–135, 148, 150–151, 182n6

Hebron/Al-Khalil, 57–58, 70, 73, 81, 86–90, 177n4, 182n3. See also Bethlehem-Al-Khalil/Hebron van route

Hilal, Sandi, 80, 128, 171n4

Hizma Checkpoint, 109

Hodkinson, Stuart, 24

humanitarian line, 21

Hussein, Saddam, 35

Hussein, Talal bin, 33

ID cards, 34, 38, 43, 103; and controlling movement, 32, 36, 41, 48, 54–55, 58–59

Ihmoud, Sarah, 15

immobilization, 2, 8, 30, 50, 55, 95, 103, 143, 145, 176n18

im/mobilization, regime of, 5, 78, 136, 154, 156, 158, 160, 174n9; challenges to, 19, 78, 81–82, 91, 95, 104, 121, 127, 151, 182n3; and checkpoints, 36, 41–43, 53, 172n7; and collective mobility, 11; definition, 7–11, 124; and diffused bordering, 25, 44, 46–48, 56, 59, 78, 91–92, 153; and enclosures, 11, 17–18, 21–44, 78, 124, 153, 176n1; and Palestinian Intifada, 8, 25, 33–39, 103, 157, 175n12, 179n1; role in Israeli settler colonialism, 21–44, 98–99, 102–103, 131, 143–144; and temporality, 124–125; uneven, 8, 32. See also mobility regime

indigeneity, 9, 117, 121, 158–159, 172n10, 173n12, 182n5; anti-, 27, 103, 157; and mobility regime, 4–5, 7, 18–19, 31, 78; Palestinian, 28, 36, 48, 56; and

indigeneity (*continued*)
  self-determination, 2, 11–14, 126–128, 163;
  and spatial knowledge, 84–91, 97–98, 153;
  and survivance, 148, 150–151
Indigenous peoples, 6, 9, 24
Indigenous studies, 2
Interim Agreement on the West Bank and the
  Gaza Strip (1995), 38
Ireeha. *See* Jericho/Ireeha
Israeli Civil Administration, 33–34, 38, 54
Israeli High Court of Justice (HCJ), 49
Israeli Labor Party, 30
Israeli Likud Party, 30
Israeli Ministry of Transportation, 109,
  113–114

Jabal Abu-Ghnaim, *29*
Jarrar, Khaled, 103, 182n3
Jeffrey, Alex, 6, 26
Jenin, 111, 129–130, 180n6
Jericho/Ireeha, 28, 57–58, 65, 70, 73, 83, *87–89*,
  129, 165. *See also* Bethlehem–Ireeha/Jericho
  van route
Jerusalem, neighborhoods: Beit Hanina, 109;
  East Jerusalem, 10, 32, 41, 54, 107–110, 129;
  Old City, 22, 41, 61, 89; Shu'fat, 109; West
  Jerusalem, 22, 60
Jerusalem International Airport, 177n12
Jim Crow, 116
Jordan, 32–33, 47, 83, 130, 148, 168, 178n15;
  and rule of West Bank, 27–29, 177n12
Jung, F. Sam, 127

Kafr Qasim, 113
Kauanui, J. Kēhaulani, 4
Kelley, Robin D. G., 120–121, 124
Kelly, Jennifer, 104
Khadamat Rafah, 103
Khalil, Al-. *See* Hebron/Al-Khalil
Khalili, Yazan, Al-, 46, 176n1, 182n3
Klein, Naomi, 35, 175n14
Knesset, 35, 116–117
knowledge networks, 18, 75, 77, 85, 98
Kotef, Hagar, 8–9, 24, 51, 84

Lebanon, 33, 178n15
Linebaugh, Peter, 6
Livni, Tzipi, 118–119

Ma'ale Adumim settlement, 45
Makdisi, Saree, 54–55, 125
Manara, al-, 70
Mandela, Nelson, *112*
Manger Square, 61, 70, 72, 90, *146–147*

mapping, 49, 130, 159, 178n4; cartographies of
  refusal, 90; and fragmentation, 10, 39–*40*;
  transit route maps, 16, 74, 80, 85–90, *86–88*,
  106, 132–136, 140, 143, 179n6
Marcuse, Herbert, 97
masha', al-, 80
Mbembe, Achille, 115
McFarlane, Colin, 6
McGahern, Una, 103
Meneley, Anne, 104
methodology of the book, 2, 4–11, 13–19,
  25–27, 60
mobile commons, 13, 26, 92, 94–98, 121, 154;
  commoning, 6, 18, 78, 80–81, 85, 88, 90–91,
  121; description of term, 80–81, 85, 172n5,
  178nn1–2; and *sumud*, 78, 179n11
mobility justice, 13–14, 16, 80, 178nn1–2
mobility regime, 16–18, 22, 26, 41, 78, 99, 104,
  180n2; and Israeli enclosures, 5, 7–8, 24–25,
  36. *See also* im/mobilization, regime of
mobility studies, 2, 47
Morrill, Angie, 127
muhafidha, 60–61, 65, 82
murabata, 15, 183n13

Nablus, 57, 70, 72, *79*, 129, 144, 182n3; siege of,
  8, 180n14
Nablus Checkpoint, 93, 179n12
Nakba, an-, 27, 133
Naksa, an-, 27. *See also* Arab-Israeli War
  (1967); Six-Day War (1967)
Nativity Church, Bethlehem, 146, 149
Netanyahu, Benjamin, 119, 162–163

Omar, Ilhan, 103
Oslo Accords, 8, 10, 12, 37–41, 45–47, 54,
  176nn19–21, 177n12; and fragmentation,
  146, 148, 157; post-, 92, 99, 102–103
Oslo II. *See* Interim Agreement on the West
  Bank and the Gaza Strip (1995)
Ottoman train system, 3, 60, 130, 133, 148
Oush Ghrab, 129, 182n8. *See also* Peace
  Park

Palestine Monitor, 114
Palestine studies, 2
Palestinian analytic, 105, 120
Palestinian Authority (PA), 38, 54–55, 114,
  161–162, 165; and public transportation,
  2–3, 45–47, 155–157, 167. *See also* PA
  Ministry of Transportation (Wizarat an-
  Naql w al-Muwasalat)
Palestinian Central Bureau of Statistics,
  177n11, 178n14

Palestinian Freedom Rides, 18, 102, 109–111, 114–115, 119
Palestinian General Federation of Trade Unions, 114
Palestinian Intifada, first, 12, 14, 173n11, 174–175nn11–13, 176n19; and im/mobilization, 8, 25, 33–39, 103, 157, 179n11
Palestinian Intifada, second, 8, 90–99, 154, 175n13, 176n21, 179n11–12, 181n1; and the Apartheid Wall, 49, 51, 158; and the Oslo Accords, 41–43, 46, 103, 176n21, 177n12; and taxis, 3, 18, 73, 159, 179n10, 180n14
Palestinian liberation, 11–12, 120
Palestinian Liberation Organization (PLO), 33, 37, 41, 175n11
Palestinian Monetary Authority (PMA), 161
PA Ministry of Transportation (Wizarat an-Naql w al-Muwasalat), 16, 61, 64, 67–68, 74, 82, 91, 154, 166–167
Papadopoulos, Dmitris, 80, 121, 172n5
paperson, la, 126
Paq, Anne, 103
Parizot, Cedric, 22
Peace Park, 129, 182n8. See also Oush Ghrab
Persian Gulf War, 35
Peteet, Julie, 8, 48, 55, 117, 123, 125–127
Petti, Alessandro, 80, 128–129, 171n4
Psagot settlement, 109
public transportation, definition of, 3–4, 171n2

Qalandiya Checkpoint, 45, 53, 56, 63, 66, 94, 144, 177n8, 177n12
Quds University, Al-, 58, 83, 155
Qumsiyeh, Mazin, 33, 37, 174n10–11
Qutami, Loubna, 26, 105, 120

racialization, 9–11, 25, 104, 181n11
racial segregation, 18, 49, 102, 104, 111–121, 175nn16–17, 181n12. See also apartheid
Rafah Checkpoint, 137
Ramallah, 81, 92–94, 109, 134, 140–141, 179n13, 182n3; Bethlehem–Ramallah route, 45, 72–74, 83, 86, 89–90; buses in, 61, 70, 178n3; and Qalandiya Checkpoint, 53, 56–57, 63, 66, 144
Ree, C., 127–128
reinhabitation, 85, 90, 182n3
repatriation, 13, 120, 125, 148, 172n10
resistance, 12, 33–34, 59, 78, 99, 142, 173n14, 174n10; and decolonization, 2, 15, 120, 157, 159–160; fragmentation's effects on, 37, 41, 91; Israeli containment of, 17, 22, 31; and sumud, 14–15, 178n1; and Ta'wwudna, 181n1; walking as, 103

resistance studies, 2, 157, 159
Reuters, 114
Reynolds, John, 116
Rifkin, Mark, 126
right of return, 15, 128–133, 137, 140, 148–150, 162
Right to Movement (RTM), 103
Robinson, Cedric, 9
Russell Tribunal on Palestine, 117

Said, Assef, 114
Said, Edward, 12, 84–85, 90, 146
Sansour, Larissa, 19, 123, 143–150
sarha, 104
Saudi Arabia, 130, 148
Seam Zone, 50, 180n6
Security Barrier. See Apartheid Wall
self-determination, 48, 172n9, 176n2, 182n10; definition, 12; Indigenous, 4–5, 13–14, 24, 127–128, 151; Israeli denial of, 4, 8–9, 23, 26–27, 34–36, 146, 153, 162–163; reclamation of, 11, 19, 44, 121; and sumud, 15, 161; temporal, 125, 127, 136, 143, 149–151, 182n10. See also self-determined movement
self-determined movement, 1–2, 15–16, 19, 46, 48, 51, 55, 78; and checkpoints, 55–56; as decolonial act, 95–98, 102, 123–133, 139, 142–143, 150–151, 154–161; and im/mobilization, 59; Israeli denial of, 8–9, 34–36, 43, 81, 102, 125, 142, 154; and mobile commoning, 80
Separation Fence. See Apartheid Wall
service. See taxis, shared/service
settlements, Israeli, 9, 17, 38–39, 50–51, 55, 174n9; as civilian occupation, 29–30; and the mobility regime, 41–42; opposition to, 33; and public transportation, 60, 74, 89, 156; and the settler bus system, 3, 105–109, 180n3, 180n7. See also Ariel settlement; Barkan settlement; civilian occupation; Har Homa settlement; Ma'ale Adumim settlement; Psagot settlement; West Bank and the Gaza Strip (WBGS)
settler colonialism, use in book, 4–11
settler indigeneity, 24, 84
shared vans. See Fordaat (shared vans)
Sharif, Lila, 9, 124, 182n6
Sharif, Yara, 8, 159, 173n4
Sharon, Ariel, 30–31, 41
Shehadeh, Raja, 9, 104, 182n6
Sheller, Mimi, 13, 16, 80, 121, 172nn5–7, 178n2
Six-Day War (1967), 5, 27. See also Arab-Israeli War (1967); Naksa, an-sociality, 77–85, 96–98, 182n3

South Africa, 111–112, 114, 116–117, 172n8. *See also* apartheid: South African
South Dakota, 105
Soviet Union, 35, 175n14
Stacher, Joshua, 103
State of Israel, declaration of, 27. *See also* Nakba, an-
staying/remaining, 14–15, 183n13; and active presence, 97, 128, 160–161; and art of presence, 96–97, 160; as self-determination, 133, 150; and *sumud*, 14–15, 97, 160–161, 178n1. *See also* active presence; art of presence
Stoler, Ann, 30, 39
sumud, 14, 172n11, 173n13; and mobility, 15, 78, 95, 97, 160–161, 178n1, 179n11. *See also* staying/remaining
Super Futures Haunt Qollective (SFHQ), 127, 182n5
Surda roadblock, 92–94, 179n13
survivance, 97, 148, 150, 160–161. *See also* active presence; art of presence; staying/remaining
Syria, 130, 148

Taba Agreement. *See* Interim Agreement on the West Bank and the Gaza Strip (1995)
Tamari, Salim, 14, 172n11
Tawil-Souri, Helga, 8, 37–38, 47–48, 125, 172n7, 176n2
taxis, private/*Tulub*, 2–3, 60, 63–64, 67, 73–74, 81
taxis, shared/*service*, 2, 21, 60, 82, 91, 144, 162, 178n14; and checkpoints, 53; definition, 64–65, 178n15; fares, 73–74; line permit numbers for, 67
Tel Aviv, 16, 35, 108, 177n12
temporality, 13, 19, 74, 78, 119, 150–151; and diffused bordering, 56, 125, 143, 150; and enclosures, 2; and im/mobilization, 124–125; reclamation of, 81–84, 103, 122, 125–128, 131, 133, 139, 142–143; role in settler colonialism, 55–59, 75, 122, 125–128, 136, 172n7; temporal self-determination, 55, 122–128, 136, 143, 149–151, 158, 182n10. *See also* waiting
Thomsen, Carly, 105
Tlaib, Rashida, 103
trains, 74, 145, 149, 171n2; British railway system, 3, 60, 148; Jerusalem light rail, 14, 60; in *A Metro in Gaza*, 19, 133–142; Ottoman railway system, 3, 60, 133, 148; in *Right to Mobility*, 130–133; stations, 130–131, *131*, 133, 182n3
Tsianos, Vassilis, 6, 80, 121, 172n5

Tuck, Eve, 12–14, 127–128, 172n10, 174n7, 182n5
Tunis, 33
Tunnel Checkpoint, 61, 107–108

United Nations Office for the Coordination of Humanitarian Affairs in the Occupied Palestinian Territory (OCHA OPT), 49, 51, 53, 176n4, 177n5
United Nations Security Council, 155
United Nations Security Council Resolution 242, 37
U.S. Civil Rights Movement, 104, 109–110, 114, 118

Vasudevan, Alex, 6
viapolitics, 1, 15–16, 19, 46, 59
violence, 75, 103, 125, 127–128, 135; colonial, 5, 14, 58–59, 111, 136, 151; Israeli, 41, 57, 157, 175n12
Virilio, Paul, 125
Vizenor, Gerald, 97, 160

Wachman, Avraham, 30
waiting, 61, 64; at checkpoints, 21–23, *56*, 66, 119, 127, 168, 173n3; for passengers, 63, 67, 69–70, 72–74, 77, 83–85, 155, 162, 166; rejection of, 137, 160; for rides, 82–83, 178n3; and roadblocks, 92–93, 168; and stolen time, 55, 125–126; weaponization of, 123, 125, 148
Walaja, Al-, 50
walking/running, 70, 72, 154; and checkpoints, 21, 53, 101; as resistance, 103–104; and roadblocks, 92–93; *sarha*, 104
Walters, William, 15–16, 46–47, 59
Weinstein, Yehuda, 119
Weizman, Eyal, 51, 80, 129, 171n4
West Bank and the Gaza Strip (WBGS), 28, 31–39, 49, 54–55, 155–157, 175n15; Areas A, B, and C, 38–*40*, 45, 81, 111; invasion of, 5, 25, 181n8; Palestinians in, 10, 42, 177n7
World Zionist Organization, 30

Ya'alon, Moshe, 114, 118–119
Yang, K. Wayne, 12–13, 127, 172n10, 174n7
Yogev, Moti, 117
Younis, Ala, 137, 139

Zaccheni, Laurent, 135
Zahzah, Omar, 26
Zapatistas, 160
Zionism, 30, 35, 105, 174n10, 175n14; and settler colonialism, 4–5, 7, 27, 84

MARYAM S. GRIFFIN is an Assistant Professor in the School of Interdisciplinary Arts and Sciences at the University of Washington Bothell.

www.ingramcontent.com/pod-product-compliance
Lightning Source LLC
Chambersburg PA
CBHW050805270326
41926CB00025B/4541